Happy 39th Birthday
From Ann & Elliott

all the best   Nov 16, 1983

AUSTRALIA
A TIMELESS GRANDEUR

AUSTRALIA
A TIMELESS GRANDEUR

PHOTOGRAPHY BY
REG MORRISON
TEXT BY
HELEN GRASSWILL

Lansdowne Press
Sydney · Auckland · London · New York

Produced by Helen and Bruno Grasswill
Photography by Reg Morrison
Researched and written by Helen Grasswill
Design, maps and diagrams by Bruno Grasswill
Geology consultant: Oliver Chalmers,
    Honorary Associate, The Australian Museum
Copy editor: Jacqueline Kent
Indexer: Joan Clarke
The author and photographer travelled by courtesy of:
THIESS TOYOTA PTY LTD
ANSETT.
ESSO AUSTRALIA LTD
BILL KING'S NORTHERN SAFARIS
Reg Morrison used Nikon equipment almost exclusively for
the photographs in this book. The main cameras, a Nikon
F and Nikon F2A, were coupled with lenses ranging in
focal length from 24 mm to 500 mm. The film stock was
Kodachrome 25 ASA and 64 ASA.

DISPLAY PHOTOGRAPHS
FRONT JACKET: The Olgas (story, page 190)
ENDPAPERS: Star trails at Chambers Pillar
(story, page 200)
HALF-TITLE PAGE: A group of Western
Australian grass-trees (Kingia australis)
and a solitary blackboy (Xanthorrhoea sp.)
PAGES 2-3 : Chambers Pillar
TITLE PAGE: Waterfall Valley, near Cradle
Mountain (story, page 56)
THIS PAGE: Dead tree, Simpson Desert
(story, page 206)
CONTENTS PAGE: Red lotus (Nelumbo
nucifera), Arnhem Land (story, page 138)
BACK JACKET: Sand dunes in the Simpson
Desert

Published by Lansdowne Press, Sydney
176 South Creek Road, Dee Why West, NSW Australia 2099
First published 1981
Reprinted 1982
© Copyright Lansdowne Press 1981
Heading typography designed especially for this book
© Copyright Bruno Grasswill 1981
Produced in Australia
Typeset in Australia by Savage and Co. Pty Ltd, Brisbane
Printed in Australia by Griffin Press Limited, Adelaide

National Library of Australia Cataloguing-in-Publication Data

Grasswill, Helen.
    Australia, a timeless grandeur.

    Bibliography.
    Includes index.
    ISBN 0 7018 1600 7.

    1. Australia — Description and travel.
    2. Australia — History. I. Morrison, Reg.
    II. Title.

919.4

Body type 11/13 pt Zapf; captions 11/12 pt Signette Italics and 9/10 pt Gill Sans;
map labels 8 pt Gill Sans and 8 pt Signette Italics; sub-headings and dropped capitals
36 pt Gill Sans; Acknowledgements, Bibliography 9/10 pt Zapf; Index 8 pt Zapf.

PREFACE

The strange . . . invisible beauty of Australia . . .
more poignant than anything ever experienced before.

D. H. LAWRENCE
Kangaroo, 1923

THE AUSTRALIAN landscape has often been described as lacking in spectacle, for it has no towering mountains such as the Himalayas or the European Alps, no mighty rivers like the Amazon or the Mississippi, and no active or even dormant volcanoes. Yet, with its vast plateaux and plains, clear blue skies and inevitable eucalypt trees, the country has great strength of character and a compelling beauty that seems almost inexplicable.

In his novel *Kangaroo,* published in 1923, the English author D. H. Lawrence wrote perceptively of the ". . . *invisible* beauty of Australia, which is undeniably there, but which seems to lurk just beyond the range of our white vision. You feel you can't *see* — as if your eyes hadn't the vision in them to correspond with the outside landscape. For the landscape is so unimpressive, like a face with little or no features . . . And yet, when you don't have the feeling of ugliness or monotony . . . you get a sense of subtle, remote, *formless* beauty more poignant than anything ever experienced before."

The "sameness" that is so often apparent in the Australian landscape arises from the sheer size of the various geographical environments and from a superficial homogeneity of vegetation, which in itself is deceptive. The country is in fact extremely varied and has numerous areas of spectacular beauty.

To discover this beauty one must take the wide view, for the attraction of an area is seldom in a single feature but in an entire surrounding . . . and it is as much felt as seen. Sometimes the beauty is dramatic and austere, often it is gentle, but nearly always it is made up of many elements that are bound into a whole by an overriding feeling of peace and solitude. Across wide distances, there is no visual intrusion by man . . . just the pristine natural environment that has changed little in thousands of years. There is a dignity about the ancient rocks and about the trees that have so resolutely stood their ground through the grinding passage of time.

In this book, our aim is to reveal the almost "secret" beauty — and true diversity — of Australia's natural landscape by concentrating on a selection of areas that have had a special impact on us. We have endeavoured to portray the intrinsic character of each of these places and hope that by their example we show the essential differences that exist throughout the continent. At the same time, we hope we have captured the strong threads that tie them together to form a total landscape that is distinctively Australian.

Many areas that have been included, such as Ayers Rock and the Great Barrier Reef, are familiar to most people. However, several places are little known . . . the magnificent treasury of Kubla Khan Cave and the severely sculptured Acropolis in Tasmania; the circular Gosse's Bluff, thrown up millions of years ago in central Australia by an exploding comet; and the dome-like stone cities of the Shark Bay Stromatolites in Western Australia, which are still being built by primitive algae.

In order to give a deeper understanding of the landscape, we have tried, wherever possible, to show the relationships between the present landforms and their origins. On the Great Barrier Reef, for example, we wanted to show not simply close-ups of colourful coral and the region's gaudier inhabitants, but also how reefs develop and build islands. This we have attempted by means of simultaneous views of both above and below the waterline, to give a unified picture instead of presenting the region as two entities.

In the text we have tried to depict the essence of each landscape area by outlining its geological structure, climate, vegetation and wildlife, and also to show man's relationship with the land, from the early Aboriginal occupation, through European invasion to the present time.

Prepared as we were by the initial research that went into compiling the fieldwork itinerary for this book, we were still unprepared for the personal discoveries that first-hand knowledge would bring. We hope that the view we give touches upon some of that subtle and poignant beauty of Australia's unique natural landscape.

Helen Grasswill and Reg Morrison
Sydney
June 1981

CONTENTS

INTRODUCTION

Australia has a strange and lonely grandeur. In a world where natural landscapes are fast disappearing, the country is fortunate in retaining vast areas of wilderness that are substantially free from the impact of man. They are peaceful places that have changed little in thousands of years and their beauty is so compelling that it is felt by all the senses.

Remoteness and solitude are inherent in the Australian landscape. Covering a vast area of 7 682 300 square kilometres, the country is both an island and a continent — a land separated from the rest of the world and possessing wide empty spaces within its shores. This isolation has led to the evolution of vegetation and wildlife markedly different from those found in other lands and it has also enabled pockets of rare plants from past climatic ages to survive in limited habitats, perhaps on only one mountain peak or in one remote gorge.

The great size of the Australian continent means that it spreads across several climatic zones, from the tropical north, through the desert lands of the centre, to the temperate south and to the cold, wet lands of the Roaring Forties in Tasmania. Nevertheless, the country's landscape is always distinctive because of its fantastic combinations of colour and form. The rich reds and rusty browns, the yellows, the ochres and the muted Australian green all seem "earthier" than in other lands. Coupled with this is the intense quality of the light, for over much of the country the sky is almost always an uninterrupted sheet of metallic blue. Usually the horizon is broken only by low mountain ranges that appear purple in the distance or by bare rock monoliths that change colour dramatically according to the light.

Age is the primary and most ubiquitous factor that binds together the Australian landscape. For longer than any other continent it has been free from the turbulence brought by earthquakes, volcanoes and other violent natural phenomena. This stability has enabled the forces of weathering and erosion to work uninterrupted, wearing the surface smooth, so that today the overwhelming characteristic of the landscape is its extreme flatness. Three-quarters of the continent consists of low plains and plateaux, and even the once-high mountain ranges are now mere blunt-topped hills. Only a little over 5 per cent of the land rises to an altitude higher than 600 metres, and no mountain peaks reach above a permanent snowline.

The lack of high mountain ranges to precipitate rain and give rise to rivers makes Australia not only the flattest and lowest of Earth's landmasses, but also the driest. It has the lowest average rainfall of all continents (470 millimetres compared with 720 millimetres for world land surfaces as a whole), as well as one of the highest rates of evaporation. More than a dozen of the world's rivers each carry more water to the sea per year than all Australian rivers combined. Even the country's most important river, the Murray, takes a year to discharge the same amount of water that the Amazon empties in a day and a half.

Yet despite its lack of spectacular contours and vigorous streams, Australia has a surprising variety of powerful landscapes — beautifully sculptured rock monuments, deep gorges, exquisite lakes and waterfalls, fantastically contoured mountain ridges, caves with dazzling crystal ornaments, shimmering salt-pans, rivers that seldom flow, and a wild coastline with grand cliffs, gigantic tidal races, magnificent coral gardens and rare rock structures still being built by primitive organisms.

The eucalypt or "gum" tree is integral to the Australian landscape. About 75 per cent of the country's trees belong to this genus, ranging from the tall, straight-trunked mountain ash (*Eucalyptus regnans*) and karri (*Eucalyptus diversicolor*) to the various small and twisted mallees that have several slender stems growing from a single rootstock. Of 400 or so eucalypt species in the world, only 7 occur naturally beyond Australia.

The characteristic scents of the Australian bush come largely from oils in the leaves and stems of the eucalypts, and the familiar dark green bush colouring is typical of their foliage. But the colour and texture of the bark of these trees varies greatly. They range from the smooth, white trunks of the ghost gum (*Eucalyptus papuana*) and the river red gum (*Eucalyptus camaldulensis*) to the rough, deeply grooved black trunk of the red ironbark (*Eucalyptus sideroxylon*), while some species, such as the little snow gum (*Eucalyptus pauciflora*), have beautifully streaked trunks of several colours caused by the shedding of the bark. The fruits and the flowers of the eucalypts also differ markedly in colour, size and time of blossoming, but almost all species are renowned for the large quantities of nectar they produce.

Side by side with the eucalypts are the acacias, more commonly referred to as "wattles". Some 700 species of acacia trees and shrubs grow in Australia — more than half the total number in the world and easily this country's largest floral genus. Like the eucalypts, the acacias vary greatly in size and habitat. The best known species are probably the lovely golden wattle (*Acacia pycnantha*), which, with its fluffy deep yellow flower balls, is the nation's floral emblem, and the common mulga (*Acacia aneura*), a small but widespread tree that imparts a silvery-greyness to much of the inland.

Other trees typical of the Australian landscape include casuarinas (commonly known as "oaks" or "she-oaks"), banksias, melaleucas (known by various names such as paperbark and tea-tree, although this last name strictly applies only to species of *Leptospermum*) and the unique grass-trees (*Xanthorrhoea spp.*), often called "blackboys" or "yaccas". In limited habitats, beautiful endemic trees such as primitive cycads, pandanus, *Livistona* palms, pines and bottle trees are also found.

Australia's wealth of wildflowers is unparalleled. There are many thousands of native species, most of which do not occur anywhere else in the world. By far the greatest number of species — including the famous kangaroo paws (*Anigozanthos spp.*) — are found only in the south-western corner of Western

Australia. However, countless other flowers are widely distributed and almost all regions have some unique plants.

Even Australia's grasses differ from those in other lands, a great many of them being characteristically golden rather than green. About 700 species are indigenous to the continent, while a further 100 or more have been introduced. Most of the native species are tufted and stand erect, although in coastal and marshy regions there are "creeping" varieties. In drier areas, some species are extremely sharp or prickly, and in the north several species are very long. The most widespread genus is *Triodia*, usually known as "spinifex" (but not true *Spinifex*, which is a maritime genus), and other grasses have popular names such as Mitchell grass, kangaroo grass and spear-grass.

Like the plants, much of the wildlife that has evolved in the isolated Australian environment is markedly different from that found in other parts of the world.

The country is famed for its endearing marsupials, which number more than 120 species, ranging from large kangaroos taller than a human to tiny possums no bigger than a garden flower. Without competition from more aggressive mammals, these essentially peaceful creatures have been able to dominate the land and they have developed in a variety of ways to suit almost all habitats that the continent offers.

Although marsupials occur in several other countries, especially in South America, nowhere do they attain anywhere near the numbers and diversity that they do in Australia. Apart from their characteristic of carrying young in a pouch, many Australian marsupials bear little resemblance to one another. Even in such a basic habit as movement they vary greatly, with some species such as kangaroos and wallabies hopping on powerful hind legs and others running, climbing, burrowing or even gliding. Food habits differ, too. Many marsupials are herbivorous, occasionally supplementing their diets with

insects, but about 40 of the smaller species, including the Tasmanian devil (*Sarcophilus harrisii*) and several little marsupial mice and cats, are fierce carnivores that will attack other animals more than twice their own size. A few species have extremely specialised diets, including the slow-moving koala (*Phascolarctos cinereus*), which lives on the leaves of certain eucalypts, and the long-tongued numbat (*Myrmecobius fasciatus*), which eats only termites.

Marsupials are not the only indigenous wildlife inhabiting Australia. The country supports a further 110 or so species of native land mammals (mostly rodents and bats, but also including the dingo and the primitive egg-laying monotremes, the platypus and the echidna), about 420 reptile species, some 720 bird species, more than 200 species of freshwater fish and countless small species such as insects, spiders, crustaceans and amphibians — some of which can survive for years without water, by means such as burrowing or existing only as eggs until sufficient rain falls to trigger them to hatch. Several thousand species of fish have also been recorded in coastal waters and there are about 30 marine mammals, including seals, whales and the vegetarian dugong (*Halicore dugong*).

The most conspicuous of these animals are undoubtedly the beautiful birds. Australia has often been referred to as the "Land of Parrots" and 60 of the world's 320 parrot species are found in various habitats of the continent. Many of these birds are unique to Australia, ranging from brilliantly plumaged galahs, rosellas and lorikeets to handsome cockatoos and the tiny budgerigar (*Melopsittacus undulatus*). Usually flying in flocks, they are an impressive and colourful embellishment to the landscape, especially in featureless areas of the inland.

Honeyeaters and numerous small birds such as wrens, thrushes and robins are also widely distributed across the continent, while beautiful waterbirds such as pelicans, herons and ibis populate lagoons and other waterways. In the north there are magnificent tropical birds, including the elegant jabiru (*Xenorhynchus asiaticus*) and the brolga (*Grus antigone*), and in the south there are penguins and albatrosses. But undoubtedly the best known Australian birds are the laughing kookaburra (*Dacelo gigas*) and the emu (*Dromaius novaehollandiae*).

The wild areas of Australia are essentially safe for man. Nearly all the country's animals are harmless — though some of the reptiles are so bizarre in appearance that they seem almost to be miniatures of prehistoric monsters. Notable among these animals are several spiky-coated dragon lizards, the fish-eating freshwater Johnston crocodile (*Crocodylus johnstoni*) and the giant perentie (*Varanus giganteus*), which grows up to 2 metres long and is reputedly the second largest lizard in the world (after the Komodo dragon of Indonesia). Only in coastal areas and the northern rivers of Australia are there predatory animals, such as the man-eating estuarine or saltwater crocodile (*Crocodylus porosus*) and several sharks. Even the venomous creatures such as certain snakes and spiders seldom attack unless provoked, though several sea animals will inflict a deadly sting. A greater danger across most of the continent is the frequent lack of fresh water and the vast areas of wilderness in which the uninformed visitor could easily become lost.

The country's first human inhabitants, the Aboriginal people, are thought to have migrated to Australia from Asia in several phases, beginning at least 40 000 years ago. Some groups probably came via land bridges that at times connected Australia and New Guinea, others perhaps came by boat. It is estimated that at the time of European settlement there were about 300 000 Aborigines, but there may have been a great many more. These people belonged to numerous "tribes" or "small nations" and spoke many different languages and dialects. However, whilst some customs differed, the basic philosophies and communal lifestyle of all tribes were similar.

The Aborigines developed a remarkable empathy with the land and their traditional knowledge reflects a deep understanding of nature and natural processes. They believe that once the country was without form or life. Then, in the time of the Dreaming, spirit ancestors undertook great journeys, fashioning the landscape and creating everything in it. Part of the creator remains with each feature of the landscape and the various creators are taken as totems by living Aborigines, who became responsible for safeguarding the land. With this sacred relationship, any artificial concept of land ownership does not arise: for the people are inseparably *part of the land* and it is part of them. Deprived of their land, Aboriginal people lose this traditional reason for living and all hope for the future is gone.

At one with nature, the Aborigines found it unnecessary to remodel the environment. They lived a nomadic life, hunting and gathering only enough food and other materials for basic needs. They were not aimless wanderers, but followed a set pattern according to the seasons and the availability of water and food. None of the native animals was suitable for herding, but sometimes the Aborigines "farmed" the land by means such as burning, both to flush out game and to stimulate the regrowth of plants. The dingo (*Canis familiaris*), which is believed to have been brought to Australia by Aboriginal people about 10 000 years ago, is the only animal they domesticated.

Although they did not have any form of writing, the Aborigines' cultural life was extremely rich. Knowledge and traditional lore were handed down verbally from generation to generation through stories, ritual and song, and important beliefs were recorded in beautifully composed petroglyphs (rock carvings) and paintings on rock and bark. In the north, these art forms have been highly developed. Arnhem Land, where traditional lifestyles still survive, contains the most extensive and most significant examples of ancient rock art in the world.

In the care of the Aboriginal people, whose presence rested so lightly on the land, the natural Australian landscape survived intact throughout the centuries that civilisations in Europe and Asia were building man-made monuments and later when Africa and the Americas were being plundered for riches of spices and gold. The only visitors to Australia during these times were traders from Macassar and other parts of south-east Asia, who came annually to collect prized items such as *bêche-de-mer* or trepang (*Thelenota ananas*), turtleshell, pearlshell and sandalwood (*Santalum spp.*).

Recorded European visits to Australia began when the little Dutch ship *Duyfken* commanded by Willem Jansz made a landfall on the east coast of the Gulf of Carpentaria in 1606, but a few stone structures and various artefacts from shipwrecks testify that Portuguese, Spanish and perhaps other navigators probably found the continent earlier. Certainly, enlightened European theorists of the early Middle Ages who believed that the world was round, not flat, postulated the existence of a large continent in the southern hemisphere, which they considered necessary to "balance" the landmasses of the north. This land appeared on maps of the period in a variety of vague outlines, some bearing a marked resemblance to parts of Australia, and came to be known as *Terra Australis Incognita*

— the Unknown South Land.

During the first half of the seventeenth century, Dutch navigators charted much of Australia's northern, western and southern coastlines. But these people were traders searching for goods to sell at a profit in Europe and to them Australia was a most uninviting place. It did not yield spices like the Indies and there was no gold-rich civilisation such as the Spanish and the Portuguese had found in the Americas. Nor was there any civilisation like those of the Far East from which they could buy silks, ornaments and exotic wares. Worse, much of the coastline was extremely treacherous, rivers and lakes were pitifully scarce, and they considered the Aboriginal people to be savages. Following two extensive voyages by Abel Janszoon Tasman in the 1640s, Dutch interest in the southern continent waned, for exploration was too costly to be continued without at least some return.

The English association with Australia began most inauspiciously when the British East India Company ship *Tryal* was wrecked in 1622 on a reef north of the Monte Bello Islands, off the Western Australian coast. By the end of the century the gloomy picture that the Dutch had painted of Australia, or New Holland as it was then called, was confirmed to the British public by the colourful buccaneer William Dampier who, after visiting parts of the west coast, wrote two books, *A New Voyage Around the World* and *A Voyage to New Holland in the Year 1699*, in which he described the continent's landscape as barren, sandy and destitute of water and the Aboriginal inhabitants as "the miserablest People in the world".

Dampier's books did much to discourage further British interest in New Holland. Not until 1770 did James Cook in HM BARK *Endeavour* sail along the east coast of the continent, which he claimed in the name of King George III of Great Britain, and report that the country's "Eastern Side is not that barren and miserable country that Dampier and others have described the Western Side to be".

Nevertheless, British impressions of Australia were still not favourable and only when the American War of Independence of 1775–83 brought an end to the transportation of convicts from England to the British colonies in North America did the remote island-continent start to be seen in a different light. In 1786, following a recommendation by the botanist Sir Joseph Banks who had been with Cook on his voyage of 1770, the British government decided to establish a convict settlement in New Holland.

Thus it was that on 26 January 1788 Australia's first permanent white settlement was founded at Sydney Cove. The presence of the French in the region from about this time did much to prompt further British exploration, and other settlements gradually appeared along the coastline. Although many free settlers began to arrive in Australia, the British continued to view the continent primarily as a prison compound.

To the early white inhabitants, Australia was a strange new land. Because the landscape was outside their former experience, most people thought that it seemed "wrong". Whole families of familiar plants and animals were missing, replaced by trees that were considered to be odd and dull and by wildlife that were regarded as curiosities. The sun was in the north not the south, the seasons were "upside-down", and there appeared to be little in the way of edible fruits, vegetables or palatable game.

Seeking echoes of Europe, the British colonists set about changing parts of the Australian landscape to colours and forms with which they were familiar and to populate the country with animals to which they were accustomed. They built towns like those of their homelands and sought timber and minerals such as gold. By the year 1840, white settlements had been firmly established in various coastal areas of Australia and it was only a matter of time before the interior began to be penetrated, too. Australia was coming to be looked upon by the white man as a land of hope.

The cost of European settlement was borne by the Aboriginal people. The white man drove them from the most fertile lands and irretrievably eroded their way of life. If the Aborigines objected to or tried to prevent the invasion of their country, the newcomers retaliated with superior weapons. Within 100 years, the white man's ignorance, brutality, diseases and "gifts" of poisoned food had eradicated numerous tribes and in Tasmania the entire Aboriginal population had gone. Elsewhere the Aborigines were herded into missions and settlements, and today traditional lifestyles are strongly maintained in only a few areas.

But the nature of much of the land has itself resisted the encroachment of the white man. Many European explorers and settlers lost their lives through thirst, starvation, exposure and shipwreck, and others were defeated simply by the vast distances and the difficulty of communication, by the ruggedness of the terrain, or by prolonged drought or flood. Today the total population of Australia is only about 15 million people, of whom some 85 per cent live in cities and towns. The greater part of the continent is virtually uninhabited by man.

Two hundred years of white settlement in Australia is but a speck in time. However, it has been long enough to consolidate a distinct national identity. Few white Australians today feel nostalgic about the neat green fields and tidy trees of their European countries of origin, for they have grown to love the wide open spaces, the golden-yellow grasses and the gnarled eucalypts of this land.

Now considered to be a rich country, Australia harbours enormous amounts of minerals such as iron ore, bauxite and uranium that are sought for modern technological developments. Without care, exploitation of the land could rapidly destroy the country's vast tracts of precious wilderness, which ultimately are of more far-reaching significance for the future well-being of mankind. □

Australia's geological background

EVER SINCE land first appeared on earth, its contours have been constantly changing. Landmasses have shifted around the globe and changed in shape and size, seas and oceans have come and gone, mountain ranges have been built and then eroded away. In geological terms, Australia — as we know it — has been only recently crafted.

But some of the rocks that make up the continent are very old. Portions of Australia rose out of the sea at least 3000 million years ago and were dry land when vast tracts of Europe and Asia were still submerged. One such area in southern Western Australia, which geologists call Yilgarnia, is one of the oldest lands on Earth, for it has not been submerged since it was first raised.

The beautifully sculptured Wave Rock lies in the heart of Yilgarnia. Other rock formations more than 2000 million years old include the rugged northern plateau country of the Kimberleys, the Hamersley Range and Arnhem Land, while rocks in the MacDonnell Ranges of central Australia are only a little younger. In fact, almost half of Australia's surface rocks were formed more than 600 million years ago — in the most ancient geological times, known as the Precambrian Era — and many scientists believe that the country's younger rocks and its desert sands probably overlie rocks of this great age.

How Australia gained its present outline and position on Earth is explained by two theories which, because of growing evidence, have in recent years become widely accepted: the theories of "continental drift" and "global plate tectonics".

According to the theory of continental drift, all the continents of Earth were joined together some 200 million years ago in one giant landmass that geologists call Pangaea.

About 180 million years ago, Pangaea began to split up at about the Equator, forming two supercontinents: Laurasia, which consisted of the present-day North America, Europe and northern Asia; and Gondwanaland, comprising South America, Africa, India, Australia and Antarctica (and possibly part of south-western China). Later, forces beneath the Earth's crust caused these two supercontinents to fragment and the continents we know today started to drift apart.

Although it is not known when Gondwanaland began to break up, most scientists agree on the sequence of events. It is thought that South America and Africa were the first continents to split away, followed by India, which slowly moved northwards until it collided with Asia, the impact causing the formation of the Himalayas. Finally, about 45 million years ago, Australia and Antarctica separated, slowly drifting to their present positions at a rate of a few centimetres per year.

The way in which the continents move across the planet is explained by the theory of global plate tectonics. It is believed that all the world's landmasses and ocean floors are carried on rigid plates of rock, about 70-150 kilometres thick, which overlie the Earth's mantle. There are about half-a-dozen big plates and a number of smaller ones, and they are thought to be propelled by slow convection currents from deep within the Earth's core. The Australian continent sits in the centre of one of the largest plates, far from the turbulent margins that are thought to create earthquakes and other traumatic earth movements when adjacent plates collide.

Compared with most parts of the Earth, the Australian landmass has been relatively stable for more than 200 million years. Nevertheless, there have been significant changes. Oceans, seas and lakes have at times filled the Centre, coastal outlines have altered, weathering and erosion have removed vast amounts of surface materials, and glaciers, volcanoes and earthquakes have disrupted the land. The last major earth movement, the Kosciusko Uplift which raised the entire eastern side of the continent, occurred only 2-3 million years ago.

When the first Aboriginal people arrived about 40 000 years ago, the face of Australia was very different from what it is now. The central deserts which today cover almost half the continent were then fertile and covered with lush vegetation and freshwater lakes. But about 20 000 years ago, the climate started to change and aridity set in. Within a few centuries the land became dusty and parched, and entire species of plants and animals died out.

At various times landbridges connected mainland Australia with Tasmania and New Guinea, and about 15 000–30 000 years ago there were glaciers in Tasmania and the Kosciusko region and ice caps over other parts of the land. When the ice melted 8000–12 000 years ago, the rising sea levels drowned countless coastal valleys, forming beautiful deep inlets.

Until about 15 000 years ago, the region of the Great Barrier Reef was also dry land. But the sea slowly inundated this area too, creating ideal conditions for corals to build their magnificent limestone structures.

In some parts of Australia, such as around Mt Gambier and western Victoria and also on Queensland's Atherton Tableland, volcanoes were active just a few thousand years ago. Minor tremors and earthquakes still occur in various regions of the continent, but they do not bring the devastation that in recent times has occurred in other lands.

Today, there are three major physiographical divisions of Australia: the Great Western Plateau, composed primarily of extremely old rocks and incorporating most of Western Australia and the Northern Territory, much of South Australia, and parts of western Queensland and New South Wales; the Eastern Highlands (or Great Dividing Range), formed of ancient igneous and sedimentary rocks uplifted by the geologically recent Kosciusko Uplift and extending from the tip of Queensland to Tasmania; and the Central Eastern Lowlands, a depressed region located between the other two and containing many rivers that no longer reach the sea. However, these classifications give only a very broad picture of the structure of the Australian landscape and there are countless variations within each region. □

The dolerite coast

TASMAN PENINSULA

I T IS a reflection of European ancestry that to most Australians the Tasman Peninsula is known only as the location of Port Arthur, site of the best preserved and most extensive ruins of our convict settlements. Buildings such as these, scarcely 150 years old, are all that Australia has to offer in terms of the type of history and background that are so inherent in a European way of life. But today attention is being focussed away from these symbols of the Old World. White Australians are becoming more aware of this vast, strange land which for more than 40 000 years the Aboriginal people have loved and understood so well. Now, even on the Tasman Peninsula, one of the strongest links with our European origins, many Australians are finding that their greatest interest and empathy lie with the natural features of the land.

This tiny peninsula on the south-eastern tip of Tasmania has a diversity of beautiful landscapes. The central areas are hilly, with lovely forests, grasslands and picturesque waterways. But the coast is wild. The sea constantly thunders in against towering grey dolerite cliffs and sandstone headlands, carving magnificent landforms such as caverns, arches and blowholes.

Visually spectacular, this coastline is one of the most treacherous of the continent. It is a last landfall before Antarctica, and apart from being persistently pounded by foaming icy seas, it is often battered by the howling winds of the Roaring Forties. There are very few sheltered beaches and coves.

The Tasman Peninsula was among the earliest parts of Australia to be mapped by European navigators. It was first sighted in 1642 by the Dutchman Abel Janszoon Tasman, after whom it is now named. Various other navigators including Admiral Bruni D'Entrecasteaux and Captain John Cox anchored in nearby bays during the latter part of the following century, but none ventured too close to these wild shores. It was not until the 1800s that Europeans considered the area for settlement, and then not because of its beauty but for its suitability as a site for a prison.

The Tasman Peninsula does not protrude directly from mainland Tasmania. It is attached by a low and narrow isthmus to another peninsula, Forestier Peninsula, which in turn is connected to the mainland. The isthmus joining the two peninsulas is called Eaglehawk Neck and at its narrowest point it is only 20 metres wide.

The basic rocks of the Tasman Peninsula are sandstones formed beneath the sea 200-300 million years ago. When the Tasmanian landmass was violently uplifted about 165 million years ago, molten tongues of black dolerite (a medium-grained igneous rock that looks much like basalt) forced their way up between the existing horizontal strata of sandstone. An interesting feature of dolerite is that as it cools and solidifies into rock it contracts severely, creating prominent vertical cracks. The ceaseless processes of weathering and erosion eventually removed much of the surrounding sandstone, exposing the dolerite in giant masses of long, dark columns. As the former coastline around the Tasman Peninsula has sunk and the sea level has risen, huge walls of dolerite now stand dramatically, sheer above the sea.

Cape Pillar at the south-eastern tip of the Peninsula is the most spectacular of these dolerite cliffs. A massive cluster of columns, it soars nearly 300 metres high. Tasman called this point South Cape but it was renamed Cape Pillar in 1789 by Captain John Cox who charted the southern and eastern coasts of Tasmania. It is a distinctive landmark that can be seen from afar by ships coming from both east and south, and it is separated from tiny, sheer-sided Tasman Island by a strait less than a kilometre wide.

The dolerite at Cape Raoul on the south-western part of the Tasman Peninsula is almost as impressive, rising in a mighty wall of vertical columns which tower up to 180 metres above the sea. The columns are compact on the western side but taper down gradually towards the eastern end, where they are craggy and appear like organ pipes. At Cape Hauy, north of Cape Pillar, several columns stand separated from the main mass. Long and narrow fingers of dolerite, they reach to incredible heights. The aptly named Needle is one of the tallest of these towers, rising to about 90 metres above the sea, and other notable spires include the Candlestick and the Lanterns.

In many parts of the peninsula, unusual contrasts in the coastal scenery occur where the dolerite gives way to sandstone and mudstone. South of Port Arthur, wave and wind erosion along a fault line at the contact zone between sandstone and dolerite has created the Remarkable Cave, a narrow and rectangular-roofed tunnel extending about 40 metres through the cliffs, from the sea to a chasm on the landward side. Waves rush in and out of the cave all year round, with the exception of a few days around Easter when the tides are at their lowest ebb and it is possible to walk right through the tunnel to the sea. At other times the fury of the waves makes it very dangerous to enter the cavern.

The powerful wave action is also responsible for many blowholes and caves in the sandstone near Eaglehawk Neck, at the head of the peninsula. Sometimes the sea has broken right through the rock, forming deep coastal gorges. The 60-metre-deep Devil's Kitchen is one of the most terrifying of these clefts, with thundering waters surging upwards as though in a cauldron about to boil over. Nearby, a massive natural land bridge called Tasman's Arch spans another rocky gorge, its ceiling looming more than 50 metres above churning waters. But the full force of the sea is best demonstrated at the Blowhole, where on a rough day huge jets of spray are flung skyward with every incoming wave.

On the marine platform at the base of Eaglehawk Neck, the work of the waves has produced a rare natural feature, the Tessellated Pavements. Looking like the work of a stonemason, these plazas of rectangular paving blocks are the result of erosion along the joint lines of a very fine-grained sandstone.

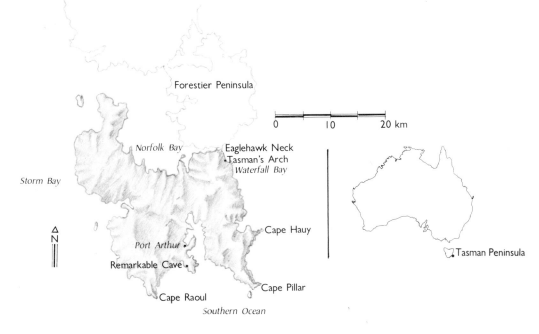

Another unusual and very beautiful section of coastal scenery is located at Waterfall Bay a few kilometres south of Eaglehawk Neck. Here the architect is not the waves, but a stream, for, as the name suggests, a waterfall cascades over the cliffs and plunges directly into the sea.

To Colonel George Arthur, the fourth Governor of Tasmania (or Van Diemen's Land, as it was then called), the physical characteristics of the Tasman Peninsula were ideal for the establishment of a convict settlement. Its rugged coastline and treacherous waters would present enormous obstacles to anyone hoping to escape by sea and the only landward escape route was the narrow strip of land at Eaglehawk Neck, which could be easily patrolled. Arthur called the peninsula "nature's natural penitentiary".

The first people Arthur attempted to confine on the Tasman Peninsula, however, were not convicts but Aborigines. In 1830 he mounted his notorious "Black Line" campaign to herd all the remaining Tasmanian Aborigines onto the peninsula, beyond a border known as the Black Line, and thereby put an end to troubles between blacks and whites. The attempt was abortive. About 2000 men were recruited to round up an Aboriginal population of approximately the same number, but after seven weeks and an expenditure of £35 000, they had succeeded in bringing in only one woman and a boy. The Aborigines, of course, were philosophically bound to their environment and it was unthinkable for those from other parts of the island to leave their own land and go to live on the Tasman Peninsula. With their knowledge of the surroundings it was easy to evade Arthur's men, but unfortunately the failure of the scheme did not save them from eventual extinction.

The Port Arthur Penal Settlement was established later in 1830 on a picturesque bay in the heart of the Tasman Peninsula, where a sawyer's camp had previously operated for a brief time. Facilities were very rudimentary at first, but during the years 1835-7 many fine stone and brick buildings were constructed. The prisoners were put to work at a variety of tasks including farming, timber-felling, mining and several manufacturing endeavours. Subsidiary stations were erected on other parts of the Peninsula, including Point Puer (Latin for "boy") across the bay from Port Arthur, where a boys' prison was established to keep young felons separated from hardened adult prisoners.

For some time Port Arthur was the industrial centre of the colony. Large shipments of goods to and from the settlement were handled at the harbour, while smaller shipments were often sent to a receiving station at Norfolk Bay, on the western side of the peninsula (nearer to Hobart Town), and from there transported overland to Port Arthur via a railway with carriages pulled by convicts.

Although life at Port Arthur was harsh, the settlement never had as great a reputation for brutality as did several other convict stations in Australia. Nonetheless, many convicts attempted

to escape. Of those who were successful, nearly all took treacherous seaward routes. Escape across the narrow strip of land at Eaglehawk Neck was practically impossible, for it was not only patrolled by soldiers 24 hours a day but was also guarded from shore to shore by a line of fierce dogs which were tethered on short chains so that there was only a few centimetres' clearance between each. This deterrent and many other aspects of the conditions at Port Arthur provided inspiration for Marcus Clarke's classic novel *For the Term of his Natural Life*.

The penal settlement at Port Arthur was abandoned in 1877, more than 20 years after transportation to the colony had ceased. By this time, free settlers had been living on the Tasman Peninsula for some 15 years. Attempts were soon made to remove the stigma of the convict days and for several years Port Arthur was known as "Carnarvon". However, when the government offered the old convict establishment for sale in 1889, little interest was generated and only a small portion was sold. Two bushfires, one shortly after the abandonment of the settlement and the other about 20 years later, destroyed most of the buildings and neglect caused the rest of them to fall into disrepair.

Attempts to encourage visitors to the area began in 1892 when a photographer named John Watt Beattie published a booklet showing interesting convict relics to be seen there. But not until the 1920s did people start to visit Port Arthur in substantial numbers.

Today Port Arthur is a historical reserve and a main attraction of the Tasman Peninsula. The remains of several buildings can still be seen, standing in a setting of neat English-style gardens and lawns. Only two buildings are still intact: the lunatic asylum, which has been restored and converted into a visitors' centre, and the Commandant's residence, now a private home. The most notable of the buildings in ruins are the four-storey penitentiary and the church, the latter being a fine piece of nineteenth-century Gothic Revival architecture designed by a convict named Mason. It was ecumenical, but had no name and was never consecrated, supposedly because a murder and a suicide occurred there during its construction.

Other convict relics elsewhere on the peninsula include parts of the man-powered railway, a farm, timber mills and coal mines. The tiny *Ile des Morts* (Isle of the Dead) in the middle of the bay at Port Arthur also stands as a grim reminder of the convict days. It is the graveyard of 1769 convicts and 150 soldiers and free settlers: the convicts were buried in unmarked mass graves, whereas the soldiers and settlers were accorded headstones.

The presence of the orderly historic sites on the Tasman Peninsula presents a fascinating contrast with the wild beauty of the surrounding countryside. Although there are now several townships on the peninsula, large areas remain as natural bushland and the grand dolerite cliffs and other spectacular coastal landforms are protected as scenic reserves.   □

. . . Narrow fingers of dolerite
reach to incredible heights

1. Cape Pillar
2. Cape Hauy
3. The Candlestick, Cape Hauy
4. The Needle, Cape Hauy

*Looking like the work of a stonemason,
these natural plazas are the result
of erosion . . .*

1–4. Tessellated Pavements, Eaglehawk Neck
5. Remarkable Cave
6. Tasman Arch, Eaglehawk Neck

2

3

4

5

6

Bastion of pink granite

FREYCINET PENINSULA

View across Thouin Bay to Cape Forestier

O N THE mid-east coast of Tasmania, the long and slender Freycinet Peninsula juts prominently into the Tasman Sea, presenting dramatic seascapes of sweeping white beaches and steep headlands set against a backdrop of precipitous pink granite hills.

Formerly part of a mountain range, the peninsula was created about 6000 years ago when the ice melted at the end of the last ice age. As the sea rose, the lower land was drowned, forming the large inlet of Great Oyster Bay and leaving the high hills standing like a protective bastion along the coast.

The most prominent landmark of the peninsula is the Hazards, a line of high granite hills which forms a mighty barricade across the width of the land. On the secluded southern side of this barrier a neck of low land separates the peninsula's most beautiful beaches: Hazards Beach on the protected western shore and the crescent-shaped white beach of Wineglass Bay on the eastern seaboard. The highest parts of the peninsula are further south, culminating in Mt Freycinet (620 metres).

A feature of the granite on the exposed coastal areas of the Freycinet Peninsula is that it is covered with fiery red lichens which contrast strikingly with the brilliant blue of the surrounding waters. In some places, especially on boulders along the beaches, different types of lichen grow near each other in concentric patches. Ranging in colour from bright yellow, orange and red to white and pale green, they give a fascinating "painted picture" effect to the rocks.

Lichens are dual organisms—an alga and a fungus living together and functioning as one. They are one of the earliest forms of plant life to colonise a bare rock surface, being preceded only by other microscopic algae that roughen the smooth rockface sufficiently for the lichens to gain a foothold. To absorb nourishment, lichens secrete acids which dissolve the cementing substances in the rock and thus loosen tiny rock granules. Eventually these granules, together with particles of humus from dead lichens, gather in tiny cracks and crevices where they provide a foothold for the next plant colonists, the mosses. The tiny rootlets of the mosses break down the rocks even further, and in time small amounts of soil build up, enabling colonisation by grasses and small shrubs. This succession of plant types is very slow in places where soil and

Coles Bay
Great Oyster Bay
The Hazards
Wineglass Bay
Hazards Beach
Promise Bay
N
Mt Freycinet
Tasman Sea
Bryan's Beach
Schouten Passage
Schouten Island
0   5   10 km
Freycinet Peninsula

water do not accumulate easily, and on the exposed steep rock surfaces on the coast at the Freycinet Peninsula, huge areas of granite are covered only by lichens.

The remainder of the Freycinet Peninsula is clothed in heaths and dry forests. Most of the trees are hardy eucalypts, with thickets of tea-trees *(Leptospermum spp.)* forming a dense undergrowth. A rare tree, the Oyster Bay pine *(Callitris tasmanica)*, is endemic to the region.

In spring and summer the heathlands are embellished by myriad wildflowers. Particularly common are the white flowers of both the wedding bush *(Ricinocarpus pinifolius)* and the pretty *Thryptomene micrantha* shrub, which is unique to the peninsula and as yet does not have a common name. Colour is brought by plants such as boronia, native indigofera, a variety of lilies, the blue-flowering kangaroo apple *(Solanum laciniatum)* and more than 100 species of orchid.

In many ways the scenery of the Freycinet Peninsula seems to have more in common with areas of mainland Australia than with other parts of Tasmania. The rocks are granite, whereas the nearby areas are primarily covered by dolerite and sandstone, and whilst temperatures are cool, the rainfall is lower than in most other parts of the island. Although there are numerous small creeks on the peninsula, there are no major rivers and fresh water often becomes scarce, especially in summer. These factors have had a marked effect on the vegetation, which is drier than that usually found in Tasmania.

Covering an area of about 6500 hectares, the peninsula was declared the Freycinet National Park on 29 August 1916. Together with Mt Field National Park, which was proclaimed on the same day, it shares the distinction of being the first of Tasmania's national parks. It was enlarged to almost 11 000 hectares in 1967 by the addition of Schouten Island, which lies off the southern extremity of the peninsula, separated from it by the narrow Schouten Passage.

With walking tracks but no vehicle access, the park is an important wildlife sanctuary, inhabited by a great variety of animals including almost all Tasmanian bird species except those endemic to rainforests and alpine moorlands.

As in all parts of Tasmania, the marsupials and other mammals in the park are sub-species of those found on mainland Australia, their primary difference being a thicker fur which they have developed to cope with the colder climate. The largest marsupial is the forester kangaroo *(Macropus giganteus tasmaniensis)*, a sub-species of the great grey kangaroo of the mainland and the only true kangaroo in Tasmania. The State's only wallabies, the Bennett's wallaby *(Macropus rufogriseus)* and the smaller rufous or pademelon wallaby *(Thylogale billardierii)*, are also found in the park.

Seabirds and marine life are important features of this coastal park. Common bird species include the muttonbird, the little or fairy penguin, cormorants, the Australian gannet *(Morus serrator)* and the white-breasted sea eagle, while the lagoons and swamps also provide breeding grounds for waterfowls such as the black swan *(Cygnus atratus)* and the coot *(Fulica atra)*.

Before the white man came to Australia, both Freycinet Peninsula and Schouten Island were inhabited by Aborigines. Today, the only traces of these people are found in middens, the most abundant of which are in the low sand dunes backing Hazards Beach. But they are also remembered in the names of landscape features, such as Lugunta Creek (meaning "tiger cat") and Malunna Creek ("bird's nest"). For the most part, however, the nomenclature used today is of European origin, commemorating the visits of various navigators and early settlers, and it tells much of the subsequent history of the area.

The first European to sight this coast was the Dutchman Abel Janszoon Tasman in 1642. Tasman named Schouten Island and called the peninsula "Vanderlyn Island", not realising that it was connected to the coast. His error was discovered in 1802 when a party from an expedition commanded by the Frenchman Nicolas Baudin explored the shore. Baudin renamed the peninsula in honour of one or both of the brothers Louis and Henri Freycinet, who were members of the expedition, and gave French names to other places along the coast.

European settlers arrived in this part of Tasmania in 1821, but their progress was very slow because of conflicts with the Oyster Bay Aborigines, considered the most hostile of the Tasmanian tribes. Much blood was shed on both sides until finally the original owners of the land were wiped out.

For nearly a century various industries operated intermittently on Freycinet Peninsula and Schouten Island including coal mining, quarrying, whaling, and sheep and cattle grazing.

Both Coles Bay and the little township of the same name, which sits at the head of the peninsula, are named after an early settler, Silas Cole, who for a time made a living by burning shells for lime. His little hut was a welcome sight to many visitors, including one Captain Albert "Black" Hazard whose whaling ship *Promise* was wrecked in the mid-1800s on a rock in what is now called Promise Bay. While his crew took refuge on a tiny island (later known as Refuge Island), Captain Hazard swam ashore and made his way to Silas Cole's hut for help. In doing so, he skirted the prominent granite hills that are now named after him.

Today, on both the peninsula and the island, only a few relics such as the ruins of old buildings, railways and jetties remain as reminders of those early days. The status of national park, however, does not entirely protect the area from commercial development. A privately owned quarry operates near Malunna Creek at the foot of the Hazards, and applications have been made for permission to commence further quarrying elsewhere in the park. Such activities would badly disfigure the landscape and damage plant and animal habitats. Conservationists have been successful, so far, in preventing these potential disruptions to the environment. □

1. Looking southward from Cape Tourville to Freycinet Peninsula
2. Hazards Beach, with Mt Freycinet beyond
3. Bennett's wallaby (*Macropus rufogriseus*)
4. Southern blue-tongued skink (*Tiliqua nigrolutea*)
5. Lichen-painted boulders, Sleepy Bay

Gem of the rainforest

RUSSELL FALLS

S URROUNDED by emerald green ferns and mosses, Russell
Falls stream down over a tiered rockface like a series of
crystalline veils. These glittering cascades are the highlight of
an exquisite temperate rainforest at the entrance to Mt Field
National Park.

Although the rainforest has none of the harshness of light
and colour normally associated with Australian scenery, its
character is uniquely Australian. The dominant trees are the
giant mountain ash *(Eucalyptus regnans)* and alpine ash
(Eucalyptus delegatensis), their long bare trunks soaring 60
metres high before branching into leafy canopies which filter
the sunlight through in a gentle, flickering glow. Beneath them
grow a variety of smaller eucalypts and other characteristically
Australian trees, such as the black-trunked Tasmanian
"myrtle" *(Nothofagus cunninghamii)* and the smooth-barked
sassafras *(Atherosperma moschatum)*.

The understorey is moist and luxuriantly green. Crystal clear
streams trickle through lovely fern-tree gullies, every so often
hastening their pace to create tiny waterfalls and mini rapids.
A great variety of smaller ferns grow in creeper-like tangles
and numerous mosses and lichens spread like soft carpets over
rocks and fallen tree trunks.

Russell Falls, with a total drop of about 45 metres, is the
most spectacular of three large waterfalls in the rainforest. At
the top the water slides over a few step-like platforms, then
it sprays down in two sheer stages of about 15 metres each
to a creek at the base of a lush, shaded valley. The lower fall
is about 12 metres wide and it is possible to walk across the
rocky bar separating it from the upper fall, which is slightly
narrower.

It seems impossible that falls of such beauty could be con-
fused with those anywhere else, but in the early days of
European settlement that is exactly what happened. The central
region of Tasmania is studded with many beautiful waterfalls
and although Russell Falls are the most grand, there are others
which, on a smaller scale, could be described in a similar manner.

The falls that we know today as Russell Falls were previously
called Browning's Falls after a settler who discovered them
around 1856. The original "Russell's Falls" are believed to be
on a tributary of the Derwent River and were named after a
member of an exploring party who crossed them "over a rocky
bar". An initial confusion between the two waterfalls is easy
enough to understand, but somehow it was perpetuated and
with the passage of time the mistaken identity remained.

A short distance beyond Russell Falls, on the same creek,
is the second and very different waterfall in the rainforest.
Named Horseshoe Falls, it flows down from two sides of a rock
ledge, meeting at the base to form an upside-down horseshoe
shape. The third waterfall in the area, Lady Barron Falls, is
located about 3 kilometres to the south-west and is similar to
Russell Falls, but much smaller. It is named after the wife of

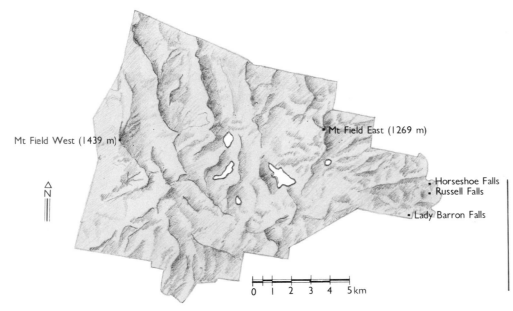

. . . At ground level the light might be reduced to perhaps one-fiftieth of that outside the forest

1. Russell Falls Creek, below the main waterfall
2. Soft tree-ferns (*Dicksonia antarctica*) form a tunnel over a pathway in the rainforest surrounding Russell Falls

Russell Falls

Sir Harry Barron, who was Governor of Tasmania between 1909 and 1913.

The waterfalls are the main attraction of the rainforest, but equally interesting is the vegetation, especially the ferns.

There are some 7000 known species of fern throughout the world, of which about 335 are found in Australia, many of them in Tasmania. They evolved about 300 million years ago and most of them require a cool, damp environment with little fluctuation in temperature or humidity. At Mt Field, conditions are ideal. The mountain slopes and the canopies of the taller trees protect the understorey from the drying effects of the sun and the wind, and the high regular rainfall (over 1000 millimetres per annum) provides the water they need. Prominent species found in the park include several fish ferns, kangaroo fern, bat's wing fern, mother shield fern, hare's foot fern and, perhaps the most interesting of all, the soft tree-fern (*Dicksonia antarctica*), often referred to as "man-fern" because of the soft mass of gingery, hair-like fibres at the top of its tall trunk.

The ferns are particularly prevalent in the sheltered, well-watered gullies, where they comprise at least 80 per cent of the plant cover. The various species have different light requirements and tend to grow almost in layers, those requiring the most light growing to the highest levels, successively shading other species that require less and less light, until at ground level the light might be reduced to perhaps one-fiftieth of that outside the forest. Other moisture-loving plants including mosses, lichens, vines and climbers need more light and grow on the trunks of taller trees, adding further to the greenness of the forest.

Above the gullies the forest is more exposed to the sun and the wind, and the ferns gradually give way to a wet "sclerophyll" forest of eucalypts and other hardy plants. The luminescent light greens become less dominant, replaced by the familiar darker greens of the Australian bush.

In the past this lovely area was inhabited by groups of Tasmanian Aborigines. Food was abundant, and delicacies relished by the Aborigines included a starchy pith which is found near the crown of the soft tree-fern and a small fungus (*Cyttaria gunnii*) that sometimes grows on the *Nothofagus* "myrtle" and in appearance resembles bunches of yellow grapes. Today the forest is the sole domain of a variety of birds and animals, all of which are protected. The most frequently seen species are the smaller birds such as the pink robin (*Petroica rodinogaster*), the satin flycatcher (*Myiagra cyanoleuca*) and the scrub tit (*Sericornus magna*), and marsupials such as the rufous and Bennett's wallabies (*Thylogale billardierii* and *Macropus rufogriseus*).

Russell Falls and the surrounding rainforest were proclaimed a reserve as early as March 1885. Thirty years later, on 29 August 1916, the reserve was enlarged to form Mt Field National Park which, with the Freycinet Peninsula, was one of the first two national parks in Tasmania. It is named after Judge Barron Field, a London barrister and *littérateur* who in 1817 took up an appointment as Judge of the Supreme Court of New South Wales. He subsequently wrote Australia's first volume of verse, *First Fruits of Australian Poetry*, published in 1819, and in June of the same year founded Australia's first bank. As Tasmania was at that time still under the control of New South Wales, Judge Field visited the island as an itinerant judge in 1819 and 1821.

Mt Field National Park originally covered an area of only a little over 2000 hectares around Russell Falls, but this was later increased to about 16 950 hectares. Unfortunately, as has all too often been the case, the status of national park did not give a permanent guarantee of preservation of the natural environment. Despite protests, a special bill put through State Parliament enabled 1490 hectares, including some of the finest stands of mountain ash, to be excised in 1949 for paper pulping. By way of replacement, 1520 hectares of mixed forest were added to the park.

Today Mt Field National Park covers an area of almost 17 000 hectares. It is composed primarily of dolerite and sandstone, although in some places, such as around Russell Falls, much of the sandstone has been eroded to expose dark mudstones. The landscape is mountainous, with the dense eucalypt forests and rainforests of the lower slopes gradually giving way, as the altitude increases, to moorlands and sparsely clad alpine scenery. The highest peaks in the park are Mt Field West (1439 metres) and Mt Field East (1269 metres), and the country between them is adorned with many lakes, mostly of glacial origin. But the rainforest is the most beautiful part of the park and Russell Falls, with its delicate falling veils, is undoubtedly its finest jewel. □

1

A unique wilderness

TASMANIA'S SOUTH-WEST

T HE South-West of Tasmania is one of Australia's—and the world's—most precious wilderness areas. Described by UNESCO as a region of "incomparable significance and value", its rugged landscape and harsh climate are formidable barriers that have prevented colonisation by imported plant and animal species. It is one of Earth's few remaining temperate environments in which the natural balance of life has not been altered by man.

Wild and remote, this region has a unique scenic grandeur with a wide range of magnificent landforms and extraordinary vegetation. Jagged mountain chains rise one after the other, their steep slopes covered with dense tangled forests. Glistening beacons of white quartzite tower over tiny glacial lakes and vigorous rivers force their way through deep ravines, forming countless foaming rapids and waterfalls. There are no foothills, and at places the mountain ridges give way abruptly to sweeping buttongrass plains and alpine moorlands. On the coast, high cliffs drop sheer to the sea, for there are few beaches and only a handful of inlets.

This scenery is markedly different from that found in other parts of Australia. Apart from a very small area of the Kosciusko Plateau in New South Wales, only the South-West and other highland areas of Tasmania were affected by glaciers during the last ice age. In the South-West the great age, resistance and contortion of the rocks has resulted in distinctive landforms which still look much as they would have done when the ice melted some 6000–12 000 years ago.

The area of the South-West wilderness is not clearly defined, but it is generally taken to mean an estimated 13 000 square kilometres of land in the south-western corner of Tasmania which is not encumbered by roads or other permanent constructions of man. Like the rest of Tasmania, it lies within the belt of the Roaring Forties, those wild prevailing winds which with the absence of land barriers blow strongly and persistently across the icy Southern Ocean, bringing rough seas and a cool, rainy climate. Fierce storms with torrential downpours and frequent sleet, hail and snow are characteristic of the region all year round, although in the summer months of January and February there is usually some relief.

Much of the South-West comprises very ancient rocks laid down as sediments more than 700 million years ago and then metamorphosed (changed under heat and pressure) into quartzites and schists. Several phases of intense folding have thrown the strata into huge mountains, which have subsequently been worn down by erosion, removing many of the schists and other softer rocks to form wide valleys and leaving the harder quartzites exposed in massive ridges of jagged vertical strata. The later glacial activity has accentuated both the cragginess of the slopes and the rounded contours of the valleys, creating a remarkably contrasting landscape.

The Western Arthur Range, the Sentinel Range and the Frankland Range are superb examples of this type of scenery, with beautiful formations of many-coloured rocks often exposed near the summits. But most impressive of all are the gigantic white towers of Federation Peak and Frenchman's Cap.

Federation Peak, a pinnacle rising to an altitude of 1223 metres at the south-eastern end of the Arthur Range, is perhaps the most spectacular landform in the South-West. Composed of whitish-grey quartzite, the pinnacle itself is more than 600 metres tall. It is flanked by several similar but blunt-topped peaks, all of which rise from the semi-circular rim of a gigantic cirque (a basin-shaped hollow formed by glacial erosion) and are separated from one another by deep, sheer gaps. At their base, virtually in the centre of the amphitheatre formed by the cirque, is lovely Lake Geeves, facing the south-east. But more intriguing is tiny Hanging Lake, sitting high amid the pinnacles at an elevation of about 1000 metres and looking almost as though it might fall over the side of the cliff. This lake is only a few hundred metres south-west of Federation Peak, but it is separated from it by an immense chasm.

Frenchman's Cap, far to the north-west of Federation Peak, is equally imposing, rising sheer on one side for more than 600 metres, the last 400 of which are composed of pure-white quartzite. Reaching an altitude of 1433 metres, it can be seen from the sea some 50 kilometres to the west and is thought to have been named in 1791 by the English navigator George Vancouver because of a fancied resemblance to the Phrygian caps commonly worn by French Revolutionaries in the eighteenth century. An obvious remnant of glaciation, the peak is ringed by cirques and tarns (small mountain-rimmed glacial lakes), while the mountain massif from which it rises is skirted almost full circle by the Franklin River and tributary streams.

This scenery dominated by quartzite peaks is typical of the central and western areas of the wilderness. However, in the far east of the region the mountain landscape is quite different, though still shaped by glaciation. Here, at places such as the Hartz Mountains, the rocks are primarily ancient folded sandstones and limestones capped by dolerite of the same age and origin as that on the Tasman Peninsula and elsewhere in eastern Tasmania.

The Mt Anne massif, a circular area of dolerite completely surrounded by ancient quartzite regions, is a magnificent example of this type of scenery. Located just east of Lake Pedder, it is a series of jagged peaks, the highest of which, Mt Anne itself, rises as a pyramidal summit to an altitude of 1425 metres. Wide glacial passes separate it from the adjacent peaks of Mt Eliza and Mt Lot. These and other main peaks are often snow-capped and hidden under a veil of cloud, giving them a misty profile that contrasts with the starkness of the dark, bare dolerite rocks. Lower down, glaciers have gouged out enormous cirques that now carry beautiful lakes, the largest and most impressive being Lake Judd, lying at the base of 300-metre-high cliffs on the southern side of Mt Eliza.

A notable feature of the Mt Anne massif is that a great deal

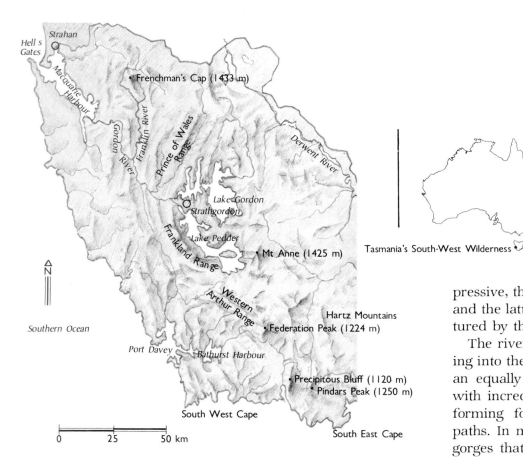

The trees and shrubs become more and more stunted as altitude and exposure to the elements increase

Looking across to the pyramidal summit of Mt Anne, from Mt Eliza

of the underlying rocks are dolomite, a very soluble form of limestone which has become honeycombed with extremely deep caves. Since many shafts are snow-filled for most of the year, very few caverns have been explored or even discovered, but because of the high relief of the massif it seems likely that the area may include Australia's deepest caves. The widely-known Hastings Caves, some distance to the south-east, also occur in a dolomite belt.

The wild South-West coast makes a fitting border to this beautiful, rugged region. During the last ice age the coast extended a further 20-50 kilometres into the sea. When the ice melted, the sea level gradually rose, drowning the former coastal plain and leaving the higher hilltops as islands, such as those of the Maatsuyker group. Today the seas pound against steep cliffs, for there are few low areas or inlets other than two large drowned river valleys, Macquarie Harbour and Port Davey. These openings contain many bays and points, and several islands, but their shores generally rise abruptly and in most places dense forests grow right to the water's edge.

One of the most panoramic sections of the coast lies to the east of Port Davey, between two low but imposing promontories known as South East Cape and South West Cape. Here the coast is indented by wildly beautiful bays such as New Harbour, Cox Bight, Louisa Bay and Surprise Bay, and in a few places the rough surf pounds in to tiny white beaches. Prion Beach, the longest beach on the south coast, is also located in this area, its 6.5-kilometre-long ribbon of sand dunes forming a buffer that protects the waters of New River Lagoon, which lies beyond, from the onslaught of the southern seas. From the pebbly shores of the lagoon the South-West's most spectacular coastal landform, Precipitous Bluff, soars to 1120 metres, its densely forested lower slopes giving way abruptly to a dramatic capping of sheer 300-metre-high dolerite cliffs. The lower portion of the bluff, composed of limestone, is believed to contain countless caves hidden beneath the forest growth. To the east a sister mountain, Pindars Peak, reaching 1250 metres, looms majestically in the distance and on a clear day the white spire of Federation Peak can just be seen far to the north-west.

Although no more than 150 metres high, the rocky promontories of South East Cape and South West Cape are also im-

pressive, the former being the southernmost point of Australia and the latter a granite intrusion that has been superbly sculptured by the elements.

The river systems that flow through the wilderness, emptying into the inlets or finding their way directly to the sea, have an equally pristine beauty. They pour down the mountains with incredible force, plunging into numerous waterfalls and forming foaming rapids wherever boulders obstruct their paths. In many places they pass through narrow ravines and gorges that tower with dramatic suddenness, sometimes several hundred metres high. In times of flood the water levels in these gorges rise by as much as 10 metres. The rivers then rush furiously from source to mouth, but during calmer periods they have many tranquil reaches.

The main artery of the South-West is the Gordon River. Rising in Lake Richmond near the King William Range, it weaves through the wilderness for some 180 kilometres, passing through great chasms and collecting numerous tributaries before emptying into the eastern end of Macquarie Harbour. In one particularly striking section of the river, known as the Splits, the waters pour through three extremely narrow gorges with 100-metre-high cavernous rock overhangs and masses of boulders that have been sculptured and polished smooth by the massive volumes of water which surge through in times of flood.

About 45 kilometres upstream from its mouth, the Gordon is joined by its most impressive tributary, the Franklin River. From its source in the Cheyne Range in Tasmania's central highlands to its junction with the Gordon, the 125-kilometre-long Franklin drops 1400 metres, passing through several major gorges, the most spectacular of which is a 10-kilometre-long winding corridor known as the Great Ravine. The largest gorge in Tasmania, it is a combination of four wild rapids and five long peaceful reaches, with contrasting names such as the Churn, Serenity Sound, Thunderush and the Sanctum. Some parts of the ravine are enclosed by tall, sheer cliffs, but elsewhere the rocky sides merge into steep, densely forested slopes which tower up to 600 metres above the level of the water. As in all the region's rivers, the floodwaters of centuries have carved deep basins and caves in the base of many of the cliff walls.

The vegetation of the South-West is among the most fascinating in Australia. The rugged environment and the wet climate have enabled only thin, infertile soils to develop over most of the region and consequently only very hardy plants are able to survive. Temperate rainforests and peat-forming heaths and sedges form the main plant cover, but there are also areas of eucalypt forest and alpine herblands. Unlike most alpine regions, however, there is no distinct treeline: instead many trees simply adapt to local conditions, becoming more and more stunted as altitude and exposure to the elements increase. Due to the isolation of the wilderness, several of the plant species

are unique to the region, while many other species are found only here and in nearby areas of Tasmania. Interestingly, a number of plants have affinities with existing or fossil species found in New Zealand, South America and other lands of the Southern Ocean.

The location of the different plant communities in the South-West is very complex and depends on a variety of factors, particularly soil, drainage, altitude, aspect and frequency of bushfires. The influence of fire seems most strange in the South-West, which, with an average annual rainfall in the highland regions of more than 3000 millimetres, is Australia's wettest region. However, the widespread buttongrass can burn within hours of rain and the eucalypt leaves, with their volatile oils, are also readily inflammable. As eucalypts need sunshine and can regenerate after burning, whereas rainforest species need shade and moisture for regeneration, the occurrence of fire has an important bearing on the types of trees that are dominant in a particular area. For example, after a fire eucalypts soon start to grow, and if there are further fires they continue to regenerate prolifically. If, however, further fires do not occur, the cover afforded by the growing eucalypts creates ideal conditions for the regrowth of rainforest species. Should there be no fire for several hundred years the eucalypts will die, leaving only pure rainforest species. Indeed, were it not for bushfires, almost the entire South-West would be covered by rainforest, leaving only comparatively small areas of alpine moorlands and sedgelands on soils too waterlogged to support tree or shrub growth. As it is, about a third of the wilderness is covered by heathlands and sedgelands, while quite large areas are taken up by eucalypt forests and flowering herblands. Nevertheless, rainforests still form the most significant plant communities, occurring in the lower and medium altitudes up to about 1000 metres.

The most common tree in the rainforests is the evergreen Tasmanian "myrtle" *(Nothofagus cunninghamii)*, also known as "Antarctic beech". A handsome tree, it grows more than 30 metres tall and has a thick, rough-barked black trunk and a dense foliage of deep green leaves. According to local soil conditions, a variety of other trees may share the forest with the myrtle including the fragrant sassafras *(Atherosperma moschatum)* and several superb endemic conifers. Ferns, mosses, liverworts and other small plants form a moist and rich green understorey.

Although now very rare, the most impressive conifer of the rainforests is the stately Huon pine *(Dacrydium franklinii)*, which grows on swampy or moist soils of the river flats. Taking several centuries to mature, this tree is renowned for the great age to which it can live. Some Huons have been dated as being 2000-3000 years old, although most surviving stands are considerably younger. The tree is usually less than 35 metres tall and has a slightly rough grey-barked trunk, dark green spindly foliage and minute fruiting cones. Other beautiful conifers of the South-West include the brown-trunked King Billy or King William pine *(Athrotaxis selaginoides)*, which is found on quite infertile soils and grows 35-40 metres tall, and the celery-top pine *(Phyllocladus aspleniifolius)*, growing 20-25 metres tall, usually on acidic soils.

The acidic regions of the rainforests also support one of the South-West's most notorious trees, the horizontal *(Anodopetalum biglandulosum)*. Named because of its peculiar growth pattern, this plant initially sends up a slender main stem which grows vertically to a height of 5-10 metres, then bends under its own weight to a horizontal position. New branches growing from the fallen stem also bend, and become very tangled. This process continues and eventually the branches of the trees become so intertwined that they form an impenetrable wall of scrub, sometimes as high as 30 metres. Thick forests of the horizontal scrub have been a major obstacle preventing man from reaching many parts of the wilderness.

Apart from the rainforests, the South-West is famed for its windswept plains of tawny buttongrass *(Gymnoschoenus sphaerocephalus)*, which are largely responsible for the characteristic tea-coloured stain of the water in rivers and lakes of the region. A large and tufted bog-rush with a distinctive round button on the end of the stalks, the buttongrass is the dominant plant in the sedgelands and heathlands of the wilderness. In poorly drained areas it grows in tall tussocks separated by muddy depressions, but elsewhere it forms small mounds that make a comparatively even ground surface. About 100 other plant species may grow with the buttongrass, the most common being the tea-tree *(Melaleuca squarrosa)* and the pale yellow-flowering silver banksia *(Banksia marginata)*. The vine-like bauera *(Bauera rubioides)*, which is almost as notorious as the horizontal, is common on the margins of the buttongrass plains and along the banks of watercourses. A sprawling shrub with a long wiry stem, it grows in a very tangled mass with other scrambling plants and is extremely difficult to traverse. It is sometimes known as "native rose" because its pink or white flowers are somewhat rose-like. In some areas walking is also made difficult by thickets of *Richea scoparia*, a tall, spiked shrub which is easily recognisable in summer by its magnificent display of crimson, yellow and white flowers.

An unusual plant often found both on the plains and in the forests of the highlands is the pandani *(Richea pandanifolia)* which, although resembling a tropical palm, is in fact a member of the heath family. Growing 4-9 metres in height, its trunk is crowned by a graceful array of slender grass-like leaves almost a metre long. Dead leaves of past seasons generally drape like a skirt around the lower part of the trunk, making the pandani seem as though it should be on a warm South Seas island rather than in the cold snow country of Tasmania's South-West.

At the very highest altitudes, the buttongrass and other heaths and sedges give way to a variety of alpine herb plants and to an intriguing form of vegetation known as cushion plants. Aptly named, the cushion plants consist of a number of diverse species—from unrelated genera including *Pterygopappus, Abrotanella, Gaimardia* and *Donatia*—which grow together in low compact mounds of intertwined shoots. These mounds may be quite small or they may spread out over a square metre or more, and they are so tightly packed that it is possible to tread on them without leaving any impression. Growing on the most exposed peaks and ridges, they tend to dam tiny streams which form when the snow starts to melt. When the water finds a new path, the cushion plants expand and grow there as well. The result is a series of miniature gardens with small waterholes and occasional sculptured rocks, intermingled with pure white snow. This garden effect is highlighted when the cushion plants are in flower, for each tiny colourful bloom is only a few millimetres in size and seems to occupy the same proportion of area against the green as flowers in a normal-sized garden.

The larger herb flowers are usually a few centimetres in size and many species grow amid sphagnum moss *(Sphagnum spp.)*, a remarkable plant which has the ability to absorb several times its own weight in water and which forms swampy bogs often a few metres deep.

Australia's smallest eucalypt, the varnished gum *(Eucalyptus vernicosa)*, is another interesting plant in the exposed highlands. Found only in the South-West and other parts of western Tasmania, it is particularly prevalent on the snow-covered mountain plateaux of the quartzite regions, where it grows no more than a metre high at maturity. The Tasmanian snow gum *(Eucalyptus coccifera)* dominates the dolerite high country, its beautifully coloured streaky bark adding to the sculptural appearance of its gnarled, dwarfed trunk.

At lower levels there are many other eucalypts, the most widespread being the hardy Tasmanian peppermint *(Eucalyptus nitida)* and the swamp gum *(Eucalyptus ovata)*. These trees adjust well to the harsh environment, growing as tall as 40 or 50 metres if conditions are suitable but being able to survive in a much smaller form on poorly drained, infertile soils. Both species are salt-tolerant, and on coastal dunes they are the largest plants amid a variety of heaths and grasses.

Several tall eucalypts—including the majestic mountain ash *(Eucalyptus regnans)*, the alpine ash *(E. delegatensis)*, the Tasmanian blue gum *(E. globulus)* and the manna gum *(E. viminalis)*—are found in many of the river valleys and in fertile areas around the margins of the wilderness, while the lovely yellow gum *(Eucalyptus subcrenulata)* grows in many sandstone areas, varying in size according to altitude.

Although an abundance of wildlife is not apparent in the South-West, the region supports a surprising number and variety of species highly adapted to cope with the wet, rugged environment. Most of these animals are small, such as tree frogs, lizards, tiny marsupials, birds, and freshwater fish and crustaceans, but others are quite large, including the Bennett's wallaby *(Macropus rufogriseus)*, the rufous or pademelon wallaby *(Thylogale billardierii)*, the wombat *(Vombatus ursinus)*, the Tasmanian devil *(Sarcophilus harrisii)*, the echidna *(Tachyglossus aculeatus)*, the platypus *(Ornithorhynchus anatinus)* and the venomous Tasmanian tiger snake *(Notechis ater)*. Many species hibernate during winter, while others emerge from their nests or burrows only to feed. Some bird species seen in the region, such as the king penguin *(Aptenodytes patagonica)* and the royal penguin *(Eudyptes schlegeli)*, are only occasional visitors, but about 50 land birds and 30 sea birds live in the area at most times. Among these species are the green ground parrot *(Pezoporus wallicus)*, which is now rare in mainland Australia, and the southern emu-wren *(Stipiturus malachurus)*. Doubtless, some fauna in the vast wilderness remain undiscovered by man.

The South-West has always been inimical to settlement by man, particularly the rainforests, where suitable food is scarce. The Aborigines confined themselves to the fringes of the region, and the white men who followed them stayed only at a few select points. Lonely explorations were made inland, but to this day no one has ever settled in the vast interior of the wilderness and parts of it have possibly never been visited.

Archaeological evidence indicates that about 20 000 years ago Aboriginal groups lived in caves along the Franklin River and that some 12 500 years ago other groups lived in the Florentine Valley—both localities being near the northern extremity of the wilderness. However, little is known about either of these groups of people, nor is it known for how long they lived there. More substantial information is available about later Aboriginal groups who lived on the coastal fringes of the South-West for perhaps 3000 years until they were driven away by the white man in the early nineteenth century. As in other parts of Australia, these people had a deep understanding of their land and never had cause to destroy the natural environment. However, in order to ensure that their food supply remained adequate, they did make a significant impact on the vegetation.

The South-West is unsuitable for the growing of crops, but the Aborigines developed a system of "natural farming". Their tool was fire and as they could not produce it artificially, each group always carried a smouldering fire-stick. By burning the land regularly over many centuries, they gradually changed parts of the coastal vegetation from rainforest to heath and sedge lands. The fires had the immediate effect of flushing out animals for food and of clearing tracks to make travelling easier. But, more importantly, fire stimulated regrowth of grasses and other plants which provided a source of vegetable food and also attracted a larger animal population. As this method encouraged natural processes, and as there was no artificial planting or wholesale destruction, the trees and other plants continued to grow in a totally wild state, as though never interfered with by man.

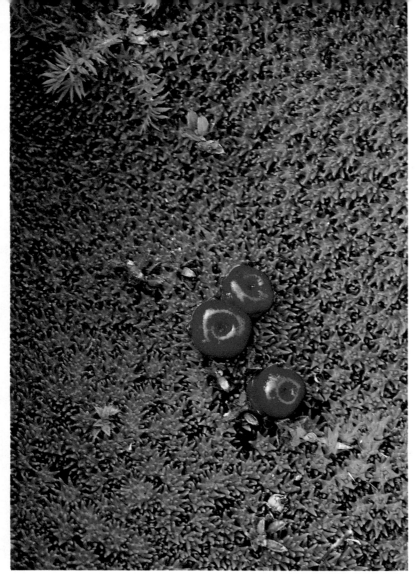

Tiny red berries (*Pernettya tasmanica*), each about 5 millimetres in diameter, growing in cushion plants

Today only middens along the coast give evidence of the Aborigines' long occupation of the land, for their lifestyle was simple. Had it not been for the arrival of the white man, they would doubtless still be living in the wilderness in exactly the same way.

Although the white man's association with the South-West has been only fleeting, his impact on some of the peripheral areas has been substantial and there is great concern today about the preservation of the remaining untouched wilderness.

Europeans first came to know about the South-West as early as 1642, when the Dutchman Abel Janszoon Tasman sailed past its shores. A visit by the French Admiral Marion du Fresne in 1772 heralded a spate of further expeditions by both French and English navigators, notable among whom were James Cook in 1777 and Bruni D'Entrecasteaux in 1793.

The most appreciative of these early visitors, however, was the surgeon and explorer George Bass, who with Matthew Flinders circumnavigated Tasmania in 1798, charting the coast and proving conclusively Bass's theory that Tasmania was an island separated from the mainland. On seeing the South-West coast, Bass wrote that it " ... presented a rugged and determined front to the icy regions of the South Pole. To a very unusual elevation is added an irregularity of form that justly entitles it to rank among the foremost of the grand and wildly magnificent scenes of Nature."

But these were the days of sail, and to other early navigators, explorers and settlers, the South-West coast meant only danger and fear. Its waters are among the roughest in the world and hide countless rocks and reefs. Over the centuries it has become the graveyard of many ships, blown to their doom by the wild winds. Even today, with the aid of charts, lighthouses and sophisticated equipment, it is a formidable coast.

Yet despite the rugged and inhospitable nature of the wilderness, the white man eventually came to see it as an area of potential economic wealth. In 1815, just over 10 years after the establishment of Hobart Town, Captain James Kelly sailed along the full length of the South-West coast during his 49-day circumnavigation of Tasmania in the whaleboat *Elizabeth*. Kelly had been commissioned by Dr Thomas William Birch, a surgeon and Hobart Town merchant, to look for timber, especially the durable Huon pine which was much prized for furniture and boat-building. He discovered Port Davey, Bathurst Harbour and Macquarie Harbour, which he named respectively after: Thomas Davey, then Lieutenant Governor of Van Diemen's Land; Lord Bathurst, British Secretary of State for the Colonies: and Lachlan Macquarie, Governor of the Colony of New South Wales, of which Van Diemen's Land was then a dependency. All three areas contained large stands of the sought-after pine.

For his contribution to Kelly's expedition, Thomas Birch was granted a year's concession to cut Huon pine at both Port Davey and Macquarie Harbour, and several lonely camps were set up at these two great inlets over the next few years.

By 1820 the colonial government was seeking to establish a convict settlement on the remote South-West coast, and both inlets were considered as possible sites. Macquarie Harbour was eventually chosen and a convict station was established there in 1822.

For security reasons further activity at Port Davey was discouraged and the few Europeans to venture there during the ensuing 15 years were mainly surveyors, prospectors, and navigators seeking a safe anchorage.

Among these visitors was George Augustus Robinson who arrived at Port Davey in 1830 during his well-meaning but disastrous Friendly Mission to relocate the Tasmanian Aborigines on government settlements, or "sanctuaries", at Flinders Island and other islands of Bass Strait. Robinson and his party of eight white men and ten Aborigines from Bruni Island made contact with the South Coast Aborigines and spent several weeks travelling with them over country which Europeans had previously regarded as impenetrable. Those Aborigines whom Robinson could not persuade to move to Bass Strait were taken by force, in the belief that it was for their own good, and by mid-1833 the only Aborigines remaining in the South-West were the groups around Macquarie Harbour. They were rounded up by Robinson the following year and he stayed with them as guardian on Flinders Island until 1835.

But the Tasmanian Aborigines were not to survive. Removed from their own land, which was integral to their life, these formerly healthy, happy and spirited people could not survive in the world that the white man made for them and within a few years most of them were dead. The last full-blooded Aborigine in Tasmania, Truganini, died in 1876. She had been one of the Bruni Island people who accompanied George Robinson on his Friendly Mission.

Macquarie Harbour was ideal for a penal establishment. An almost landlocked expanse of water, it is about 34 kilometres long and between 6 and 11 kilometres wide, and covers an area of approximately 290 square kilometres. It is fed by two

1. The ruins of the penitentiary on
Sarah Island, Macquarie Harbour
2. A gully on Sarah Island where some
of the last West Coast Aborigines are
believed to have died due to
ill-treatment by convicts and guards

mandant was Lieutenant John Cuthbertson and the total population, including soldiers and their families, was 110.

The main settlement was built on Sarah Island (often called Settlement Island), which lies deep inside the harbour. A two-roomed building was also erected on the tiny nearby Grummet Island to segregate the women convicts. This building covered the entire surface of the island and a cave underneath was also utilised. The women, however, were not kept at Macquarie Harbour for very long and Grummet Island was soon used as a place of banishment for the very worst male prisoners. It became known as the "Isle of the Condemned" and there are stories telling of up to 50 men being kept there at a time. There was no stream on either island, so fresh water had to be carried daily from the mainland.

The major industries of the penal station centred around the Huon pine. The most hardened convicts were set to work as timber-getters, in what must have been among the most appalling conditions of any convict settlement in Australia. They laboured hard from sunrise to sunset, felling the huge trees, sawing and splitting them, and then tying the logs together into rafts which they floated to the settlement. Often they worked waist-deep in freezing water for most of the day.

Working conditions for the less dangerous prisoners were not quite so bad, although still harsh. These men were employed in a variety of jobs, including ship-building, tanning, bootmaking, constructing and maintaining buildings, and vegetable-growing. Much of the Huon and other timber taken from the area during the first few years was used in the settlement, but later the majority of the wood was sent to Hobart Town, where it was sold.

During the 11 years that the penal station remained in operation, the number of convicts living at Macquarie Harbour generally ranged between 250 and 350. Sentences were long and punishments of up to 100 lashes were common for misdemeanours. There was a shortage of food, especially fresh fruits and vegetables, and scurvy was always a problem. Dysentery and rheumatism caused by the cold and wet conditions were also rife, but the men had to be extremely sick before they were admitted to the settlement's small hospital. James Backhouse, a Quaker missionary who visited Macquarie Harbour in 1832, reported that 85 deaths had occurred in the settlement up to that time. Of these, 35 were attributed to "natural causes". The others died more violently: 27 drowned, 8 died in other accidents (mostly by being crushed by falling logs), 3 were killed by soldiers, and 12 were murdered by comrades. It is said that many prisoners considered hanging to be preferable to staying at Macquarie Harbour and that some of the murders were committed so that the murderer himself would then be sent to the gallows at Hobart Town.

Despite its isolation from other settlements, escape attempts from this "Western Hell" were frequent. However, relatively few were successful. James Backhouse noted that of 112 men

rivers, the King and the Gordon, and is surrounded by a soaring barrier of virtually impassable mountains. Furthermore, the entrance to the harbour is a treacherous, narrow channel through which the tides race in and out. A dangerous sandbar at the mouth creates eddies and fierce surf, and over the years many vessels have foundered in the rough, shallow waters. The convicts called this channel Hell's Gates, for once inside there was little hope of escape.

The first convicts arrived at Macquarie Harbour on 2 January 1822. They numbered 74 in all, consisting of 44 hardened male convicts, 8 females, and 22 other males who were skilled in various trades necessary for building the settlement. The com-

who had managed to get away from Macquarie Harbour before 1832, well over half perished in the bush, mostly of starvation but sometimes by more sinister means.

Particularly horrific was the escape in September 1822 by a depraved ex-pieman, Alexander "Bolter" Pierce, and seven other men. One by one, members of the party were killed and eaten—for there was no other food—until only Pierce remained alive. He was eventually captured and sent back to Macquarie Harbour, only to escape again and kill another accomplice before finally being sent to Hobart Town and hanged. Pierce was rather sardonically known as "The Pieman", and the Pieman River north of Macquarie Harbour, where he was apprehended during an earlier escape attempt, is named after him.

By the time the convict settlement was abandoned in 1834, conditions had improved considerably, and it seems a fitting end that the last ship to be built there, the brig *Frederick*, should be seized in a bloodless mutiny by 10 convicts, who then escaped to South America. Nonetheless, the notorious reputation of the penal station endured and even the famous settlement at Port Arthur, which replaced it, was regarded as humane by comparison. Today a few stone ruins remain on Sarah Island, ominous reminders of the miserable men who were once forced to live on its shores.

The closure of the convict settlement at Macquarie Harbour awakened new interest in the commercial possibilities of the wilderness, especially for the trade in Huon pine, and a number of official explorations were made into the interior of the region. George Frankland and a Captain Heniker explored the lower Huon River in the late 1820s, W. S. Sharland explored the region around Frenchman's Cap in 1832, James Calder and John Helder Wedge discovered Lake Pedder in 1835, and the following year George Frankland found Mt Anne.

By the mid-1830s free settlers were working the Huon stands on the lower Gordon and Franklin rivers, upstream from Macquarie Harbour, and others moved in to Port Davey and to the Huon and Cracroft rivers south of Mt Anne. Whaling stations also operated for a few years at Bramble Cove in Port Davey and at New Harbour, Cox Bight and De Witt Island, but indiscriminate slaughtering of the animals brought an early collapse to this industry.

The most significant settlement was the community established at Port Davey to cull the Huon pine. The first timber-getters arrived in the mid-1830s and the population reached a peak in 1875, with about 50 people living at Settlement Point and a few others at the Spring River. But the felling of the Huon was uncontrolled and by 1880 all accessible stands had been cut out, so the settlement was abandoned. The same fate befell the age-old Huon in other parts of the South-West and by the early 1900s almost all the large stands of this precious tree were gone.

Many tracks were slashed through the wilderness during these years, not only for the settlers but also to provide an

escape route to inhabited country for people shipwrecked on the wild South-West coast. In the 1850s there was even an ambitious scheme to build two roads to Port Davey, one from the Huon River via Lake Pedder and the other from Dunrobin Bridge on the Derwent River via the Gordon River. Work on the latter was actually commenced in 1850, but by 1856 it reached only as far as the Gordon Bend—a mere 60 kilometres—and the project was abandoned because of excessive costs.

After the timber-getting community left Port Davey, a new wave of tracks were cut in an effort to reduce the isolation of the region. Federation Peak, which had been named the "Obelisk" by the surveyor James Sprent in the mid-1800s, was given its present name by one of the best-known track cutters, Thomas Bather Moore, who saw it in the distance in 1901, the year of the Federation of the Australian States.

The tracks, however, did not open up the South-West to further settlement.

Attempts to utilise the wilderness for agricultural purposes were even more short-lived than the efforts of the timber-getters and whalers. Since the late 1840s until as recently as 1949, farmers and graziers have periodically tried their luck at various places on the edge of the wilderness, but none has been successful. Indeed, surveys and studies over the years have shown that the soils of the South-West are unsuitable for any form of agricultural development.

Even mining, which developed with extraordinary fervour on the mid-west coastal region north of Macquarie Harbour, spread only to isolated fringe areas of the South-West.

Tin was mined at Cox Bight, near Port Davey, from about 1892, extending to Ray River in 1926 and to Moth Creek in 1936. This last claim was taken over in 1941 by the legendary Charles King, who was joined a few years later by his son

Denis. The King family home, Melaleuca—built in 1945 and named after the purple-flowered *Melaleuca* tea-trees that grow along the banks of the creek—soon became a landmark and a welcome haven for bushwalkers and other visitors to the area.

Despite the fact that small-scale mining has been in operation in the Cox Bight–Melaleuca area for more than 80 years, the population has never been large and no town has ever been built there. By contrast, osmiridium mining operations in the north-east of the wilderness reached boom proportions, albeit short-lived.

Osmiridium, a naturally occurring alloy used for various industrial purposes, was discovered near the Adams River south of the Florentine Valley in 1909 by the surveyor William Hope Twelvetrees. When mining began in 1925, the metal was fetching five times the price of gold. A town, Adamsfield, soon sprang up and within 12 months it boasted a population of 2000. However, before another year had passed, the heyday of Adamsfield was over. By the end of 1926 a decreasing demand for osmiridium had caused its market value to fall dramatically. This, together with the fact that the best and most accessible deposits at Adamsfield had already been worked, led to a rapid decline in population and by the following year only about 100 miners remained. The town lingered on for another 10 years or so, but has since been overgrown by the bush.

Other mining operations in the South-West were on a much smaller scale, and equally short-lived. Notable among these was a makeshift gold-mining settlement at the Jane River south of Frenchman's Cap. More than 30 men were working there in 1935, but as elsewhere in the South-West the difficult weather and the rough terrain precluded mass exploitation of the region and numbers soon dwindled. However, at Recherche Bay on the south-eastern edge of the wilderness, there was a major resurgence of the timber industry for several decades earlier this century and coal was also mined quite extensively. But it was of low-grade quality, so when the trees gave out and the timber-getting community left, mining was abandoned too.

The only permanent town to be built in the wilderness during these years of industrial activity was Strahan, tucked inside Macquarie Harbour on its far northern shore. Founded in 1878, it rose to importance as a port for mines at Zeehan and Mt Lyell, further north. Later, the minerals were transported to more accessible ports, especially Burnie on the north coast, and Strahan gradually fell into decline. Today it is a tiny centre for crayfishing and tourism, but it is best-known because it is the only town on Tasmania's bleak west coast.

Strahan marks the north-western corner of the wilderness. Little trace remains of the other settlements which once dotted the edge of the region, and most of the early tracks that criss-crossed the interior have long been reclaimed by the bush. Today, while there are still enough tracks to cater for the bush-walker, the majority of the region is retained in a true wilderness state.

But, for how long will it remain that way? Until the 1960s the South-West wilderness encompassed almost one-quarter of Tasmania. However, that area has been severely reduced by the first stage of the controversial Gordon River hydro-electric scheme, which in 1972 drowned Lake Pedder. The remaining wilderness is now seriously threatened by further hydro-electric development, as well as by mining and forestry.

The drowning of Lake Pedder focussed world-wide attention on the South-West. The original Lake Pedder was an exquisite glacial lake with a pure-white quartz sand beach, set amid a circle of impressive mountain peaks. It was widely acknowledged as being Australia's most beautiful lake, and since 1955 had been proclaimed the showpiece of a 23 800-hectare Lake Pedder National Park. Furthermore, its ecology was known to be unique and much of it had barely been studied.

But the argument in favour of saving the lake went beyond its individual beauty and value. It was a vital and central part of the magnificent wilderness which until then still included all the land south and west of the Lyell Highway in central Tasmania. The aesthetic, spiritual and ecological importance of such a large region functioning in an entirely natural way is incalculable.

Man's desire to tame this wilderness, on the other hand, is highly questionable. There is no necessity to touch it: indeed, man's own survival may ultimately depend on the continued existence of natural areas such as this. From an economic viewpoint, many people claim that in recent years hydro-electricity has been losing its cost advantage over other forms of power, largely because of the high cost of construction in the more remote and less easily dammed areas that remain since the completion of the first stage of the Gordon scheme. Moreover, Tasmania's hydro-electricity potential could not anywhere near meet the State's present energy demands, let alone those of the future, so other forms of power will always be needed. Bearing these points in mind, arguments normally advanced in favour of hydro-electricity, such as the fact that it is relatively pollution-free and does not operate on non-renewable fuels, fade into insignificance, and numerous individuals and organisations advocate the development of alternative sources of energy now, rather than waiting for a few years and allowing the precious wilderness to be destroyed.

The conservation movement to save Lake Pedder and the Gordon River system was one of the largest and best-organised in Australian history. Apart from individual activists, several action committees were set up to increase public awareness of the issue and to lobby governments and the powerful Tasmanian Hydro-Electric Commission.

The depth of feeling for the South-West is shown in the story of one of the greatest battlers for its preservation, Olegas Truchanas, a post-World War II Lithuanian immigrant who explored much of the wilderness alone. In 1958 Truchanas became the first person to canoe down the Gordon River from Lake Pedder to Macquarie Harbour. Before the flooding of the lake and the Middle Gordon River, he visited the area more than 30 times and took magnificent photographic slides which he showed to thousands of people at functions in the Hobart Town Hall. These showings were significant in stimulating public support for preserving the wilderness, but tragically when bushfires ravaged Tasmania in 1967 Truchanas's house was among those burned and most of his slide collection was lost. In 1972 he returned to the Gordon River to take more pictures, which he planned to use in the fight to prevent further hydro-electric development in the region. The quest was to cost Truchanas his life. It seems that in trying to reach a calm patch of water he tripped on a slippery boulder and fell into the river just above a waterfall.

Despite its status as a national park and numerous protests from conservationists and international scientific bodies, the flooding of Lake Pedder went ahead. But even then the "Save Pedder" activists did not give up hope. For a year or so after the flooding there were Federal governmental enquiries into the possibility of deflooding the lake and trying to return it to its former condition; however, this did not eventuate.

In any case, the damage to the South-West as a whole was irreversible. The Gordon River Road, which was constructed to service the project, effectively cut the wilderness in half. It was built without any consideration for aesthetic values and together with a town, Strathgordon, which was built to accommodate workers, it stands as an ugly scar in what should be the heart of the wilderness. The new man-made Lake Pedder, and also adjacent Lake Gordon, were claimed to be "bigger and better" than the original lake. Bigger, certainly; but they could never be better. The International Biological Programme of UNESCO described the decision to flood Lake Pedder as "the greatest ecological tragedy since European settlement of Tasmania", and the result bore out this claim.

There is a gloominess about the area today. In the lakes, the tops of dead trees drowned by the flooding are like grey ghosts of the past, and elsewhere there are unsightly roads, buildings, huge power lines and other man-made encumbrances. These intrusions not only destroyed many rare and unique native species but also enabled alien plants and animals to live in areas that they could neither have reached nor survived in previously.

Although the first stage of the Gordon River scheme has drastically reduced the size of the true wilderness, it is not too late to save the valuable areas that still remain. To this end, a number of conservation groups amalgamated in 1976 to form the Tasmanian Wilderness Society, and support for the movement has been growing steadily ever since.

Today the main issue causing concern is the likely further development of the Gordon River scheme. Proposals regarding this project have been the subject of bitter debate over the last few years and have included suggestions that Tasmania's last wild river system, the Franklin, be harnessed for power. The Tasmanian Government for the present has decided against flooding this river, but until it is declared a wild river national park and thoroughly protected by law, it is not safe. Pressures to flood the Gordon above its junction with the Olga River, however, are of more immediate concern, especially as such an eventuality would drown the remarkable Splits. Also at risk of being drowned by this scheme is the Truchanas Huon Pine Reserve. Located on the Denison River and containing the South-West's last significant stands of 1000-year-old Huon pines, it was named posthumously as a tribute to Olegas Truchanas who in 1970 was instrumental in saving the trees from timber-getters.

Other areas threatened by possible future hydro-electric schemes are the Davey River and, to a lesser extent, the Huon and Arthur rivers. In addition, the roads built for hydro-electric projects give access for potential mining and forestry operations. Indiscriminate mining is also a potential threat in some coastal areas. In recent years, for example, applications have been made to mine high-grade limestone at and near Precipitous Bluff. Such mining, if it were allowed, would not only destroy the scenic beauty and pristine values of the area, but would also damage and endanger the rare and remarkable forest cover of Precipitous Bluff, which rises from sea level to alpine altitudes and on the western side has not been burned for several hundred years.

The preservation of the South-West is not simply a Tasmanian or even an Australian question. It is of world-wide importance, being one of the few remaining temperate wildernesses of substantial size left on this planet. Although a 403 200-hectare portion of this region has been proclaimed as the South West National Park (which incorporates the old Lake Pedder park), and other smaller areas have also been set aside as national parks and reserves, the survival of the South-West as a significant untouched wilderness can be assured only by uncompromising preservation of the entire region. □

From the coast, chains of jagged mountains rise one after the other, giving birth to countless rivers and streams

1. The windswept western approach to Mt Lot
2. Frankland Range, with the new Lake Pedder in the foreground
3. The Gordon River
4. Frenchman's Cap, from Macquarie Harbour
5. South Cape, with South East Cape beyond

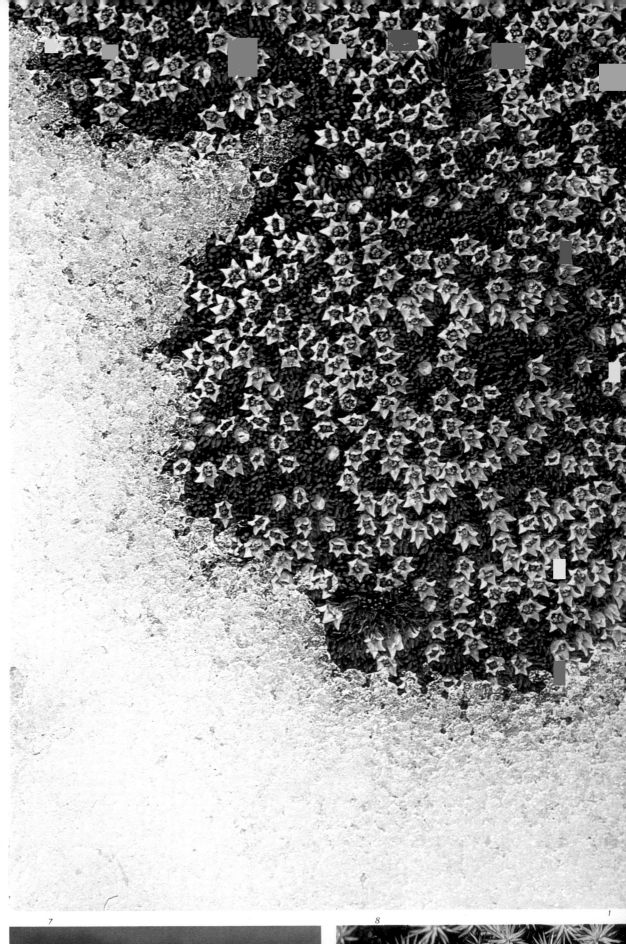

. . . Delicate alpine vegetation blossoms amid the ice and the snow

1. Cushion plants (*Donatia novae-zelandiae*)
2. Spear-like icicles hanging from alpine shrubbery (*Archeria serpyllifolia*)
3. Pandani (*Richea pandanifolia*)
4. A steadfast clump of sphagnum moss growing amid a variety of cushion plants
5. Sphagnum moss
6. Tiny pale pink petals of *Pimelea sericea* peep through a blanket of summer snow
7. Tasmanian waratah (*Telopia truncata*)
8. A giant moss (*Polytrichum sp.*)
9. Mountain rocket (*Bellendena montana*)
10. Alpine berries (*Cyathodes abietina*)
11. Sprays of *Gentianella diemensis*

7

8

A glacial masterpiece
LAKE ST CLAIR

A CROSS the whole of Tasmania's central highland region, the thick dark forests are dotted with hundreds of lakes. The most beautiful of these waterways is Lake St Clair, at the southern end of the Cradle Mountain–Lake St Clair National Park.

Lake St Clair is Australia's deepest natural lake. Lying in a long valley, its floor was scooped out about 15 000 years ago by a massive glacier. When the ice melted, waters converged upon the valley, filling it to depths of more than 200 metres.

The lake, the largest created by a glacier in Australia, extends approximately 17 kilometres from north to south and averages some 2-3 kilometres in width. Mt Olympus (1430 metres) stands about 1.5 kilometres back from the western shore and rises to such towering heights that its slopes are reflected in the deep, dark waters. On the eastern bank the tree-covered slopes of the Traveller Range rise almost sheer from the water's edge, reaching an average altitude of about 850 metres but culminating in Mt Ida at 1253 metres.

Shady rainforests dominated by the lovely Tasmanian "myrtle" (Nothofagus cunninghamii) extend along the lake's shores, giving way in places to tall forests of eucalypts including the giant mountain ash (Eucalyptus regnans). The "myrtle", sometimes known as "Antarctic beech", is one of the prettiest trees in the region, its spreading branches being densely covered by deep green foliage. Unlike the beech trees of Europe, which are deciduous, the "myrtle" is an evergreen. In early spring, bronze and chestnut younger leaves contrast strikingly with the green of the older foliage. Another Nothofagus species, the tanglefoot (N. gunnii), grows on high mountain tops to the north and is Tasmania's only native deciduous tree. Its leaves turn golden in autumn and drop to the ground when the first winter snows fall.

1. View across Lake St Clair towards the Du Cane Range
2. Roots of dead Tasmanian "myrtles" (*Nothofagus cunninghamii*), on the western shore of the lake

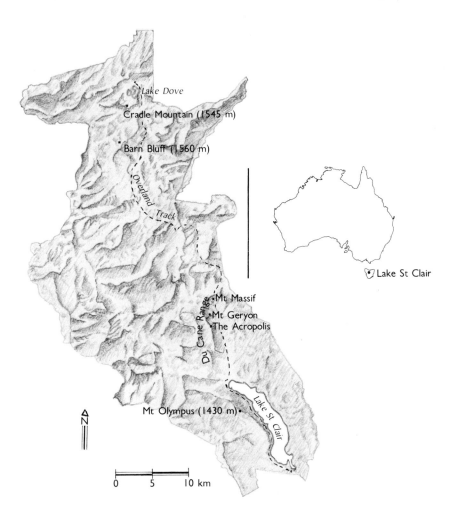

Lake St Clair is fed by the melting snows of the surrounding mountains. Standing 737 metres above sea level, it is the source of the Derwent River, which flows 190 kilometres in a south-easterly direction, passing through Hobart before finally emptying into the sea at Storm Bay. The river has been extensively developed for hydro-electricity and Lake St Clair is a major catchment area, its water level having been raised artificially to provide a storage capacity of about 2 million megalitres.

The first European to see Lake St Clair is thought to have been an eccentric Dane, Jorgen Jorgenson, whose colourful life as an artist, writer, sailor, spy, explorer, convict and police constable—to name just a few of his numerous occupations—brought him to Australia in 1801 and again in 1826. The second of these visits was as a convict, transported for petty theft. Earning his ticket-of-leave within a year, Jorgenson was assigned to the Van Diemen's Land Company, which had been granted 350 000 acres (about 140 000 hectares) of unexplored country in the north-west of Tasmania to open up for development. During an exploration for this company in 1826-7, Jorgenson is said to have discovered Lake St Clair but was unable to explore the area thoroughly due to dwindling food supplies and the hindrance of snow and mist. Five years later, in 1832, the Surveyor-General of the Van Diemen's Land Company, W. S. Sharland, reached the lake and claimed to have discovered it. For thousands of years before these white men came, it had been known to the Aboriginal people of Tasmania, who called it *Leeawulena*.

The name by which the lake is now known was given to it in 1835 by the government Surveyor-General George Frankland, after the St Clair family of Loch Lomond, Scotland. Several other places in the area were also named by Frankland, some honouring famous people whom he admired, including the English poet Lord Byron and the French naturalist Baron

Cuvier, others, such as Mt Olympus and the Narcissus River, reflecting his interest in Greek mythology. This latter derivation of names became a tradition emulated by later visitors to the region, and today the majority of the nomenclature has romantic allusions to the classics.

Both the Lake St Clair and the Cradle Mountain areas were gazetted as scenic reserves in the 1920s. They were united in 1947 to form the Cradle Mountain–Lake St Clair National Park, which covers an area of about 126 000 hectares of uninhabited mountain country famed for its magnificent alpine scenery.

Vehicle access to the park is restricted to two short roads, one leading to Lake St Clair near the southern perimeter and the other to Cradle Mountain in the north. In the vast wilderness between these two ends of the park, there are walking tracks which attract bushwalkers from all over the world. Of particular note is the 80-kilometre Overland Track, opened in the mid-1930s, which runs from Cradle Mountain to Cynthia Bay on Lake St Clair, passing through scenery ranging from eucalypt forests and rainforests to jagged mountains, buttongrass plains and alpine moorlands. Snow covers the area throughout winter and blizzards may occur without warning, even in summer. There are stormproof shelter huts, however, at various points along the way.

The climate at Lake St Clair is cool and wet all year round, with an average annual rainfall of about 1500 millimetres. In summer, when conditions are mildest, the smaller flowering plants bloom in a profusion of colour. The larger shrubs and trees—such as wattles, sassafras and needlebushes—flower a little earlier, usually in late spring, while the mountain berries are out in autumn.

Animal life around Lake St Clair is most obvious in the warmer months. The Bennett's wallaby (*Macropus rufogriseus*) and the rufous wallaby (*Thylogale billardierii*) are common near the shores of the lake. Two other interesting inhabitants of the area are the platypus (*Ornithorhynchus anatinus*) and the echidna *(Tachyglossus aculeatus)*, the world's only egg-laying mammal species. The platypus is particularly numerous in the Narcissus River, which runs into the northern end of the lake, but the animal is shy and seldom seen.

In winter the animals and plants are less conspicuous. The scenery at Lake St Clair, however, is still extremely beautiful, with the mountains often clothed in a mantle of snow. □

2

*Tiny touches of contrasting
colour decorate the green mantle
of the rainforest . . .*

50

1. Tasmanian "myrtle" (*Nothofagus cunninghamii*)
2. Fir club moss (*Lycopodium fastigiatum*)
3. A "coral" fungus (*Cladia retipora*)
4. Mushroom-sized fungus (*Hygrophorus sp.*) in a sphagnum bog
5. Mossy creek near Mt Olympus, Lake St Clair
6. Cephissus Falls, on the Narcissus River
7. Narcissus River, north of Lake St Clair
8. An array of "myrtle" and sassafras leaves on the forest floor

Nature's ancient architecture

THE ACROPOLIS

THE commanding edifice of the Acropolis, north of Lake St Clair, stands like a massive ancient citadel overlooking virgin rainforest and buttongrass plains. Composed of hard dolerite, it is a mighty natural fortress of pillars and jagged towers, and its beautiful bare rock surface makes it look like a man-made construction.

But the building of the Acropolis began long before man first appeared. About 165 million years ago earth movements upheaved the Tasmanian landmass and hot tongues of dolerite magma intruded into existing sandstones, where they solidified into extensive dykes, sheets and sills deep under the Earth's surface. When subsequent erosion removed the overlying sandstones, the resistant dolerite of the Acropolis became exposed in a wall of tall, closely-packed columnar formations. This unusual appearance, characteristic of dolerite, was caused by contraction cracks which developed as the mass cooled. An ice-capping some 15 000 years ago modified the landform to its present shape.

Together with adjacent Mt Geryon and Mt Massif, which are also composed of dolerite, the Acropolis forms an imposing arc-shaped barrier at the head of the Narcissus River valley. The three mountains are part of the Du Cane Range, named after Charles Du Cane who was Governor of Tasmania from 1869 to 1874, and they were probably first visited by Europeans during his term of office.

The names of the Acropolis and triple-peaked Mt Geryon were given to the mountains in the 1930s and their derivation from classical Greece perpetuates a place-naming tradition started a century earlier by the surveyor George Frankland when he explored the Lake St Clair area. The name Acropolis was inspired by the mountain's resemblance to an ancient Greek acropolis, especially the famous Acropolis of Athens on which the Parthenon was built. Geryon was a mythological monster with three heads who ruled over an island named Erytheia. The tenth of the Twelve Labours of Herakles (or Hercules), son of the Greek god Zeus, was to capture Geryon's wonderful herd of oxen.

The magnificent natural structure of both the Acropolis and Mount Geryon engenders a feeling of awe and inspiration which is quite independent of their romantic nomenclature. Nonetheless, the very sculptural appearance of the bare rock is surprisingly reminiscent of ancient Greek architecture, and the Greek names seem appropriate. Certainly they are an improvement on earlier names that Europeans had given to the mountains. The Acropolis was previously called the "Porcupine" in fancied and rather unflattering reference to the spike-like appearance of the dolerite, and Mt Geryon was known by the prosaic names of the "Rifle Sight" and "Precipice Mountain". For a time Mt Geryon was also referred to as "Tarpeian Rock", after the Tarpeian Rock on the Capitoline Hill in Rome from which murderers and traitors were hurled in ancient times. However, the Greek name survived.

2

The Acropolis, Mt Geryon and other peaks of the Du Cane Range lie within the Cradle Mountain–Lake St Clair National Park and are very popular rock-climbing sites. There is no vehicle access to the area, but it can be reached on foot via offshoots from the Overland Track, which passes from the north to the south of the park. The walk to the Acropolis and Mt Geryon from Lake St Clair takes approximately 1-1½ days each way and there are unobtrusive campsites and shelter huts near the track. Other notable landmarks in the vicinity of the Acropolis include Mt Eros, the Parthenon, the Labyrinth and Walled Mountain. There are also various small glacial lakes and a pretty waterfall, Cephissus Falls.   □

Sculptured by ice

CRADLE MOUNTAIN

Cradle Mountain, with Lake Dove in the foreground

"THIS must be a National Park for all time. It is magnificent. Everyone should know about it, and come and enjoy it."

These enthusiastic words spoken by Gustav Weindorfer from the top of Cradle Mountain in 1910 were the genesis of what was to become one of Australia's finest reserves.

Weindorfer is generally considered to be the founder of the Cradle Mountain–Lake St Clair National Park. An Austrian by birth, he migrated to Australia and settled on a farm at Kindred in north-western Tasmania. A holiday in the remote montane bushland around Cradle Mountain sparked a lifelong passion which soon put an end to his farming days and led to his becoming one of Australia's legendary mountain bushmen.

Weindorfer was captivated by the raw virgin beauty of these rugged highlands, where on a clear day one can see wide panoramas of row after row of finely chiselled mountain peaks stretching far to the distant horizon. The mountains are snow-capped for most of the year and when it is sunny the white contrasts sharply with the blue of the sky. But usually their mood is ethereal, with the peaks merging into a floating blanket of mist and cloud.

Cradle Mountain, rising to an altitude of 1545 metres, is the highlight of this glorious alpine country. A jagged arc of precipitous columnar dolerite that dips deeply in the centre, it was sculptured by ice about 15 000 years ago, during the last ice age. Huge glaciers plunged down the mountainside, hollowing out semicircular valleys known as cirques and pushing the rocky debris before them to create moraines (mound-like rock piles). When the ice melted, the moraines acted as dams, holding back the water to help form beautiful lakes, the largest of which is Lake Dove. Other impressive waterways nearby include Crater Lake, Hidden Lake and many smaller tarns. (The name "Crater Lake", suggesting a volcanic structure, is a misnomer: the lake is solely of glacial origin.)

A few kilometres to the south-west of Cradle Mountain, a slightly taller pillar of dolerite known as Barn Bluff (1560 metres) also rises starkly, dominating the landscape. But its beauty is more severe than the intricately contoured Cradle for, although covered by a sheet of ice during the last ice age, it was not affected by glaciers.

The climate at Cradle Mountain is cold and wet, with a high average annual rainfall of around 3000 millimetres. The weather is very changeable and although rain falls most days, the sun frequently shines between the drifts of low cloud. Mists, fogs and icy winds are common and blinding snowstorms can occur at any time, without warning. But the atmosphere is seldom bleak: for the most part, the unpredictable weather is an attractive characteristic of the mountains.

The persistent rain is integral to the beauty of the highlands. There are countless rushing rivers and creeks, numerous picturesque waterfalls, dense rainforests festooned with mosses and ferns, and swampy moorlands covered by buttongrass. High on the mountains, flowering herb plants grow in clumps across watercourses formed by melting snow and several species of the hardy and unusual "cushion plants" form floral clusters on exposed ridges.

In the densely forested valleys of the highlands there are two impressive conifers, the big King Billy or King William pine (*Athrotaxis selaginoides*) and the celery-top pine (*Phyllocladus aspleniifolius*). A smaller relation of the King Billy pine, the rare pencil pine (*Athrotaxis cupressoides*), grows around many of the lakes and tarns on the high open moorlands, while a fourth conifer, the creeping pine (*Microcachrys tetragon*), grows in dense mats near the summit of most peaks.

The King Billy pine takes several hundred years to reach maturity and grows about 35-40 metres in height. It has an attractive reddish-brown bark with longitudinal furrows, and its spirals of dark green, sharp-pointed leaves are often sprinkled with snow. Although once common in Tasmanian rainforests, the King Billy pine is now quite scarce because of heavy demands for its valuable softwood timber. The celery-top pine grows 20-35 metres tall and is notable for its lobed, leaf-like branchlets. The true leaves appear like tiny scales on the edges of these branchlets.

Another interesting tree of the high forests is the pandani (*Richea pandanifolia*), a heath plant which looks deceptively like a tropical palm and seems out of place in this cold environment. It grows to about 9 metres in height and is crowned by slender leaves nearly a metre long. Dead leaves of past seasons often drape like a skirt around the trunk.

Tasmania's only deciduous native tree, the shrub-like tanglefoot or fagus (*Nothofagus gunnii*), is also found high on the mountains. It is particularly pretty in autumn when its leaves change colour, passing through shades of yellow to chestnut and bronze. With the first winter storms the leaves fall, forming a carpet across the ground, but this will soon be buried in snow.

Despite the cold, wildlife is plentiful in the highlands. Species range from wallabies and smaller marsupials to birds, snakes, leeches, insects and numerous alpine aquatic creatures.

An interesting inhabitant of both the lakes and the streams is the primitive mountain shrimp (*Anaspides tasmaniae*), which is unique to Tasmania. Thought to have evolved about 200 million years ago, it measures up to 5 centimetres in length and unlike other shrimps has a straight rather than a curved body.

The most intriguing land animal is the Tasmanian devil (*Sarcophilus harrisii*), a stocky little carnivorous marsupial with a large head and powerful jaws that can crush bones. Slow in their movements, they often scavenge rather than hunt for food and they will eat almost the entire carcass of any animal they find. They have a reputation for ferocity because of their screeching call and their habit of attacking tethered or weak animals up to twice their size.

With the Tasmanian Aborigines long gone, it is not known what significance Cradle Mountain had for man before Europeans came to this land. The first recorded visit to the locality was made by a Van Diemen's Land Company surveyor, Joseph Fossey, in 1826. It is thought that the mountain was named at that time for its likeness to a baby's cradle, not, as is sometimes suggested, to a miner's cradle, which did not come into use in Australia until 25 years or so later. Another Van Diemen's Land Company surveyor, Henry Hellyer, made the first known ascent of Cradle Mountain in March 1831.

Later in the nineteenth century and into the early twentieth century, prospectors, hunters, trappers and timber-fellers penetrated the region and various tracks were cut. Prospecting was the most active of these enterprises and several minerals including copper, tin, coal and oil shale were found. But they were only in small quantities and after a few mining attempts the area was abandoned in favour of less elusive sites.

In 1912 Gustav Weindorfer and his wife, a Tasmanian girl named Kate Cowles, leased an area of Crown Land in Cradle Valley, directly north of Cradle Mountain. The only access to the region at this time was a packhorse trail, but Weindorfer's plan was to open a holiday chalet and then urge the Tasmanian government to construct a road, thereby making the area accessible to carriage vehicles.

Work on the chalet began in March 1912. It was built of King Billy pine from the forest nearby, the trees being selected very carefully to minimise disturbance to the environment.

Weindorfer named the chalet Waldheim, meaning "forest home". The original three-roomed building was opened for visitors at Christmas 1912 and the following year Weindorfer started to build extensions to cater for more guests. By 1914 the chalet had grown to eight rooms and there was also a small hut plus a number of tents. Despite the fact that there was still no road, Waldheim was becoming very popular. Visitors could drive in horse-drawn carriages as far as the Middlesex Plains, about 15 kilometres to the north, and from there they would have to walk or ride on horseback. With assistance from the local council, a road was built by the 1920s to a point a little over a kilometre from Waldheim, but it did not reach the chalet until many years later.

Until 1916, Weindorfer continued to work on his farm at Kindred as well as operating Waldheim Chalet. However, the deaths of his wife, his father and his brother in that year prompted him to lease the farm and to move permanently to Waldheim.

Since his visit to Cradle Mountain in 1910, Gustav Weindorfer had dreamed of having the area proclaimed a national park. In 1921 he started an active campaign to achieve this goal. He gained the support of various members of the Tasmanian government and the following year a scenic reserve of 63 940 hectares was declared. The area did not, however, achieve national park status until 1947 when it was finally combined with Lake St Clair to form the 126 000-hectare Cradle Mountain–Lake St Clair National Park.

Today, as Gustav Weindorfer had wished, thousands of people visit Cradle Mountain each year to enjoy the superb alpine scenery. Several more cabins have been built in the forest behind Waldheim and there is also a camping ground. Apart from numerous one-day walks, the area is the usual starting point for people undertaking the 80-kilometre walk along the famous Overland Track, which runs between Cradle Mountain and Lake St Clair through spectacular wilderness.

Sadly, Gustav Weindorfer died 15 years before Cradle Mountain was declared a national park and consequently he failed to see his dream come true. But his efforts to preserve this beautiful country which he loved so well have not been forgotten. Special permission was granted to bury him near Waldheim, and on New Year's Day each year many nature lovers make a pilgrimage to the chalet to attend a memorial service in honour of this dedicated founder of one of Australia's finest mountain parks. □

The numerous waterfalls and
lakes are integral to the beauty of
the mountains. . .

1. Lake Dove, at the foot of Cradle Mountain
2. Waterfall Valley, near Barn Bluff
3. Lake Hanson, east of Lake Dove
4. Artists Pool, tucked in the curve of Cradle Mountain . . . the tall trees fringing the lake are the rare pencil pine (*Athrotaxis cupressoides*)

59

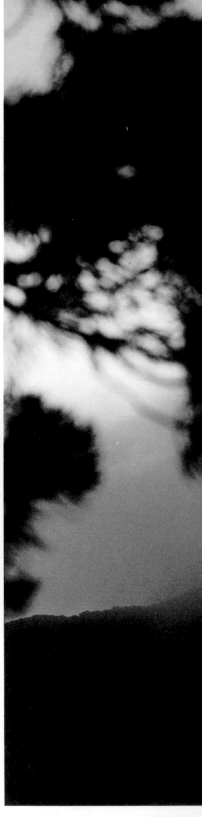

The peaks merge into a floating blanket of mist and cloud . . .

1. Eroded dolerite columns near the summit of Cradle Mountain
2. Barn Bluff
3. Fallen dolerite columns decorated by lichens, Cradle Mountain
4. Mats of hardy alpine flora *(Aciphylla procumbens)* near the summit of Cradle Mountain
5. Cushion plants *(Donatia novae-zelandiae)* growing on the exposed ridge of a cirque, Cradle Mountain
6. Mountain rocket *(Bellendena montana)* in fruit
7. Paper daisy *(Helichrysum milliganii)*

2

4

5

6

7

Treasury in darkness

KUBLA KHAN CAVE

Kubla Khan Cave

In Xanadu did Kubla Khan
A stately pleasure-dome decree:
Where Alph, the sacred river, ran
Through caverns measureless to man
Down to a sunless sea.

SAMUEL TAYLOR COLERIDGE
From *Kubla Khan*, 1816

IN THE darkness of a magnificent cave system in the Tasmanian highlands, nature has fulfilled the wildest dreams of the laudanum-drugged English poet Samuel Taylor Coleridge. Known as Kubla Khan Cave, it is the most impressive cave system in Australia—perhaps in the world. Everything about it is on a grand scale. The caverns are bigger than cathedrals and contain fallen boulders the size of houses, and the fantastic treasures they hide are many times richer and larger than those found anywhere else.

The most spectacular formation is the Khan, a massive stalagmite standing 17 metres high in the centre of a dome-shaped cavern called the Xanadu Chamber. Formed drop by drop by rainwater impregnated with minerals leached from the soil above, this mighty tower has taken at least 350 000 years to reach its present size. Over its entire surface it is embedded with calcite crystals that glitter like sequins when light shines on them. At one side of the chamber an even bigger formation, a 24-metre-high column called the Begum, reaches from the sloping ceiling to the floor. Displayed with regal grandeur, these two gigantic monuments are the only major decorations in Xanadu.

By contrast, other parts of Kubla Khan Cave are lavishly decorated. The enchanting Dulcimer Chamber, entered by crawling through a body-sized hole at the base of a narrow wall, is almost totally encrusted with cave formations. Needle-like crystals and frosted flowstone in hues of chocolate, tan and white cover the walls, a profusion of stalactites and straws hang from the ceiling, and jewel-like aragonite and calcite crystals sparkle all around. The walls of several little side grottoes are iced with crystalline formations and decorated by clusters of helictites—curious formations about the thickness of straws that twist in all directions like blown glass ornaments.

In another superbly decorated chamber, the Forbidden City, the formations are bigger and bolder, ranging from rows of stalagmites known as the Khan's Army to a magnificent array of more than 20 giant shawls draping down like a theatre curtain. Coloured in streaky bands of translucent white, reds and tans, these shawls hang in gentle folds with delicately frilled edges. Each shawl is several metres long and up to half a metre wide and the whole array stretches some 6-7 metres across. Above the shawls, spires of stalagmites in a variety of colours, from white and tan to chocolate and gun-metal grey, rise from a central plateau formed by rockfalls.

Much of the floor of the Forbidden City is composed of sparkling miniature rimstone pools—formations of pinkish-tan calcite that look like overlapping basins. Some larger rimstone pools in the middle of these small formations are edged by wafer-thin calcite, concealing deep hollows beneath.

Other impressive chambers in Kubla Khan include the echoing Cairn Hall, cut by the River Alph, and the dazzling Pleasure Dome, noted for its vast expanse of rimstone pools and sparkling flowstone. The most notable of numerous smaller grottoes is the exquisite Jade Pool, an almost enclosed recess with walls of streaked, creamy-white flowstone rising from a clear turquoise pool lined by scalloped pancakes of crystalline material. Another small grotto with a completely different character is the Opium Den, where delicate brown-stained helictites grow in an extraordinarily tangled mass.

Located near the little farming settlement of Mole Creek, north of Cradle Mountain, Kubla Khan Cave began to form some 2-3 million years ago in a belt of limestone laid down in a shallow seabed some 450 million years ago and then uplifted and folded about 70 million years later. Other cave systems in the same limestone have been dated as being at least 370 million years old.

The existence of the cave is believed to have been known to local farmers since about 1900, but it was not entered until 1948 when a team from the Tasmanian Caverneering Club discovered Cairn Hall, the River Alph and the fabulous Pleasure Dome. The Xanadu Chamber was discovered in December 1966 and a second entrance to the cave—allowing easier access to Xanadu, the Forbidden City and the Dulcimer Chamber—was found in 1970. However, the cave system is very complex and there are still many unexplored leads. To date, approximately 2700 metres of Kubla Khan have been surveyed. Another cave, the Genghis Khan, discovered nearby in 1971 and containing beautiful calcite crystal formations, has also been surveyed for 1200 metres and it is possible that the two caves may be joined.

For aeons nature has hidden the stunning treasures of Kubla Khan far away from cataclysm and destruction. There are only two known entrances to the cave, both of which involve abseiling down 20–30 metre vertical pitches and a great deal of difficult climbing. The cave is too large and too inaccessible to be developed for general viewing. Nevertheless, it is a national treasure and must be protected from any potential harm—a situation that has yet to be achieved. □

The Khan (foreground) and the Begum, Xanadu Chamber
OVERLEAF: Main corridor, the Forbidden City

"*For he on honey-dew hath fed,
And drunk the milk of Paradise.*"

SAMUEL TAYLOR COLERIDGE
From *Kubla Khan*, 1816

1. A spiky cluster of aragonite crystals
2. Aragonite crystals (detail)
3. Stalagmites in the Forbidden City

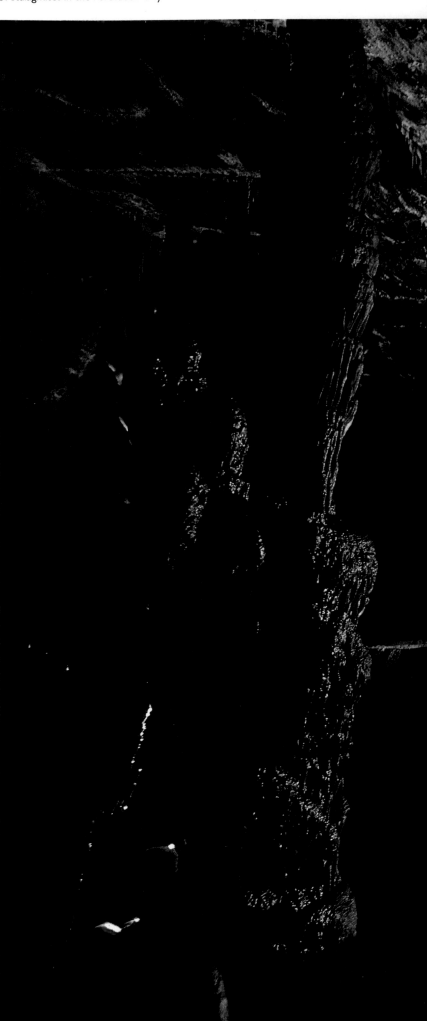

1

2

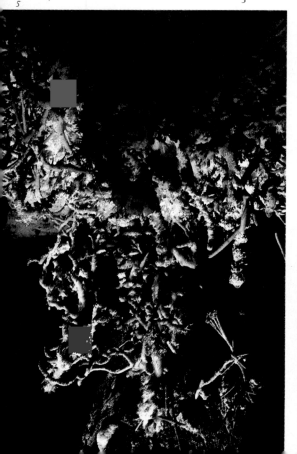

1. A section of the Dulcimer Chamber
2. Curtain formation, the Forbidden City
3. Chandelier of aragonite crystals
4. Array of giant shawls, the Forbidden City
5. A tangle of helictites, the Opium Den
6. The Jade Pool

Cornerstone of the continent

WILSON'S PROMONTORY

The south-eastern coastline of Wilson's Promontory, with Rodondo Island beyond

Rising boldly from the low and sandy Yanakie Isthmus, Wilson's Promontory forms an impressive cornerstone of the Australian continent. Reminiscent of Mediterranean islands such as Corsica, it is renowned for the beauty of its steep forested slopes, smooth grey rock outcrops and secluded white beaches surrounded by a turquoise sea.

The promontory is the southernmost part of the Australian mainland. Composed of granite formed about 370 million years ago, it was once the northern rise of a mountain ridge that extended to Tasmania. At the end of the last ice age some 6000–12 000 years ago the sea level rose by about 55 metres, forming Bass Strait and leaving only the higher peaks of Wilson's Promontory and islands such as the Flinders, Kent and Furneaux groups standing as giant stepping stones across the sea. At this time the promontory was a group of islands, but the prevailing south-westerly winds eventually caused a build-up of sand between the various islands and the mainland, creating the hook-shaped bastion of today.

Although not very high, Wilson's Promontory—or "the

Prom", as it is familiarly known—is striking because of the graceful shape of its indented coastline and the superb contrast between its sandy white beaches and precipitous dark headlands and slopes. Beautifully sculptured tors and boulders are a feature of both the beaches and the peaks, the tallest of which is Mt Latrobe (754 metres). Some of the rivers and creeks on the promontory are tidal, making their way to the sea across the sandy beaches or across swampy lowlands, while others such as the Roaring Meg Creek, at the southern end of the Prom, enter the sea through gorge-like estuaries bordered by huge granite boulders. Tea trees (*Leptospermum* and *Melaleuca spp.*) grow profusely along the banks of many of these streams, staining the water a deep yellow, and the seascape is also enhanced by several islands lying close offshore, notably Rodondo Island, a sharp-peaked monolith of red granite that soars 450 metres sheer above the water.

The dense, almost jungle-like bushlands that cover most of the Prom often extend right to the water's edge and contain a rich variety of plants from many different habitats. Of 700

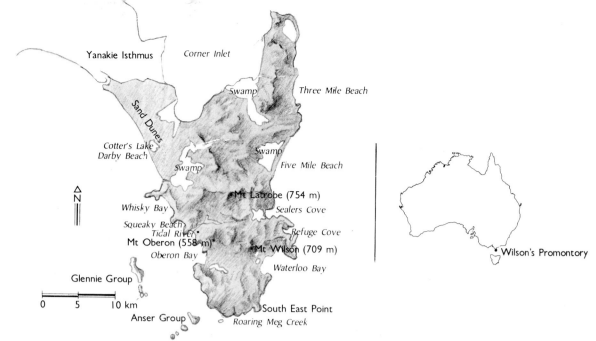

recorded species, the most common near the coast include the coastal tea-tree (*Leptospermum laevigatum*), the coast banksia (*Banksia integrifolia*), the drooping she-oak (*Casuarina stricta*) and the coast wattle (*Acacia sophorae*). Corner Inlet, on the eastern side of the Yanakie Isthmus, is also fringed by muddy salt marshes where the grey mangrove (*Avicennia marina*) and numerous delicate wildflowers grow.

Back from the water are heathlands and forests with trees such as manna gum (*Eucalyptus viminalis*) and bluegum (*Eucalyptus globulus*), while in the gullies between the peaks there are beautiful patches of rainforest containing ferns, mosses, tree-ferns, the tall "myrtle beech" (*Nothofagus cunninghamii*) and the lovely glossy-leaved lilly-pilly tree (*Eugenia smithii*), which grows up to 20 metres in height and has distinctive hanging clusters of bright pink berries.

These varied habitats provide food and shelter for a wide range of wildlife, from marsupials such as the koala (*Phascolarctos cinereus*) and the common wombat (*Vombatus ursinus*) to birds including the emu (*Dromaius novaehollandiae*), the rainbow lorikeet (*Trichoglossus haematodus*) and seabirds such as gulls and terns.

The plentiful plant and animal life made Wilson's Promontory an attractive home for Aborigines belonging to the Brataulong sub-group of the large Kurnai tribe from neighbouring Gippsland. These people called the Prom *Wamoom*. They lived there for several thousand years, but today they are remembered only by middens and artefacts left around the coast.

The first European to officially explore the region was the adventurous British surgeon and explorer George Bass, who in 1797-8 made an extraordinary journey from Port Jackson to Western Port (now Westernport) in an 8.5-metre, six-oared open whaleboat. Bass described the Prom as ". . . a lofty hummocky promontory of hard granite . . . Its firmness and vast durability make it well worthy of being, what there is great reason to believe it is, the boundary point of a large strait and a corner-stone of this great island, New Holland. It is joined to the mainland by a great neck of sand, which is nearly divided by a lagoon that runs in on the west side of it, and by a large shoal inlet on the east."

Mistakenly believing that the Prom had already been sighted by Captain Tobias Furneaux in HMS *Adventure* in 1773, Bass named it Furneaux Land. Later it was discovered that Captain Furneaux had seen a group of islands to the south (the Furneaux Group) and the name of Bass's discovery was changed to Wilson's Promontory, after Thomas Wilson, a London merchant who was engaged in trade with the colony and who was a friend of Bass and Matthew Flinders.

Bass, however, was not the first white man to visit this part of Australia. The day after he arrived at the promontory, he noticed smoke coming from a nearby island of the Glennie Group and went to investigate, expecting to find Aborigines. Instead he was astonished to find seven half-starved white men —convicts who had escaped from Sydney in a stolen boat three months earlier.

Various industries operated on the Prom during the nineteenth century including sealing, timber-getting, cattle grazing and tin mining, and occasionally scientists such as the famous botanist Ferdinand von Mueller visited the area to obtain specimens. The jutting promontory was also an important landmark for navigators and in 1859 convicts erected a lighthouse on its South East Point, using local granite and also basalt.

As early as 1884 naturalists J. B. Gregory, A. H. Lucas and G. W. Robinson began a campaign to have the Prom preserved as a national park. Opposition from various factions, including land developers who wanted to subdivide the region and sell 1000 small farms to crofters from the Isle of Skye, delayed the declaration of the park for more than 20 years. But finally members of several conservation-oriented organisations, led by the eminent biologist and anthropologist Sir Baldwin Spencer, roused so much public support and put up such a convincing case that the Victorian government in 1905 set aside 30 350 hectares of the Prom as a national park. At that stage a strip of land nearly a kilometre wide around the entire coast of the promontory was omitted from the park; however, this was added in 1908.

For many years the only access to the park was by sea or by undertaking a rugged overland journey. But scientists and others who visited the Prom were so enthusiastic about the region that by the mid-1920s a chalet was operating at Darby River and there were huts at Sealers Cove and Tidal River.

The widespread popularity of the park, however, came about as a result of World War II. Because of its isolation, rugged terrain, good water supply and abundant wildlife the promontory was considered ideal for commando training and in 1941 it was closed to the public. After the war, army buildings at Tidal River were acquired by the national park and over the years the settlement was enlarged, an army road was upgraded and extended, and walking tracks were cut or improved to give access to remote areas of the Prom.

Today Wilson's Promontory National Park incorporates part of the Yanakie Isthmus and several offshore islands, and covers an area of 48 920 hectares. Apart from Tidal River, popular and readily accessible areas include Whisky Bay, Squeaky Beach (named because the fine sand squeaks sharply when walked upon) and Lilly Pilly Gully, all of which are on the western side of the Prom. Bushwalkers also often trek to campsites on the eastern and southern shores, where the main attractions are the convict-built lighthouse at South East Point and secluded beaches at Sealers Cove, Refuge Cove, Waterloo Bay and Five Mile Beach.

Conservation of the natural environment remains an important aspect of the park, with special attention being paid to minimising the risk of bushfire, which in the past has devastated several thickly wooded areas of the promontory. □

1

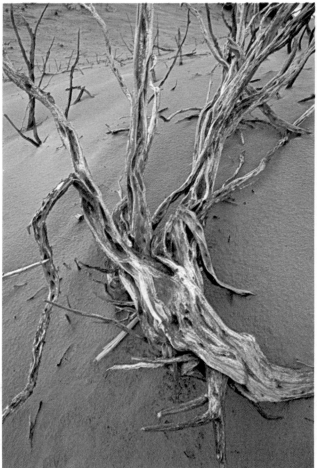

2

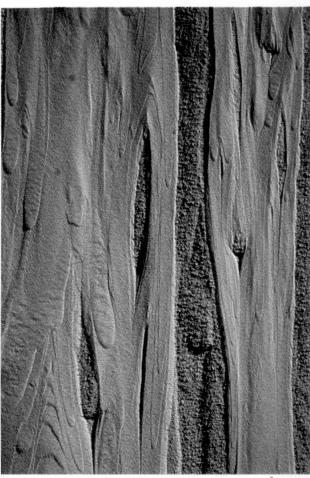

3

. . . The early morning sun dries the crests of the dunes and teardrops of sand flow down

1. Twilight at Whisky Bay, looking across to islands of the Glennie Group
2. Skeletal remains of vegetation suffocated by shifting sands
3–4. Weeping sands, Yanakie Isthmus

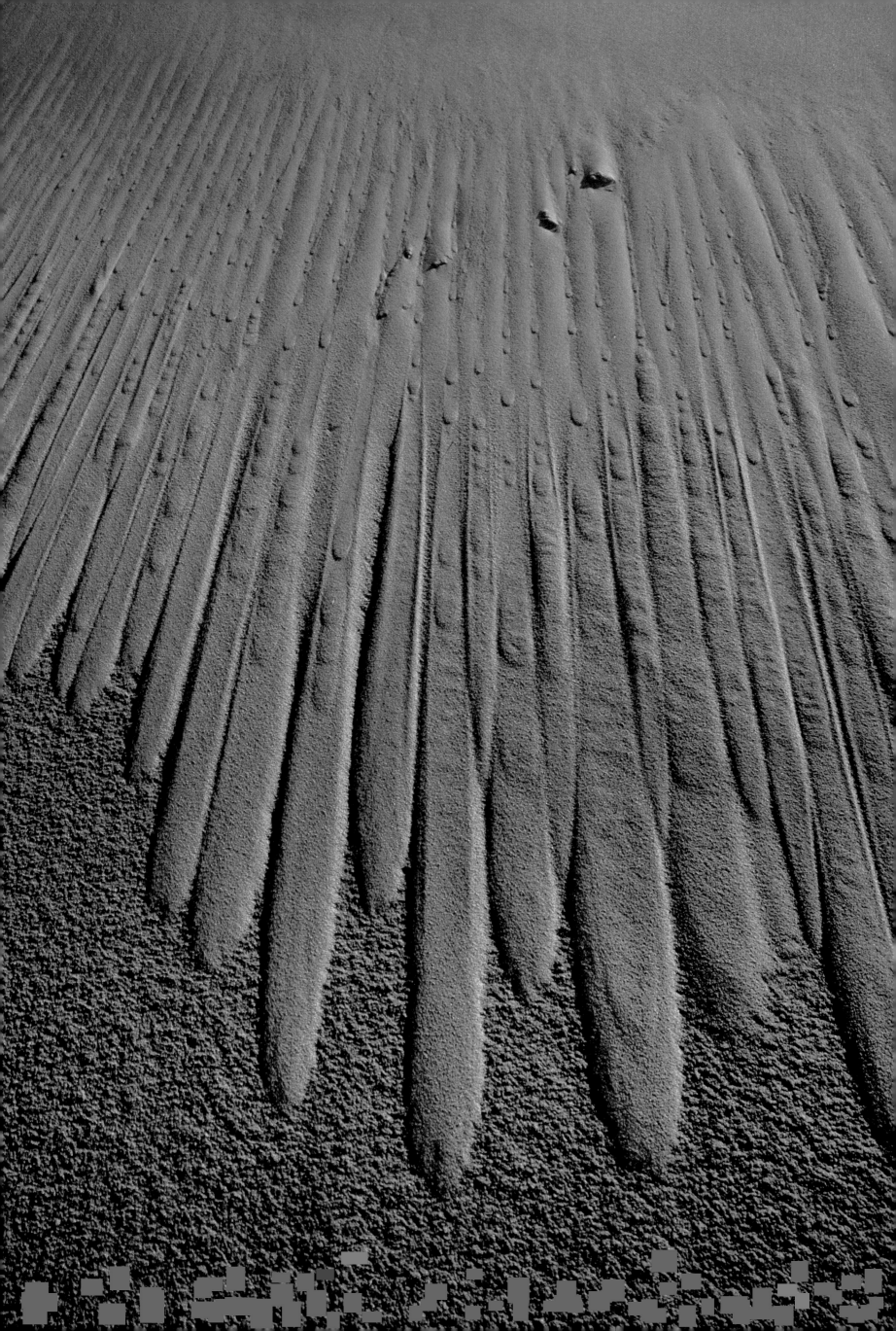

3

4

*Secluded white beaches
contrast with precipitous dark
headlands . . .*

1. The convict-built lighthouse,
South East Point
2. A ferny gully, Roaring Meg Creek
3. North Waterloo Beach
4. Waterloo Bay
5. View across South Point to
islands of the Anser Group
6. Rodondo Island

Artistry of the sea

THE PORT CAMPBELL COAST

THE 32 kilometres of dramatic coastline bordering the Port Campbell National Park in south-western Victoria present some of the most awesomely beautiful scenery in Australia. Driven by angry winds and tides, the ice-blue southern seas thunder in to a spectacular wall of tall perpendicular cliffs, carving numerous sea caves, blowholes, gorges, arches and isolated pillars of rock.

Whereas most of the Australian landscape is peaceful, this part of the coast is both dramatic and frightening. The cliffs, which are up to 150 metres in height, drop sheer to furiously boiling waters with foaming whirlpools, treacherous rips and billowing spray. On a rough day the waves may swell as much as 30 metres and even when the weather is mild the roar of the sea can be heard.

The cliffs and the country behind are composed principally of very fine-grained limestone laid down on an ancient seabed about 25 million years ago and then uplifted high above sea level. As the rock is of varying hardness, the ceaseless processes of weathering and erosion have etched away at differing speeds, producing the highly sculptural seascape. However, none of the rock is particularly resistant and as a result the Port Campbell cliffs are being worn away at a faster rate than any other part of the Australian coastline.

The various features of the coast are formed by combinations of wind, rain and wave action. Waves work along joint planes and weak rock strata, undermining the cliff and forming sea caves. The sheer strength of the water, together with its leaching effects, is sufficient to eat into the rocks, but sand, gravel and debris won from the land are also used as abrasive tools to hasten the process. If rainwater also works down through a joint or crack at the top of the cliff, a deep cleft is gradually created behind the cliff face. Eventually the undermined sections of cliff become top-heavy and topple over in great blocks into the sea below, leaving a new vertical cliff face. Any rough

1. The Twelve Apostles
2. Sunset near Loch Ard Gorge

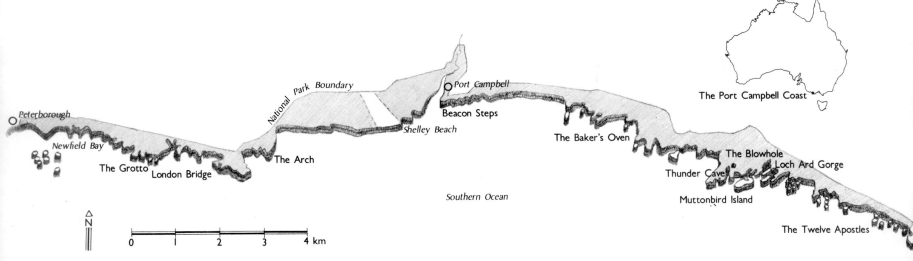

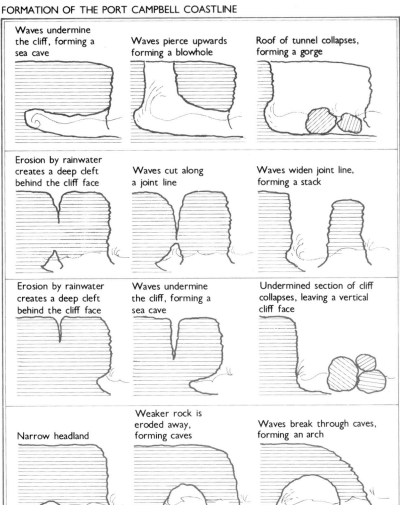

FORMATION OF THE PORT CAMPBELL COASTLINE

Waves undermine the cliff, forming a sea cave	Waves pierce upwards forming a blowhole	Roof of tunnel collapses, forming a gorge
Erosion by rainwater creates a deep cleft behind the cliff face	Waves cut along a joint line	Waves widen joint line, forming a stack
Erosion by rainwater creates a deep cleft behind the cliff face	Waves undermine the cliff, forming a sea cave	Undermined section of cliff collapses, leaving a vertical cliff face
Narrow headland	Weaker rock is eroded away, forming caves	Waves break through caves, forming an arch

patches are soon smoothed by the wind and the spray.

In some places, however, the waves cut back many metres into the cliff, forming tunnel-like caves and sometimes piercing upwards through the roof to form a blowhole. If the remainder of the roof collapses, a gorge is formed. As time passes, the waves continue to remove the softer rocks, widening the gorges into rocky bays and leaving the harder rocks as narrow headlands. Weaker areas at the base of the headlands are gradually eaten away, forming caves, and if caves on both sides of a headland meet, an arch is formed. Eventually the bridge span of the arch may collapse, leaving an isolated pillar of rock (called a "stack") standing offshore.

There are many spectacular features formed in this way along the Port Campbell coast. Among the most awe-inspiring are the deep cleft of Loch Ard Gorge, the seething Blowhole, and London Bridge, a beautiful double-arched headland standing 15 metres above the water.

The most impressive stacks are the Twelve Apostles. Narrow pillars of rock, they tower defiantly above the attacking sea, some reaching as high as 100 metres. But more than any other feature along the coast, they are old and worn. In time the

tireless aggressor will win and one by one they will topple down into the churning waters below.

Such will be the fate, eventually, of all other landforms holding out against the sea. But in the ever-changing way of things, the rest of the coastline will be altered too, and doubtless there will be new stacks, new caves and new arches elsewhere along the coast to replace those that fall.

In the days of sail the Port Campbell coastline was an ominous graveyard for ships. With treacherous surf and hidden rocks, the water is completely unnavigable and at least 30 large vessels were battered to an untimely end.

A shipwreck along this coast meant almost certain death for the passengers, for the vertical cliffs are smooth and impossible to climb. Just occasionally, however, one or two people were lucky enough to survive.

One such case involved the three-masted iron clipper *Loch Ard*, outward bound from Glasgow, which was wrecked on the coast shortly after 4 a.m. on 1 June 1878. It was winter and the weather was at its worst, but miraculously the *Loch Ard* had foundered near one of the few gorges that can be climbed. A young midshipman, Tom Pearce, managed to fight his way

*The ice-blue southern seas
thunder in to a spectacular wall
of perpendicular cliffs . . .*

1. The Twelve Apostles coastline
2. A giant wave, London Bridge
OVERLEAF: Cliffs near the Baker's Oven

2

through the surging waters to a tiny beach and soon after he dragged a girl named Eva Carmichael to safety too. The other 52 people aboard the ship drowned, including Eva's parents and six brothers and sisters.

Once ashore Tom took Eva to a cave, where she sought shelter while he went for help. Fortunately he found horses' tracks on top of the cliff and followed them until he met two stockmen from a nearby station. Later Tom was awarded the Royal Humane Society's gold medal for saving Eva. The following year he survived another shipwreck, this time off the coast of Ireland, and went on to command ships himself. Eva returned to Britain shortly after the disaster and never saw him again.

Looking down at the Loch Ard Gorge on a clear day it may at first seem quite idyllic. But the appearance is deceptive, for there are treacherous undertows and cross-currents in the water and the beach is constantly swept by noisy, eerie winds. This foreboding atmosphere is accentuated at the Eva Carmichael Cave, the entrance of which is fringed by a grotesque curtain of huge, dry stalactites.

When there are big seas there is no doubt about the dangers of the gorge. The waves crash through the narrow entrance and nearby they rush furiously through a long natural tunnel before escaping in a surging fountain from the gaping Blowhole, which is about 40 metres wide and 15 metres deep. Before it was fenced off, several people lost their lives by venturing too close to this hole.

But while man must tread cautiously along this coast, the cliffs and many of the beaches, islands and stacks provide sanctuary and nesting sites for seabirds and other animals. Little or fairy penguins (*Eudyptula minor*), for example, live in a rookery at London Bridge beach (this area has now been fenced off and safeguarded by the national park rangers) and muttonbirds (*Puffinus tenuirostris*) nest in close-packed colonies on a large, vegetated stack called Muttonbird Island. These remarkable birds migrate 24 000 kilometres each year, arriving at Port Campbell and other areas of Bass Strait in late October and leaving the following April, after mating, to spend the northern summer around the Bering Sea, near the Arctic.

The vegetation along the sea front is fairly sparse. Most of the plant species are low, salt-resistant heaths, often with smoky foliage and tiny, brightly coloured flowers. There are also many bright green, fleshy succulents and in a few places, such as in a deep recess called the Grotto, vines and other hanging plants stream luxuriantly down the sides of the cliffs.

Although this plant life enhances the beauty of the Port Campbell coast, the spectacle of the sandy-orange cliffs dropping sheer to a clear blue sea is always overwhelming.

The inlet of Port Campbell itself provides the only relatively safe anchorage along the entire length of the national park, but it is accessible only to very small craft. It was probably first used by sealers and whalers early last century and is named after Captain Alexander Campbell who was in charge

of a whaling station at Port Fairy and in the early 1840s sheltered in the little bay during a storm.

Pastoral runs were taken up near Port Campbell in the 1840s but the first permanent settlers did not arrive until the 1870s and the town's population has never exceeded 150. In the early days the main products of the district were oats and peas, but crayfishing and tourism are now more important to the town's economy.

About 700 hectares of coastal frontage east and west of Port Campbell make up the Port Campbell National Park, and this area includes nearly all of the most spectacular cliffs and other landforms. □

. . . Creating a highly sculptural seascape

1. The Twelve Apostles
2. Muttonbird Island
3. The Arch
4. Deeply etched coastline, east of Loch Ard Gorge
5–6. London Bridge
7. The Grotto
8. Coast near Loch Ard Gorge
9. Cliffs near London Bridge
10. The mouth of Loch Ard Gorge
11. A sea cave, Loch Ard Gorge

6

10

5

11

7

A noble range

THE GRAMPIANS

THE EXPLORER Thomas Livingstone Mitchell called the Grampians "a noble range of mountains" with as "bold and picturesque an outline as ever a painter imagined". To countless Aborigines who walked there before him, they were sacred grounds containing numerous ceremonial sites and figuring prominently in legends of the Dreamtime.

Located in western Victoria, the Grampians have a character that is both mellow and grand. Visible for vast distances, they present an imposing profile of sheer rocky ridges, chiselled peaks and thick forests that contrasts dramatically with the broad plains of the surrounding Wimmera district. The scenery within the ranges varies from wide panoramas of long escarpments overlooking flat pastoral valleys to narrow vistas of barren gorges and ferny gullies with fast-flowing streams cascading into beautiful waterfalls. Throughout the region there are superbly sculptured natural rock formations, many appearing like the work of man, and an extraordinary range of vegetation from past climatic ages.

Although separated from the mountains of eastern Victoria and consisting of different and younger geological formations, the Grampians are considered to form the south-western extremity of the Great Dividing Range, which runs from Cape York Peninsula down the entire east coast of the continent. They comprise three main sets of ranges and several smaller ones, running roughly north to south over an area about 100 kilometres long and 55 kilometres wide. The central ridge, which is the longest, itself consists of two distinct major sections—the Mt Difficult Range and the Serra Range—and stretches from the Grampians' northernmost peak, Mt Zero, to their southernmost peaks of Mt Abrupt and Mt Sturgeon. To the east, the main ridge is flanked by the shorter but higher Mt William Range—containing the Grampians' tallest peak, Mt William (1166 metres)—and to the west is the lower Victoria Range, renowned for its flora and Aboriginal rock painting sites.

The building of the Grampians began about 395 million years ago. Over a period of about 50 million years, vast amounts of sandy sediments were deposited in a great lake (or perhaps a sea) and eventually they became compacted, forming a huge mass of alternating beds of very resistant quartzose sandstone and less resistant siltstones and mudstones, about 6000 metres thick. Subsequent folding and weathering resulted in a series of ranges which in many places exposed gently dipping strata of sandstones and shales with intrusions of grey granite. Further erosion then wore down the land and widened the valleys, removing the weak shales at a relatively fast rate and leaving the resistant sandstones in asymmetrical ridges that feature spectacular steep escarpments facing to the east and gentle dip slopes backing them to the west. This attractive formation, known as a cuesta, can be clearly seen from the Boroka Lookout which affords magnificent views of the Fyans Valley between the Serra and Mt William ranges.

Nestling between these two major ranges is the small but enchanting Wonderland Range. Just 6.5 kilometres long and very narrow, it is a masterpiece of scenic beauty and one of the loveliest places in the Grampians.

Among the main attractions of the Wonderland is a gorge known as the Grand Canyon. Although much smaller than its name suggests, it has been deeply eroded along both the horizontal bedding planes and the vertical joint lines of its steel-grey walls and seems like a stately edifice constructed of square-cut building blocks. The gorge is located on the lower slopes of the range. It climbs quite steeply and a lovely stream trickles through it.

Near the top of the range, another attractive gorge leads to the rocky summit. Known as Silent Street, it is reminiscent of a narrow Spanish lane, with the eroded grey walls appearing like tall apartment blocks. As if to complete the image, a few lonely shrubs grow at the end of the gorge like trees on the pavement of a street and smaller plants grow on the walls as though in window boxes. They are particularly pretty in summer when the foliage is embellished by masses of flowers.

The aeons of weathering and erosion have left a craggy imprint throughout the Wonderland Range and in many places the rocks have been intricately sculptured into effigies that have earned names such as the Lady's Hat and Mushroom Rock. Interesting rock formations are also found on the edge of the Wonderland escarpment, including the Fallen Giant, a huge slab of sandstone that has broken away from the cliff, and the Nerve Test, a narrow rock projection about half a metre wide and 10 metres long. Magnificent views of the valley below can be gained from a bare rock ledge known as the Pinnacle and from Sundial Peak, so-named by early settlers who were able to tell the time of day by the sun's play of light and shadow on its rocky face.

Other impressive rock formations of the Grampians occur in more rugged regions than the Wonderland and include the aptly named Castle Rock located in a remote part of the Victoria Range, the terraced Mt Rosea in the Serra Range, the table-topped Major Mitchell Plateau in the Mt William Range, and the remarkable Balconies, a group of overhanging ledges in the small Mt Victory Range which is an extension of the Grampians' main central ridge. Of note also is Hollow Mountain, a semicircular spur of Mt Stapylton (at the northern end of the Mt Difficult Range), which has been hollowed out by erosion on the inner side and features many wind-scooped arches and open-roofed caverns.

As well as the rock formations, the Grampians contain many areas of softer scenery.

The region's rivers and creeks have cut many deep gorges along joints in the rocks, and beautiful waterfalls have been created in places where erosion by the waters has been arrested by harder beds of rock. Particularly spectacular is a series of four falls in the MacKenzie Gorge, where the MacKen-

1

2

4

5

*Thick forests and chiselled
mountain peaks. . .*

1. Silent Street, Wonderland Range
2. Hollow Mountain, Mt Difficult Range
3. Snow-draped blackboys
(*Xanthorrhoea sp.*), Mt Difficult Range
4. MacKenzie Falls
5. Tree-ferns (*Todea barbara*),
Wonderland Range
6. Moss (*Thuidium sp.*) growing on a
lichen-encrusted tree trunk,
Wonderland Range
7. Koala (*Phascolarctos cinereus*), near
Fyans Creek

THE AUSTRALIAN ALPS

To those who think of snowfields as steep white expanses with fir trees and sharp mountain peaks, the Australian Alps must seem very strange indeed. Not only is the most dominant tree a eucalypt—the smooth-barked snow gum (*Eucalyptus pauciflora*)—but the highest points are simply hummocky mounds rising from a continuous mountain ridge. Nowhere do they stand above the permanent snowline, so depending on the time of year there might not even be any snow. Yet despite this lack of usual alpine characteristics, the snowfields of the "alps" have a unique fascination, with seasonally changing scenery, remarkable alpine flora and a surprising abundance of animal life.

The Australian Alps are part of the Great Dividing Range, which extends along the entire east coast of the continent. They are a series of highland plateaux curving in a wide sweep across the south-eastern corner of the continent, from a little north of Kiandra in New South Wales to Mt Buller in Victoria. Although by far the highest mountains in Australia, they are extremely low by world standards: the highest point, Mt Kosciusko, reaches only to an altitude of 2228 metres, a mere quarter the height of the world's tallest mountain, Mt Everest, which soars more than 8840 metres.

The highest peaks of the Alps occur in the centre of the region on a wide, arc-shaped main ridge that stretches about 120 kilometres and is completely surrounded by rugged lower mountains covered with thick forests of tall eucalypt trees. The northern end of this ridge is occupied by the Snowy Mountains, where Mt Kosciusko and several other peaks top 2000 metres, and the southern end is marked by Victoria's tallest mountains: Mt Bogong (1986 metres), Mt Feathertop (1922 metres) and Mt Hotham (1859 metres). West of these three peaks is the slightly lower plateau of Mt Buffalo, standing isolated from the main range. Reaching a height of 1723 metres, it is an impressive horst (or block mountain) bounded on all sides by steep-sided faults.

The Alps have an extremely complicated geological structure, being made up of various types of rock including granites, slates, schists, limestone and basalt. Essentially they are remnants of a 500-million-year-old mountain range which aeons ago was eroded down to an almost flat plain. Their present elevation is due to a general uplifting of the eastern edge of the continent about 2-3 million years ago. As the uplift was greatest in the Kosciusko region, where the mountains reached heights of perhaps 3000 metres above sea level, it is commonly referred to as the "Kosciusko Uplift". Extensive folding and faulting during this time resulted in a pattern of north-south running mountain ridges separated by corridors of almost parallel rift valleys.

These changes had an important effect on the paths of the many rivers of the alpine region and created the drainage pattern we know today. Formerly eastward-flowing rivers were blocked by the new mountains and diverted inland to join up with what is now known as the Murray-Darling system, while those that still emptied into Bass Strait or the Tasman Sea became shorter and swifter as they plunged down the Alps' steep eastern slopes.

Since then, the Alps have been altered and lowered to their present relief only by weathering and erosion, especially by frost, ice and snow. Of particular interest is an area of about 50 square kilometres in the Snowy Mountains, between Mt Kosciusko and Mt Twynam (2196 metres), which was the only part of the Australian mainland to be affected by glaciers during the last ice age, some 15 000–30 000 years ago. The glaciers were much smaller than those which formed in Tasmania during this period, the longest one extending only about 20 kilometres along the upper Snowy River valley. Today, evidence of the glaciers can be seen in several cirques and small lakes near the top of the plateau. The largest and deepest of these lakes is Blue Lake, which lies at the foot of Mt Twynam. Four other glacial lakes—Hedley Tarn, Club Lake, Lake Albina and Lake Cootapatamba—are located a little to the south and the remains of two former lakes can also be seen in small valleys where morainal dams (composed of rock debris deposited by glaciers) were not strong enough to continue to hold back the waters. Here and in other high parts of the Alps there are also impressive piles of boulders which have been polished smooth by ice and snow.

The scenery in the Alps today differs dramatically from season to season, passing from the white of winter, through the fresh greens of spring, to the multi-coloured floral displays of summer, and finally changing to the golden hues of autumn before the cycle starts again.

In winter as much as 7000 square kilometres of the high country may be covered with a thick blanket of snow, forming the most extensive snowfields in Australia. The Alps are particularly beautiful during these months, especially when the smooth, silhouetted curves of the white-capped mountain tops are illuminated by a full moon or by the radiant alpine glow of sunrise and sunset. However, the mountain weather is very unpredictable and snowfalls vary from year to year. In some years there may not be much snow, even during winter; at other times sudden blizzards in midsummer may result in some snow remaining on the high tops all year.

Usually the first snows fall around June. By July the snow has accumulated in deep drifts in the valleys and gullies, with a thinner covering on the windswept summits. This white mantle will stay until at least the end of August, sometimes lasting through to October.

As the prevailing snow-bearing winds are strong and come from the south-west, they tend to blow the snow off the exposed mountain ridges so that it settles thickest on the sheltered east-facing slopes, where it forms steep cornices (masses of hard-packed snow). In places such as hollows, which are shaded from direct sunlight for most of the day, patches of

Snow gum (*Eucalyptus pauciflora*), Falls Creek

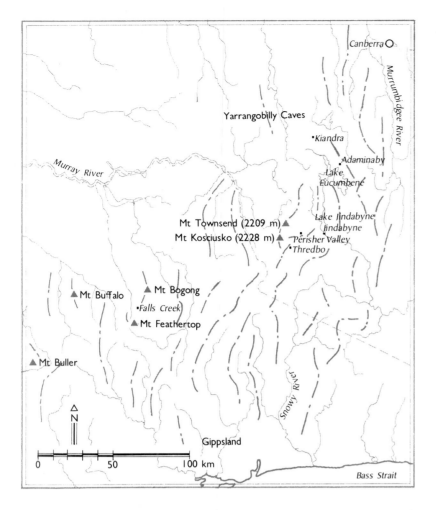

• The Australian Alps

the cornices may last well into summer. Eventually they break away from the slopes and on the underside of overhanging snow ledges, intriguing combinations of various algae species, dust and the refraction of light produce superb many-coloured patterns reminiscent of abstract art. In some places red-pigmented algae growing in the snow also create a "wine-stained" or "red snow" effect.

For alpine plants, an ability to cope with the extreme seasonal fluctuations is essential. Winter temperatures (which have been known to drop as low as –22°C), together with the strong winds, are too severe for trees to survive at altitudes above 1850 metres, although a variety of smaller plants thrive even on the peaks.

The snow gums (Eucalyptus pauciflora), which give the Alps their distinctively Australian identity, are exceptionally attractive trees with a mallee-like ability to develop in radically different ways according to the harshness of the environment. They grow in areas between 1200 and 1850 metres above sea level, and are most spectacular in the exposed higher regions, especially after fire, when they become grotesquely gnarled. Often several trunks grow from a single rootstock, twisting and turning tortuously into weird, contorted shapes.

At milder, lower levels the snow gums grow to a height of 5-8 metres, with a slender, crooked trunk and a broad crown of foliage, although in particularly well-sheltered places they may stand quite erect, reaching as high as 10 metres. Up to an altitude of about 1650 metres, the trees grow fairly close together in forests which may also include thickets of the related species, black sallee (Eucalyptus stellulata), and an occasional patch of the shrub-like alpine wattle (Acacia alpina).

As altitude increases, the forest thins out and only the snow gums remain, becoming more and more stunted. Above about 1800 metres there are very few snow gums, though a few weather-beaten trees hold out in sheltered niches.

Despite its various forms, the snow gum is easy to recognise, being distinguished by a magnificent smooth white bark streaked with green, gold, brown or red. In summer the tree flowers profusely with beautiful white blossoms.

Above the treeline the Alps are vegetated by many hardy herbs, heaths, grasses and other low plants which spend much of the year buried in snow. The herbs are particularly prolific and have developed a variety of means of coping with the harsh environment, some hugging boulders for maximum warmth, others forming tight mats for protection from the winds. The foliage is small to conserve heat and usually it has a protective waxy or hairy surface. Yet the flowers are extremely delicate.

One of the earliest herbs to flower is the alpine marsh marigold (Caltha introloba), its rosettes of white and pink petals expanding in October amid tiny icicles at the edge of snow-drifts. It is soon followed by yellow buttercups (Ranunculus spp.), white alpine daisies (Brachycome spp.), golden billy buttons (Craspedia spp.), purple eyebrights (Euphrasia spp.) and several paper daisies (Helipterum and Helichrysum spp.). By the summer months of January and February the ground is a profusion of colour.

Many plants live in swampy bog areas, where some of the massive volume of water released when the snow thaws is held back by the remarkable sphagnum moss (Sphagnum cristatum). The spongy tissues of this plant enable it to absorb several times its own weight in water, providing a constantly moist habitat for plants such as sedges, ferns, heaths and orchids. Common flowering plants in the bogs include the creamy-yellow candle heath (Richea continentis), the silvery-brown edelweiss (Ewartia nubigena) and the carnivorous white alpine sundew (Drosera arcturi), which has a sticky fluid on the tips of its leaves to trap insects such as flies and moths.

The windswept rocky ridges of the alpine summits are clothed in lichens and mosses, interspersed with snow grass (Poa spp.) and rock-clasping plants such as the carpet heath (Pentachondra pumila), which has tiny star-shaped flowers and crimson berry-like fruit. At lower levels the snow country is well-endowed with flowering shrubs of about 1-2 metres in height. These plants include the white-flowering daisy bush (Olearia alpicola), the fragrant purple-flowered alpine mint bush (Prostanthera cuneata) and the mountain pepper (Drimys lanceolata), whose distinctive bright green leaves borne on red stems contain oils that have a hot peppery taste.

Below altitudes of about 1500 metres, the small alpine species gradually give way to dense eucalypt forests dominated by the giant mountain ash (Eucalyptus regnans) and the slightly smaller alpine ash (Eucalyptus delegatensis). In a few deep valleys there are also pockets of native "pines", reminders of a time more than 5 million years ago when rainforests of beeches, conifers, ferns and mosses covered much of this part of the continent.

The Alps provide a home for a wide variety of animals, from birds, reptiles and mammals to insects, amphibians and fish. As with the plant species, adaptability is the key to survival in the high country. Some animals, such as kangaroos and wallabies, are warm-weather migrants, spending the winter at altitudes below the snowline and moving higher up with the onset of spring. Many species, however, stay in the highlands all year round, coping with the cold winter by living underneath the snow, which acts as an insulator and keeps the temperature warmer than it is above. Most of these species—for example, snakes and the echidna *(Tachyglossus aculeatus)*—hibernate to conserve heat and energy, but some remain active all year. A few insects also regulate their body temperature by changing colour, notably the alpine grasshopper *(Acripeza reticulata)* which turns black in cold weather to absorb maximum warmth and changes to brilliant blue to reflect radiant heat when the temperature climbs above 15°C.

One of the most successful permanent inhabitants of the snow country is the mountain pygmy possum *(Burramys parvus)*, which stays active all year, in winter living on insects and small plants that grow under the snow. This tiny animal was first known to Europeans through fossil bones found at the Wombeyan Caves, north of the Alps, in 1894 by the naturalist and palaeontologist Robert Broom. The name Broom gave to his find is derived from *Burra*, the Aboriginal name for the Wombeyan region and *mys*, a scientific term meaning mouse-like. For more than 70 years the burramys was thought to be extinct, but in 1966 two Victorian holidaymakers accidentally discovered living animals at Mt Hotham. The possum has since been found to be fairly widely distributed in remote parts of the Alps, between altitudes of 1500 and 2000 metres. Several other small marsupials and native rodents also adapt to life under the snow, such as the fluffy, dark-brown broad-toothed rat *(Mastacomys fuscus)*, which was once more widespread but is now found only in a few colonies in the Alps and in the high country of Tasmania.

Another intriguing animal that can survive beneath the snow is the tiny corroboree frog *(Pseudophryne corroboree)*, which in summer lives in the sphagnum bogs. It measures only 2-3 centimetres in length but is conspicuous because of its vibrant yellow and black markings. With little webbing on its feet, it is a poor swimmer and tends to crawl rather than hop. The name "corroboree frog" was bestowed on this small animal in 1953 by an American scientist who fancied that its colourful skin patterns resembled body markings used by Aboriginal people in corroborees.

The bird population of the Alps is highly varied, ranging from small wrens, swallows and martins to large eagles and the flightless emu *(Dromaius novaehollandiae)*. Owls and waterbirds are very common, but as in most parts of Australia the colourful parrots attract most attention. Of particular note is the gang-gang cockatoo *(Callocephalon fimbriatum)*, whose common name resembles its rasping call. The female is completely grey, but the male is grey only on the body and has a magnificent red head and crest. The gang-gang is found only in the south-eastern highlands of mainland Australia and its diet includes the seeds of the snow gum. However, it occasionally visits northern Tasmania and the islands of Bass Strait.

The icy mountain streams and lakes also teem with animal life. Australia's famous egg-laying mammal, the platypus *(Ornithorhynchus anatinus)*, is the most endearing aquatic creature, although the male has a spur that can inflict a venomous wound. Indigenous fish include the small "native trout" *(Galaxias findlayi)*, which seldom grows larger than 6-7 centimetres and has no body scales and only one dorsal fin. Unfortunately its numbers have been depleted significantly by the introduction of predatory brown and rainbow trout *(Salmo trutta* and *S. gairdnerii)*.

Although located between Australia's two main population centres, Sydney and Melbourne, the Australian Alps remained surprisingly remote until the late 1940s, when the Snowy Mountains and Kiewa hydro-electric schemes brought roads and large numbers of people to the region.

Before the white man came to Australia, the winter snows prevented the Aboriginal people from permanently inhabiting the high country, although various areas were visited annually by large groups in quest of the greyish-brown bogong moth *(Agrotis infusa)*, which migrates to the mountains in spring when the plains country becomes too hot. These abundant insects remain almost inactive throughout the summer, living off fat stored in their bodies. Easy to catch, they were an important food source for the Aborigines, who singed them over fire to remove the hard wings and scales and then pounded the soft bodies into a paste. Mt Bogong in Victoria and the Bogong Range in New South Wales are just two of many alpine areas where the Aborigines gathered. Their long association with the region is also reflected in other present-day place names including Kiewa (meaning "sweet water") and Lake Cootapatamba ("crystal clear waters where eagles drink").

The first white man to see any part of the Alps was an ex-convict named Joseph Wild who discovered Lake George in 1820 and then, guided by Aborigines, climbed a hill near Bungendore and saw what he referred to as "Snowy Mountains" in the distance. Possibly because of his convict past, Wild's sighting of the Snowys is rarely acknowledged, although his descriptive name for the range fell into popular usage and was eventually gazetted. In 1823 Wild accompanied Captain Mark Currie and Brigade-Major John Ovens on an expedition to the Monaro district on the eastern side of the Alps, and the party travelled to within 20 kilometres of the site of present-day Cooma.

The following year, on the other side of the mountains, the explorers Hamilton Hume and William Hovell became the first Europeans to see the main range, viewing it in the distance from the Tumut River. They were also the first to refer to the mountains as the "Australian Alps".

Before the end of the decade, squatters made headway into the grassy plains of the Monaro, where they found good grazing lands for sheep and cattle. It seems likely that these men explored the high country of the Snowy Mountains while looking for summer grazing lands, but no records were kept as entry into the area was at that time prohibited by the colonial officialdom, which wanted to confine settlement to nineteen counties established around Sydney.

A detailed journal was kept, however, by the first scientist to visit the area, Dr John Lhotsky. Born in Poland of Czech parents and raised in Germany, Lhotsky was a brilliant man who was highly educated in the disciplines of medicine, botany and geology. But he antagonised the government authorities and in the course of time many of his writings were either lost or suppressed. As a consequence Lhotsky has been much ignored by both his contemporaries and later generations of Australians, but from records that do survive it is known that in 1834 he climbed several high peaks in the Snowy Mountains—"the very heart of the Australian Alps"—and it is possible that Mt Kosciusko may have been among them.

In the absence of certainty about Lhotsky's exploration, the first European ascent of Mt Kosciusko is generally attributed to the Polish explorer and geologist, Count Paul Edmund de Strzelecki, who climbed to the summit early in 1840. Strzelecki was struck by the similarity in configuration between the mountain and a memorial tumulus erected in Krakow for the great Polish patriot Tadeusz Kościuszko. Being in a country of "free people, who appreciate freedom", he wrote that he could "not refrain from giving it the name Mount Kosciusko", which would " . . . serve as a reminder for future generations upon this continent of a name dear and hallowed to every human, to every friend of freedom and honour".

Strzelecki did not leave a cairn to mark his climb and many years later there arose some controversy as to whether he had climbed the highest peak or the slightly lower peak now known as Mt Townsend (2209 metres). The doubt seems to have originated from an error made by staff of the Victorian Survey Department, who in 1870 placed a trigonometrical cairn on Mt Townsend but marked it Mt Kosciusko. The mistake was perpetuated, and often still persists, despite the fact that the first map of the area (made in 1851 for the New South Wales Department of Lands) and all subsequent maps show Strzelecki's mountain as the highest peak, as we know it today.

Before returning to Sydney, Strzelecki and his party explored part of what is now the Victorian section of the Alps. They were not the first Europeans to penetrate this region, for the route they followed—travelling south to Omeo, then along the Tambo River to Gippsland—had been pioneered the previous year by a Goulburn station overseer, Angus McMillan, who had been prompted by drought to look for new pastures. Details of McMillan's discoveries had been withheld by his employer, Captain Lachlan Macalister, who wanted to avoid a land rush so that he could utilise the area himself. However, soon after Strzelecki's journey, a number of graziers obtained leases to large areas of land in and around the Alps, including the Kosciusko high tops.

Strzelecki also reported finding traces of gold in the Alps, but he complied with a request by Governor George Gipps to suppress the information for fear that it would precipitate a convict uprising and cause economic turmoil. After Gipps's resignation in 1846, further geological explorations were made and inevitably prospectors struck it lucky. In the mid-1850s boom towns sprang up at places such as Bright, Omeo and Harrietville in Victoria, and a few years later at Kiandra in the Snowy Mountains.

The Kiandra gold rush was sparked in 1859 by the discovery of good alluvial deposits by two brothers named Pollock, who were stockmen but did a little prospecting in their spare time. By the end of the year quite a number of miners were working in the area, and the following year the fever really hit. The population grew in 1860 to some 10 000 people in Kiandra, who worked the "magic mile" on the bed of the Eucumbene River, and a further 5000 in the surrounding district. But the deposits of alluvial gold, while easily won, were soon worked out and by March 1861 only about 200 people remained to brave the coming winter. However, in May the population received a boost by the arrival of about 400 industrious Chinese, who diverted the waters of the river and eked out a living from the gold that the white diggers had left behind.

During the next 10 years there were several rushes to outlying goldfields, and other small townships such as Adaminaby came into being. Deeper gold and other minerals, notably copper, continued to be mined around Kiandra and other areas of the Snowy Mountains until about 1937.

In a country which today is barely associated with the sport of ski-ing, it is surprising to learn that early in the 1860s some of the first officially organised ski races in the world were held at Kiandra and that around 1870 one of the world's first ski clubs, the Kiandra Snow-Shoe Club, was formed there. Some years later the office bearers of this club were to include a young Sydney solicitor named Andrew Barton Paterson, whose epic ballad, "The Man from Snowy River"—first published in the *Bulletin* magazine in April 1890 under the pseudonym "The Banjo" and released in book form in 1895—was destined to become a classic of Australian bush literature.

Telling about the pursuit of a colt that escaped to join the wild bush horses, the poem immortalised the skill of the Australian mountain men. But it portrayed only the romantic side of life in the Alps, and the story of many stockmen and miners is told in the place names they left behind—World's End, Hell Hole, Dead Horse Gap, Siberia. Deaths through being caught in blizzards or flooded rivers were not uncommon, and squatters and goldseekers were often raided by escaped convicts, bushrangers and other desperadoes who hid out in remote alpine valleys.

For many years Paterson's poem was to achieve far greater popularity than his sport of ski-ing. In the early 1900s various ski clubs were formed in the Snowy Mountains and a hotel

A silky mantle of winter snow, Falls Creek

was established in 1909 near Mt Kosciusko. Further accommodation became available over the years, notably a chalet built by the New South Wales government at Charlotte Pass in 1930, but the lack of good roads and insufficient facilities kept ski-ing in the area on a small scale until the development of the Snowy Mountains Hydro-Electric Scheme after World War II.

The Snowy scheme—begun in 1949 and completed in the early 1970s—is generally considered to be Australia's greatest engineering achievement. As far back as 1884 people had recognised the potential of the Snowy Mountains for the development of an irrigation scheme to water the thirsty but otherwise fertile lands to the west. The country's major river, the Murray, and some of its tributaries including the big Murrumbidgee River, not only pass through these dry lands but also have their source in the Snowys, where huge masses of snow are stored frozen during winter, melting later when rainfall is at its lowest. The only hitch to the scheme was that most of the melting snow ran into Bass Strait and the Tasman Sea. To utilise the waters it would be necessary to store them in huge reservoirs near the sources of the Snowy and its main tributary, the Eucumbene, and then divert them via tunnels through the mountains to storage areas between the Murray

and Murrumbidgee rivers, from which they could be released as required. It was financially impractical to redirect the waters purely for irrigation, and there the matter rested until the 1940s, when a plan was evolved for a Snowy Mountains hydro-electric power scheme which was economically viable and which incorporated irrigation as an ancillary project.

Today there are 16 major dams, 7 power stations, 145 kilometres of tunnels and 80 kilometres of aqueducts associated with the scheme. The largest reservoir, the artificial Lake Eucumbene, covers an area of 145 square kilometres and can hold 4 798 000 megalitres of water—eight times the capacity of Sydney Harbour. The lake drowned the old town of Adaminaby and another reservoir, Lake Jindabyne, inundated the tiny town of Jindabyne. Both towns have been relocated on higher land a few kilometres from their original sites.

Some 1600 kilometres of roads and tracks built in the course of the scheme's construction have opened up the area to visitors and led to the establishment of many popular ski resorts such as Thredbo, Perisher Valley, Smiggin Holes and the less-developed Guthega, all offering modern facilities. The old Kosciusko Hotel no longer exists, having been destroyed by fire in 1951, but the original chalet at Charlotte Pass is still operat-

The smooth, silhouetted curves
of the mountain tops . . .

Winter, the Bogong High Plains
OVERLEAF: Star trails disappear behind
the moonlit snowfields of the Bogong
High Plains

ing. Kiandra, now in ruins, is of great historical interest but the snowfalls are now considered too unreliable for ski-ing.

In Victoria, European infiltration of the Alps followed a similar pattern. The cattlemen who had followed the trails blazed by Angus McMillan established isolated settlements across the region, especially on the Bogong High Plains. Within a few years they were followed by prospectors and scientists, including the famous German-born botanist and explorer, Ferdinand von Mueller. Almost immediately after his appointment as Government Botanist of Victoria in 1853, Mueller explored the Mt Buffalo and Mt Buller areas. Later that year he made his way to Omeo, penetrating northward deep into the Snowy Mountains, where a peak is now named after him, and the following year he discovered Mt Hotham. During these journeys Mueller named and collected specimens of more than 1000 plant species, providing the first significant and detailed information on the fascinating alpine flora.

The earliest ski-ing enthusiasts venturing to the Victorian Alps came in the 1860s from the goldrush towns that had sprung up the decade before at Bright, Omeo and Harrietville. Initially they favoured the slopes around Mt Hotham, which separated the latter two towns, but by the 1890s there was organised ski-ing at Mt Feathertop and Mt Bernard, with more adventurous skiers exploring further afield.

An alpine club was started at Bright at the turn of the century, and ski-ing was given a significant boost in 1908 when the Victorian Railways (which earlier had constructed a railway track to the town) cut a road through to Mt Buffalo and two years later opened a chalet. Further developments in the 1920s increased the popularity of the sport, especially at Mt Hotham and Mt Buffalo, but by the late 1930s Mt Buller (1804 metres) had become Victoria's most developed ski resort, having the advantage of being closer to Melbourne than other centres.

The development of a ski resort at Falls Creek, east of Mt Hotham, came about shortly after World War II through the Kiewa Hydro-Electric Scheme which impounds water from the Bogong High Plains for both irrigation and the generation of electricity. The resort started out in a small way in 1946 when the State Electricity Commission gave its workers permission to build a ski hut to cater for recreational needs, but by the late 1950s it had been transformed into a highly organised tourist operation. Today it shares with Mt Buller, Mt Hotham and Mt Buffalo the distinction of being among Victoria's main alpine ski resorts.

In both Victoria and New South Wales, the hydro-electric schemes have brought profound changes to the landscape and character of the Alps. For more than a century before the schemes, overgrazing on the high tops had destroyed much of the fragile plant cover. However, the success of the hydro-electric projects depends on the conservation of the plant communities, which protect the soil from erosion and thereby prevent siltation of the reservoirs. As a result, grazing is no longer permitted in the catchment areas, bringing to an end the era of the legendary mountain men.

In 1944, with the Snowy scheme imminent, the New South Wales government proclaimed a large area of the mountains as the Kosciusko State Park. It was renamed Kosciusko National Park in 1967 and today encompasses an area of 627 200 hectares. All the major ski resorts and hydro-electric stations lie within the park boundaries, as do two spectacular series of limestone caves—the Yarrangobilly Caves and the Cooleman Caves—and great care is taken to balance the conservation requirements of the environment and its use for recreation, education and research.

Most visitors to the park come during the 4-month-long ski season, but the wealth of flora and fauna, and activities such as bushwalking, are bringing a growing number of people to the high country in summer. Other people are attracted to the lakes, especially Lake Eucumbene and Lake Jindabyne, where boating and trout-fishing are popular. The Yarrangobilly Caves, discovered in 1834, are also open for inspection and nearby there is a natural thermal pool, the waters of which maintain a constant temperature of 27°C and are thought to rise from a depth of 900 metres. Fortunately, soil conservation measures introduced to the mountains jointly by the park and hydro-electric authorities in the 1940s are taking effect and many plants that were almost eaten or trampled to extinction are now slowly regenerating.

In Victoria, only a very small part of the high country has been reserved: the 11 000-hectare plateau of Mt Buffalo National Park and the 4097-hectare Mt Buller Reserve controlled by the Victorian Forests Commission. Mt Buffalo, named in 1824 by the explorers Hovell and Hume (who thought that a broad rock mass now known as the Hump and a nearby thrusting peak, the Horn, resembled a buffalo), has been protected since 1908, but was not declared a national park until 1956. It includes some of Australia's most beautiful alpine scenery—a magnificent gorge, waterfalls, huge granite tors and rare alpine vegetation—and today there is great concern as to whether or not the natural environment can be preserved in the face of increasing demands placed upon it by skiers and other visitors. Certainly recreational needs are well catered for in other Victorian alpine resorts, which offer activities ranging from winter ski-ing to summer canoeing and horse-riding.

Although human intrusion is obvious in many parts of the Australian Alps, there are still substantial areas of primitive landscapes, disturbed only by simple walking tracks. The most spectacular of these wilderness areas is traversed by a 400-kilometre track from Mt Erica (near Mt Baw Baw in Gippsland), passing through ruggedly beautiful alpine and forest country to Tom Groggin in the Kosciusko National Park. But even where the hydro-electric schemes have transformed the landscape, the man-made structures are generally in harmony with the surroundings. □

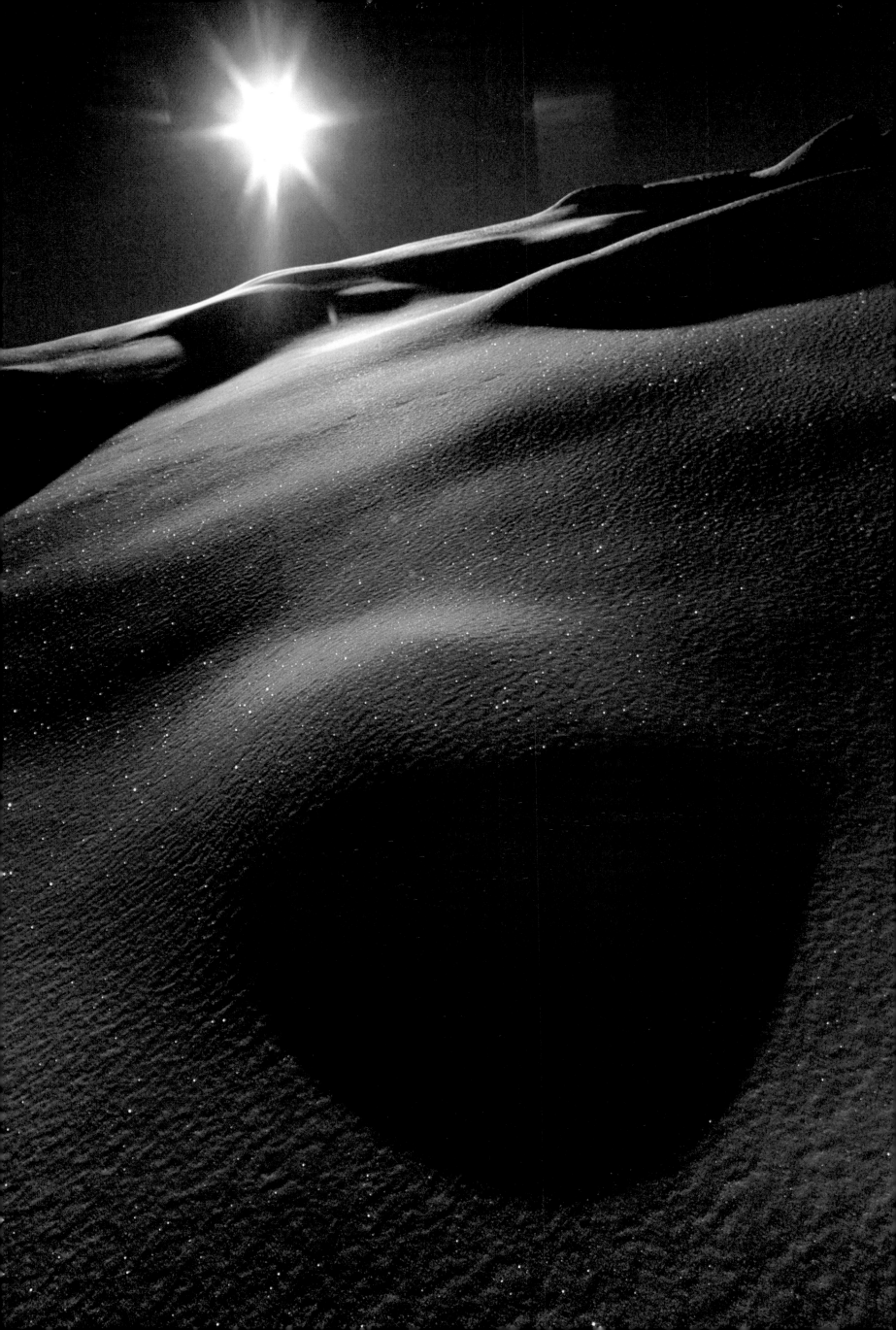

The cornices of snow break away from the slopes and patches may last well into summer . . .

1. Melting snowdrift, Snowy Mountains
2. Red-pigmented algae stain the summer snow, Mt Twynam
3. Algae, dust and sunlight accentuate abstract patterns hollowed out by wind eddies on the underside of a snowdrift, Mt Twynam
4. A snow-fed stream above Blue Lake, Snowy Mountains
5. Sunlight filters through to the ferny understorey of a eucalypt forest, Mt Buffalo
6. Alpine paper daisy (*Helipterum albicans*), Snowy Mountains
7. Alpine mustard (*Cardamine sp.*)

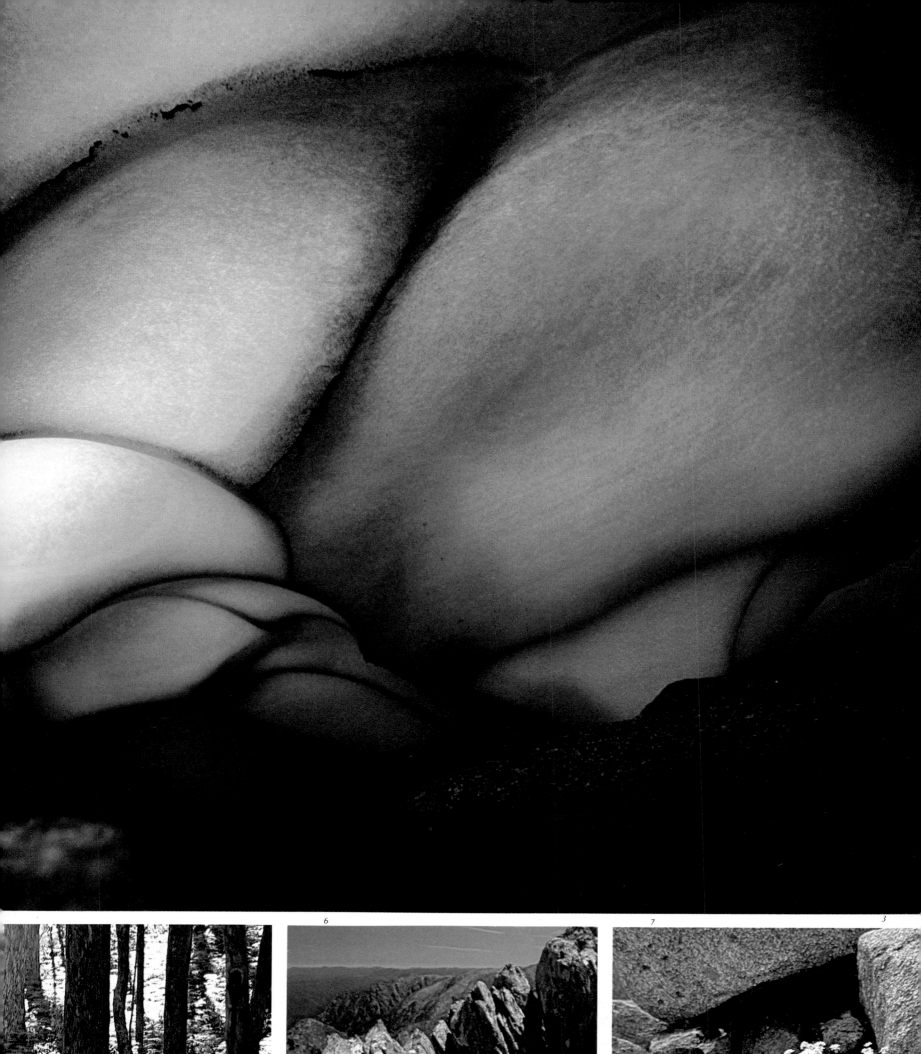

An enigmatic maze

THE BLUE MOUNTAINS

WHILE exploring the country north of Port Jackson in April 1788, just three months after establishing Australia's first convict settlement at Sydney Cove, Governor Arthur Phillip saw a long ribbon of low mountains stretching across the western horizon. A valley seemed to divide them into two parts, the northern of which Phillip named Carmarthen Hills and the southern Lansdowne Hills, after the Marquesses of Carmarthen and Lansdowne. But the misty blue aura that seems to emanate from the mountains when viewed from a distance suggested to the settlers the more romantic name, the Blue Mountains.

From those early days of European settlement in Australia, the Blue Mountains have held an enigmatic attraction. Located 65 kilometres west of Sydney, their tree-covered slopes rise abruptly from the broad, gently undulating coastal plains and form part of the Great Dividing Range that extends along the entire east coast of the continent.

But their first appearance is deceptive, for although they do not reach to great heights they are an extraordinary maze of rugged sandstone ridges and deep valleys clothed in dense forests and scrub. Seemingly impenetrable, they were to prove to be a barrier to expansion which was to defeat the colony's most able explorers for almost 25 years.

As early as December 1789 attempts were made to cross the Blue Mountains, but one by one men such as William Dawes and George Johnston, William Paterson, Henry Hacking, George Bass, Francis Barrallier and George Caley returned, unable to find a passage through to the other side. Always, they complained of being blocked by tangled masses of vegetation or by valleys that terminated in sheer cliffs hundreds of metres high. At one stage it was even suggested that the legendary Mungo Park be brought out from Africa to try his luck, but that did not eventuate.

By 1804 Governor Philip Gidley King, the third administrator of the New South Wales colony, was convinced that the mountains were impassable. He wrote to his superiors in London that ". . . as far as respects the extension of agriculture beyond the . . . mountains, that is an idea that must be given up, as the rocks to the west of that range wear the most barren and forbidding aspect, which men, animals, birds and vegetation have ever been stranger to." Persevering with attempts to cross the mountains, he declared, would be "as chimerical as useless".

For several years there were no further serious or official attempts to cross the Blue Mountains, and the colony expanded north and south along the coastal plains. Although the settlers found the soils poorly suited for grazing or for the growing of crops, they managed for a time to eke out an existence.

But the mountains remained as intriguing as ever. When convicts escaped and never returned, the myth grew stronger that a paradise inhabited by white men lay on the other side of the range. Alternatively, many convicts believed that the colony was an outpost of Asia and in their dreams of freedom imagined that they would find China on the other side.

Even the better-informed free settlers—who did not share the more extreme beliefs—thought that beyond the mountains there might be a land of milk and honey.

From about 1810, there were compelling incentives to find such a land. Overgrazing had intensified the need to find new pastures for sheep and cattle, the colony was suffering from the effects of droughts and caterpillar plagues, and several wheat crops had failed. The arrival of the fifth governor of New South Wales, Lachlan Macquarie, in December of 1809 had also rekindled the desire for exploration, for he was an army officer and interested in the hinterland whereas his predecessors had all been navy men. Not content simply to receive reports from others, Macquarie himself undertook expeditions to inspect his domains.

By 1812 the economic situation had worsened and it became imperative that new agricultural and pastoral lands be found. Some people were even saying that the colony's food supply was so seriously depleted that the settlement at Sydney might have to be abandoned. Knowing that the survival and future prosperity of the colony depended on finding a way across the Blue Mountains, Governor Macquarie offered his patronage "to every effort to surmount these obstacles".

The following year, with relative ease, Gregory Blaxland, William Lawson and William Charles Wentworth, accompanied by four servants, pioneered a route across the mountains and opened the way to the rich Western Plains.

Why their journey should have been so comparatively simple and those of their predecessors so difficult is explained by the geological structure of the region. The Blue Mountains are not mountains at all, but a skeletal remnant of an enormous sandstone plateau which was raised about 3 million years ago. They would more accurately be called the "Blue Canyons", for approximately two-thirds of the plateau has been eroded away so that the valleys now take up much more area than the ridges. These ridges are flat-topped and predominantly narrow, although there are still some solid blocks such as King's Tableland and the island-like Mt Solitary. All, however, fall away into broad canyon-like valleys walled by sheer-sided rocky cliffs that rise from huge tree-covered talus slopes. Explorers before 1813 made the mistake of trying to find a way through the mountains by following these valleys, simply to find that they terminated in the cliffs. Blaxland, Lawson and Wentworth took a route over the top of the ridges instead.

It is not clear who formulated the theory of crossing the mountains via the ridges. Probably it evolved from discussions among several people, notably Blaxland, Lawson, and George Caley, who had previously attempted a crossing himself. It is possible, also, that information may have been gained from

Jamison Valley, from Sublime Point

led by the explorer and government surveyor George William Evans to survey the route taken by the Blaxland party and then to explore further west. Evans travelled more than 150 kilometres beyond Mt Blaxland, discovering the Bathurst Plains and the big Macquarie River. He was elated by the richness of the land, calling it the "handsomest Country" he had ever seen.

Macquarie was so delighted by Evans's favourable report that he granted Blaxland, Lawson and Wentworth each 1000 acres (about 400 hectares) of land in the colony and granted George Evans £100 and 100 acres of land in Van Diemen's Land, where he was about to take up an appointment as Deputy Surveyor. Within a few months he commissioned a retired army officer, William Cox, to build a road over the two mountain ranges to the Bathurst plains ". . . so as to permit two carts or other wheel carriages to pass each other with ease".

With 30 convicts and eight soldiers, Cox began work in July 1814 and just six months later, on 21 January 1815, the 160-kilometre-long road was completed, following much the same route as that taken by Evans and by the Blaxland party before him. The achievement of constructing a road over such difficult country in such a remarkably short time—using only the simple pick-axes, gunpowder and other equipment available in those times—was largely attributable to the outstanding ability and humanity of William Cox.

Cox gave the workmen good food, took precautions to prevent scurvy, and made a detailed sick list every day. The convicts were not chained, they were given the best quality tools obtainable, and their shoes and clothing were kept in good repair and replaced as soon as they wore out. As a result of this consideration, not only was the road built in such an exceptionally short time, but also there were no deserters, no deaths and no serious accidents.

Macquarie immediately organised a tour of inspection of the road and recalled George Evans from Van Diemen's Land to act as guide. The government party left Parramatta on 25 April 1815 and on 7 May the governor conducted a ceremony which led to the founding of Bathurst, the first European settlement west of the Blue Mountains.

The most difficult part of Cox's Road, both to build and to traverse, was the descent to the west from near Mt York on the edge of the main Blue Mountains plateau. Known as Cox's Pass, it was so steep that horses and carts had to be unharnessed and transported to the bottom one by one. This pass remained in use until 1823 when it was superseded by a route suggested by William Lawson; but this, too, was abandoned a few years later in favour of Victoria Pass, opened in 1832. Built under the direction of the then Surveyor-General of the colony, Thomas Livingstone Mitchell, this new pass was a considerable engineering achievement involving the throwing down of part of the mountain slopes near Mt Victoria to

the Aborigines of the region, who had at least four routes across the mountains. In retrospect it seems astounding that such knowledge was not acquired from the Aboriginal people years earlier, but the colonists mainly came in contact with the tribes inhabiting the plains, who knew their own country intimately but would have known little about the hills.

Strictly, the boundaries of the Blue Mountains are the Colo and Wolgan rivers in the north, the northern shore of Lake Burragorang in the south, the Hawkesbury and lower Nepean rivers in the east, and the Cox River in the west. Often, however, the term is used to encompass older highlands to the north, south and west of the main plateau.

The Blaxland, Lawson and Wentworth expedition travelled only 90 kilometres across the mountains, reaching as far as present-day Mt Blaxland on the bare-walled western edge of the Blue Mountains plateau. Another and more rugged mountain range of the Great Divide had still to be crossed before the vast Western Plains would be found; nevertheless, it was their journey that broke down the barrier to expansion and, as Blaxland reflected in later years, ". . . changed the aspect of the colony from a confined, insulated tract of land to a rich, extensive continent".

This achievement, however, was not officially acknowledged until almost a year after the crossing. When the explorers first returned from their journey, Governor Macquarie was sceptical about their claims to have found a route across the mountains and wanted confirmation. He also did not want to publicise details of their expedition for fear that such information might suggest an escape route for convicts or precipitate an exodus from the coast by land-hungry settlers.

Instead, in November 1813, he sent an official expedition

Pulpit Rock, Grose Valley

lessen the steepness of the descent. Even so, the pass was not negotiable by the earliest horseless carriages and other routes were built at about the beginning of the twentieth century. However, when cars became more powerful Victoria Pass came back into use.

Although the road across the mountains has been improved considerably, the present-day Great Western Highway still substantially follows the route taken by Cox, twisting and plunging through the mountains with numerous sharp and narrow bends. Since World War II an alternative highway, Bell's Line of Road, has also been built across the main plateau, taking a shorter route discovered in 1823 by Archibald Bell and later used for many years as a stock route.

The railway across the Blue Mountains also closely follows the route taken by Cox's road. Built in stages between the years 1850 and 1869, and reaching Bathurst in 1876, it too was a remarkable engineering achievement. As with the road, the most difficult part of the construction was over the precipitous descent to the west from the main Blue Mountains plateau and this task was complicated by a lack of finances available to build an extensive system of tunnels. The Engineer-in-Chief of Railways, John Whitton, solved the problem by devising a zigzag railway system that involved only one short tunnel, three viaducts and a simple Z-shaped line with two reversing points that enabled the trains to descend gradually to Lithgow. A smaller zigzag was also built at Lapstone Hill on the eastern approach to the mountains. Opened in 1867, the Lapstone line was replaced after 25 years by a tunnel route, while the more impressive Lithgow zigzag, built in 1869, remained in use for 40 years until it too was superseded by a tunnel system.

With road and rail access available, European colonists soon settled in the Blue Mountains and in the country to the west. The discovery of payable gold at places such as Ophir, north-west of Bathurst, brought an increase of traffic over the mountains in the 1850s and 1860s, and oil shale was also mined from the main plateau. Then in the 1870s, coal began to be won on quite a large scale at a mine known as the Crushers in the Jamison Valley, in the Blue Mountains.

At about the same time, the "hills" became fashionable with wealthy members of Sydney society, several of whom built mansions there as mountain retreats. By the end of the decade a township had been established around the Crushers railway station, which was renamed more attractively as Katoomba — said to be derived from an Aboriginal word, *Kattatoonbah* or *Kedumba*, meaning "falling waters" or "the falling together of many streams". The names of other railway stations were also changed: for example, Pilgrim Inn became Blaxland, Blue Mountain became Lawson and the Weatherboard Hut became Wentworth Falls, honouring the three explorers who first crossed the mountains. Towns grew up around these stations too, and also at other places in the mountains such as Leura and Blackheath.

Early in the new century the region was being promoted for the quality of its air, which was said to have health-giving properties "... coming as it does for hundreds of miles through the eucalypt trees ... from the Pacific Ocean". Several holiday establishments operated in the area, notably the Medlow Bath Health Resort (now the Hydro Majestic Hotel complex). Owned by Sydney retail tycoon Mark Foy, it was advertised as a "hydropathic" centre and offered a variety of treatments such as massage, sun baths, mud baths and sand baths, as well as fresh food supplied from its own farm in the nearby Megalong Valley. A number of prominent artists and writers were also attracted to the mountains around this time, including the cartoonist Phil May, who lived at the elegant Carrington Hotel at Katoomba, and Norman Lindsay, who bought Mark Foy's former home at Springwood in 1912 and a few years later wrote *The Magic Pudding*, his enchanting story about a debonair koala named Bunyip Bluegum, which has since become a classic of Australian children's literature.

But from the time William Cox's road was first opened, many people came to the area simply to see for themselves the character of the little mountain range that had hemmed in European settlement on the coastal plains for almost a quarter of a century. A number of distinguished visitors to the colony visited the mountains, among them Charles Darwin, who stayed at Wentworth Falls in 1836.

Darwin was immensely impressed by what he saw and suggested that the precipitous cliffs must be an ancient coastline. In his *Geological Observations* published in London some 40 years later, he wrote of the mountains with admiration:

"It is not easy to conceive of a more magnificent spectacle than is presented to a person walking on the summit plains, when without any notice he arrives at the brink of one of the cliffs. They are so perpendicular that he can strike with

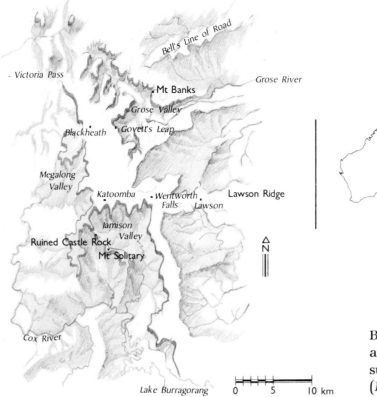

a stone (as I have tried) the trees growing at a depth of a thousand and fifteen hundred feet below him; on both hands he sees headland beyond headland of the receding line of cliff, and on the opposite side of the valley, often at a distance of several miles, he beholds another line rising up to the same height with that on which he stands, and formed of the same horizontal strata of pale sandstone . . . When one reflects on the enormous amount of stone which on this view must have been removed in most of the above cases through mere gorges or chasms, one is led to ask whether these spaces may not have subsided."

Looking down into the broad valleys of the Blue Mountains, it is easy to appreciate Darwin's questioning; and, especially when the valleys are filled with low cloud, the cliffs and headlands do appear remarkably like features of a coast. But the Blue Mountains have not subsided, nor have they been carved by a sea. The extraordinary amount of rock that has been carried away has been removed primarily by ordinary river erosion.

The formation of the Blue Mountains began about 280 million years ago when most of the area lay beneath the sea, lakes and swamps. For about 50 million years, rivers and creeks deposited vast amounts of sediment in the sea and the lakes, and gradually these materials compressed into sandstone and shale. About the same time, dead plant matter settled and decayed in the swamps, creating large coal seams. Some 230 million years ago, further quantities of sediment were laid down. Eventually they consolidated into beds of hard sandstone up to 700 metres thick, which were elevated to form dry land. Then, between 15 and 20 million years ago, basalt lavas erupted from fissures and spread over large areas of the sandstone surface.

About 2-3 million years ago, earth movements elevated the sandstone, forming a vast plateau. The long eastern face of the Blue Mountains was formed by folding at this time, and other folding movements further to the west elevated the plateau to its maximum height, in the region of Blackheath, which is today about 1050-1100 metres above sea level.

The erosion of the Blue Mountains has been greatest on the western side of the plateau where the biggest canyon-like valleys are located, whereas on the eastern side most of the openings are smaller and gorge-like. The wearing away of the plateau is, of course, continuous, as was evidenced by a huge landslide at Katoomba in 1931. If there are no major earth movements in the next few hundred million years, the ridges will completely fall, leaving only an undulating plain.

The types of vegetation growing in the various parts of the Blue Mountains is determined largely by the underlying rocks and soil. The sandstone ridges are dominated by eucalypts such as stringybark (*Eucalyptus eugenioides*), peppermint (*Eucalyptus piperita*) and red bloodwood (*Eucalyptus gummifera*), with an understorey of beautiful flowering shrubs including the crimson waratah (*Telopea speciosissima*) and the pale pink boronia (*Boronia floribunda*). Handsome blue gums (*Eucalyptus deanei* and *E. saligna*) are notable among the tree cover on the sandstone areas of the valleys, turpentine (*Syncarpia glomulifera*) is dominant in the shale areas, and lush rainforests of tall coachwood (*Ceratopetalum apetalum*) and golden sassafras (*Doryphora sassafras*), with a ferny understorey, grow on the basalt-covered slopes. Ferns, mosses and other water-loving plants are also common along the rivers and streams of the region, especially around the many waterfalls. Wildflowers are most prolific in the sandstone areas and include more than 100 native orchids and a distinctive scarlet honeyflower (*Lambertia formosa*), sometimes known as the "Blue Mountains devil" because its fruit looks like a miniature gargoyle.

Viewed at close quarters, the dense vegetation is, of course, predominantly green in colour. The deep blue distant haze for which the mountains are named is caused by a common optical phenomenon known as "Rayleigh Scattering", after Lord Rayleigh who investigated it in 1871. The term refers to the diffusion of light rays by particles of dust and minute droplets of water in the atmosphere, which makes all distant objects appear to be some shade of blue. In the Blue Mountains this effect—and therefore the intensity of the blue—is accentuated by tiny droplets of oil constantly exuded by the leaves of the eucalypt trees. Interestingly, there is probably considerable truth in the claims made by the early advocates of the "healthy fresh mountain air", because the eucalypt oils are thought to help retard the propagation of germs. However, the oils are also extremely volatile and the risk of bushfire is a serious threat, especially in the hot summer months.

The major valleys of the Blue Mountains are the densely forested Jamison, the open and grassy Megalong, and the magnificent bottle-necked Grose, all of which can be viewed from numerous lookout points.

Charles Darwin was most impressed by the Jamison Valley, where 200-metre high cliffs drop to a steep slope of talus that continues downward to the valley floor some 700 metres below the cliff rim. Some of the most famous scenic attractions of the region are found here, including the Three Sisters, a group of sandstone pillars that according to an Aboriginal legend were three sisters named *Meenhi, Wimlah* and *Gunedoo* who were turned into stone for running off to a forbidden rendezvous with three tribesmen. Other features of the Jamison Valley are the Ruined Castle Rock, the two-tiered Wentworth Falls, the picturesque Leura Falls, and the Valley of the

Govett's Leap waterfall, Grose Valley

"It is not easy to conceive a more magnificent spectacle . . ."
CHARLES DARWIN, 1836

1. Castle Head from the Ruined Castle Rock, Jamison Valley
2. The bole of a giant blue gum (*Eucalyptus deanei*) in the Blue Gum Forest, Grose Valley
3. Brush-tailed rock wallaby (*Petrogale penicillata*) with joey, near the Jenolan Caves
4. Base of Govett's Leap waterfall, Grose Valley
5. Hanging "swamp" growing on the cliff face at Govett's Leap
6. Sundew (*Drosera binata*), Grose Valley
7. Rock patterns, Narrowneck Peninsula

4

5

2

3

6

7

1

5

The Jenolan Caves . . .

1. The Grand Column, River Cave
2. A grotto in a small undeveloped cave
3. Aragonite straws and helictites in a passage leading to the grotto
4. A cluster of stalactites, River Cave
5. The Indian Canopy, Orient Cave

Waters, where several waterfalls cascade amid ferny gullies.

Access to the floor of the valley can be gained via a "giant staircase" near the Three Sisters or via a scenic railway which was originally used to transport coal miners and to bring up coal from the valley floor. Reputed to be the steepest railway in the world, it was built in the 1880s by the Katoomba Coal Mine Company and is 445 metres long, of which 230 metres are at a 45° angle of descent. Views of the valley can also be gained from the cable car of a scenic skyway, which was built in 1958 and extends some 350 metres, passing such features as the Katoomba Falls and Orphan Rock.

The Megalong Valley, which is separated from the Jamison Valley by the aptly named Narrowneck Peninsula, is predominantly rural in character although it includes superb areas of rainforest. Today it is very popular for activities such as horse-riding, but the scenery is gentle and less spectacular than the densely forested areas.

With the Jamison Valley partly developed for tourism and the Megalong Valley used for pastoral purposes, the most awe-inspiring of the main Blue Mountains canyons is the pristine Grose Valley. Thickly wooded and with sheer pinkish cliffs, it contains numerous impressive waterfalls, rock overhangs and forested areas.

The best known of the Grose Valley waterfalls is Govett's Leap, which plummets more than 300 metres in a single drop and is the largest fall in the Blue Mountains. However, the waterfall does not flow all year, and in the 1870s a legend grew that the cliff face had been named after a bushranger named Govett who had leapt to his death there when being chased by police. In fact, it was named after a government assistant surveyor named William Romaine Govett, who discovered it in 1832, and the word "leap" is a term from northern England and Scotland, meaning a sudden waterfall.

Across the valley from Govett's Leap is the stately Blue Gum Forest, where the smoky bluish-grey trunks of two eucalypt species—the round-leafed gum or Deane's blue gum (*Eucalyptus deanei*) and the Sydney blue gum (*Eucalyptus saligna*)—soar perhaps 30 metres or more before branching into a leafy canopy. Widely recognised as being one of the loveliest areas in the Blue Mountains, the trees grow right to the banks of the valley streams, their long straight trunks being reflected in the clear waters. In the 1920s plans were drawn up to log this forest, but it was saved by devoted conservationists. Since then, serious overuse of the forest for recreational purposes has destroyed much of the understorey, including blue gum seedlings. However, measures are now being taken to enable the trees to regenerate.

Today some 200 000 hectares of the Blue Mountains are set aside as the Blue Mountains National Park, while highland areas to the north and south have been declared as the Wollemi and Kanangra-Boyd national parks—the latter being renowned for its long line of tall, golden-orange sandstone cliffs known as the Kanangra Walls and for several series of undeveloped limestone caves. Another and more famous cave system, the Jenolan Caves in the rugged folded mountain range directly west of the Blue Mountains plateau, has also been reserved.

From the time they were first opened for public inspection more than 100 years ago, the Jenolan Caves have attracted more visitors than any other cave system in Australia. The caves are of two types: bold natural archways known as the Grand Arch, the Devil's Coachhouse and Carlotta Arch; and numerous decorated underground caverns, of which the Orient Cave, the Temple of Baal and the River Cave are the most impressive.

With numerous walking tracks but few roads, the rugged wildernesses of the Blue Mountains and the surrounding ranges provide safe refuges for wildlife, ranging from parrots, goannas and snakes to possums, wallabies and kangaroos. Some species, however, are less numerous than they were before white settlement. The superb lyrebird (*Menura superba*), for example, which was formerly known as the Blue Mountains pheasant, was killed both for food and for the tail feathers of the male which were used for decoration.

Little evidence remains of the Aboriginal people who once inhabited the region, but at the Red Hands Cave near Glenbrook, on the eastern side of the mountains, there are silhouettes of hands in red ochre outline and nearby are relics of grinding grooves used for sharpening implements such as spearheads and stone axes. They are thought to have been the work of the Daruk tribe, which lived in the area for at least 12 000 years.

There are many places of European historical interest in the mountains. The oldest of these is the Explorer's Tree on the Great Western Highway, near Katoomba, which was marked in 1813 by Blaxland, Lawson or Wentworth to mark their crossing. Further north on the highway, at Mt Victoria, a Toll House built of sandstone in 1849 still remains and just west of the main plateau several buildings in the little village of Hartley, dating to the 1830s, have been restored to their original state. Relics of old road passes can still be seen on the western margins of the main plateau and since late 1976 steam train enthusiasts have periodically been running a tourist train on the old Lithgow zigzag, using a restored steam locomotive and old-style carriages. Other places of note include Norman Lindsay's home at Springwood, which since his death in 1969 has been converted into a gallery and museum of his works and memorabilia, and the beautifully landscaped Everglades garden at Leura, covering 5.3 hectares and containing both native and exotic trees and shrubs.

These and many other historical relics enhance the appeal of the mountains, but the greatest attraction is the wonder and extraordinary natural beauty of the vast maze of steep-walled canyons shrouded in blue haze. □

Born of volcanoes

THE WARRUMBUNGLES

Although Australia stands near the Earth's most prominent volcanic belt – the so-called "Ring of Fire" that loops around the Pacific Ocean – the country is extremely fortunate in being the only continent that is not threatened by the possibility of volcanic eruption. But despite the fact that there are no active or even dormant volcanoes, the Australian landscape does contain numerous relics of extinct volcanoes from past geological ages.

The Warrumbungle Range in northern New South Wales gives spectacular evidence of volcanic activity some 13–17 million years ago. A spur of the Great Dividing Range, it appears as a jumble of bulky hills and jagged rocky outcrops that contrasts dramatically with the gentle curves of the mountain country to the east and with the seemingly endless plains stretching far beyond the western horizon. Generally rising only to about 600 metres above sea level, the Warrumbungles are not tall, but their many isolated spires, domes, bluffs, turrets and walls reach almost twice as high.

It is not known how many volcanoes were involved in the creation of the Warrumbungles, for the main craters were eroded away many millions of years ago. The remaining rocks indicate that there were many volcanic vents and that volcanoes erupted spasmodically over a period of approximately 4 million years, with the periods of activity interspersed with dormant phases during which newly solidified rocks were worn down by weathering and erosion.

The pre-volcanic landscape was an eroded plateau of ancient sandstones and shales. The birth of the volcanoes was heralded by earthquakes, which created hundreds of fissures along lines of weakness in the valley floors. From these great gashes flowed huge volumes of boiling, liquidy lava that spread out over the land, blocking the rivers, filling the deep valleys and forming a thin capping over the peaks. Gradually the lava flows built up and solidified into a gigantic mound of basalt.

Then came an explosive period of volcanic activity during which the lavas became thicker and carried congealed volcanic debris such as bombs, breccias and tuffs. Innumerable dykes of volcanic rock cut transversely into the thick sandstone strata and huge amounts of glowing pumice and other debris were thrust skyward, amid explosions caused by incandescent gases. Lighter dusts and ashes lingered in great dark clouds, but much of the heavier material fell immediately, building up as a series of cones along fault lines.

As time progressed, some of the lava pouring out through the newly-formed vents became very viscous, periodically solidifying in the cones and forming plugs. Later many of these plugs were removed by cataclysmic explosions caused by the pressure of steam trapped beneath. During these throat-clearing explosions, millions of tonnes of debris were flung across the countryside and the remaining rocks of the cones were severely shattered, making them weaker and less resistant to erosion. Often further lava flows followed, which cemented the debris that littered the land.

In the final stage of the volcanic activity, the lavas were slow-flowing, fast-cooling trachytes that oozed out like a thick paste and did not travel far. Consisting primarily of silica (quartz) and alkali feldspar, they eventually became so sluggish that they congealed and solidified in the cones. By this time all the steam from beneath had escaped, and in the absence of any explosive component to remove the hard rocks, the volcanoes died, their vents remaining permanently plugged.

When the eruptions ceased, the mountains were much higher than they are now. But over millennia, the forces of weathering and erosion gradually reversed the contours of the former sedimentary landscape, with the thin volcanic cover over the former high peaks being worn away, enabling the rapid removal of the softer underlying sandstones and shales, while the resistant volcanic materials now filling the ancient valleys withstood the excavation and remained as mountains. In time nearly all the shattered and softer volcanic rocks were broken down to form rich soils, which spread across the adjacent plains, leaving little more than the once-enclosed plugs and dykes of incredibly strong trachyte standing as towering pinnacles, walls and domes. As trachytes range in colour from silvery-green to red and smoky white, the rock formations are often beautifully patterned, with various combinations of texture and colour.

Most of the major peaks in the Warrumbungles occur on a huge amphitheatre-like rim overlooking the valley of Wambelong Creek. The highest point in the range is Mt Wambelong, a huge monolith built of volcanic debris cemented by lava flows, which stands 1205 metres above sea level.

But the most spectacular volcanic remnant is the Breadknife, a narrow wall of trachyte which on the western side towers 100 metres above the valley and tapers to a crest less than 2 metres wide that resembles the edge of a serrated knife. It is the remnant of a dyke formed in the same crater as the large plug of Crater Bluff (1094 metres), which lies beyond, while another trachyte tower, Belougery Spire (1061 metres), once plugged a subsidiary volcanic neck. Nearby, an impressive ridge known as the Grand High Tops offers panoramic views to other volcanic rock formations, including the massive dome-shaped Bluff Mountain (1200 metres) and the basaltic Tonduron Spire (1130 metres). To the north a white trachyte dome known as Belougery Split Rock (770 metres) dominates the lower mountain country, and to the east a bluish-tinted trachyte mound called Timor Rock (730 metres) is prominent because of its attractive bare, columnar face.

The Warrumbungles are often described as the place where plant and animal species of the dry inland plains meet those of the moist east coast. Indeed, there is a wide and diverse range of plant communities. Although the borders of the dif-

Crater Bluff

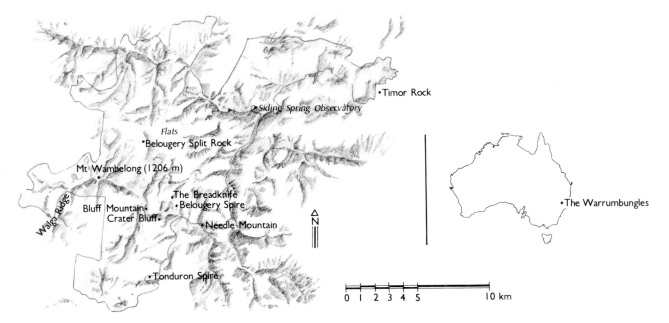

A narrow wall
towering
100 metres
above the
valley . . .

The Breadknife

ferent habitats are usually very clearly defined, fascinating contrasts and incongruities occur, such as gnarled snow gums (*Eucalyptus pauciflora*) growing near ancient blackboys (*Xanthorrhoea arboreas*) on some of the high slopes.

One of the most attractive and widespread trees of the region is the red ironbark (*Eucalyptus sideroxylon*), with a deeply grooved black trunk and pale green leaves. Also conspicuous over large areas is the grey-trunked kurrajong (*Brachychiton populneum*), which has a dense foliage of glossy olive green leaves and creamy bell-shaped flowers. Tall eucalypts, especially the white box (*Eucalyptus albens*), dominate the cool damp eastern slopes, while on the hotter and drier western slopes there are desert trees and shrubs such as the quandong or "native peach" (*Santalum acuminatum*) and the desert lime (*Eremocitrus glauca*).

The Warrumbungles were included in the territory of the Kamilaroi Aboriginal tribe. Tragically, the coming of the European destroyed these people and their culture, and their knowledge of the land is now lost for all time. It seems unlikely that they lived permanently in the rugged mountain heights, preferring an easier life on the fertile river plains which, throughout their long occupation of the land, teemed with wildlife and provided an abundance of vegetable foods such as berries, roots and herbs. However, markings in a cave on a mountain overlooking the Grand High Tops give evidence that these people did visit the Warrumbungles.

The beautifully rhythmical name *Warrumbungles*, meaning "little broken mountains", is also a legacy from the Kamilaroi people. Its survival is fortunate, for the rolling and mystical qualities of the word seem to portray the character and atmosphere of the mountains. Certainly it is more appropriate than the name given to the range by the first European visitors.

In 1818 the New South Wales Surveyor-General John Oxley came upon this "most stupendous range of mountains" which he "distinguished by the name of Arbuthnot's Range, after the Right Hon. C. Arbuthnot, of His Majesty's Treasury". Happily, control of the King's coffers did not guarantee the perpetuity of the English gentleman's name in the colony of New South Wales. By the late 1830s and early 1840s various map-makers had replaced it with versions of the more romantic Aboriginal name, initially "Warrabangle" or "Warranbangle" range and later "Warranbangles". The spelling used today appeared on maps a decade later and quietly slipped into the official nomenclature in its singular form, the Warrumbungle Range, although the plural form is more commonly used.

For the colonists, Oxley's journey was of great importance, for his discovery of the rich Liverpool Plains was to lead to further exploration and to the eventual infiltration of the area by white pastoralists.

The credit for the discovery of the Warrumbungles and the plains, however, cannot go entirely to ex-naval lieutenant Oxley. With him was the very talented and able bushman,

surveyor and explorer, George William Evans, who among other achievements had previously explored and surveyed the route for the road across the Blue Mountains.

The first European settlers to move into the area were squatters, who arrived in the early 1830s, defying government restrictions to confine settlement to nineteen counties that had been established within 250 kilometres of Sydney. Conflicts with the Kamilaroi people were commonplace, until eventually the better-armed newcomers completely took over the land. Unable to control the squatters, the government in 1836 allowed them to acquire legal sanction by imposing a licence fee of £10 for the right to graze their animals on Crown Land. These licences were replaced in 1848 by leaseholds, and with the passing of the Crown Lands Act in 1861, freehold titles became available.

Like the Kamilaroi people, the white settlers chose to live on the fertile plains around the Warrumbungles. A few ventured to the valleys beneath the stony ramparts, but the mountain heights remained untouched. So, as the white man cleared the lower land, creating rural landscapes, the "little mountains" became a refuge for wildlife. Today there are numerous indigenous species, from the great grey kangaroo (*Macropus giganteus*) to the tiny superb blue wren (*Malurus cyaneus*), but they have to compete with equally large numbers of feral animals, particularly rabbits and goats.

On 1 July 1937, the National Parks and Primitive Areas Council—an association of nature lovers—lodged a design with the New South Wales Department of Lands advocating that the most scenic portions of the Warrumbungles be set aside as the "Warrumbungle National Monument". Such a proposal was destined to receive opposition from those with conflicting interests, such as some of the farmers who owned part of the land. In the absence of roads and tracks, it was difficult to gain public interest in the project, but fortunately local councils added their support. Two important moves which gave impetus to the conservationists' requests were the generous offer by a local farmer, A. J. Pincham, to donate a large area of his property on the upper Wambelong Creek to the proposed park and the publication in October 1939 in the journal *Home Annual* of photographs by the famous Australian photographer Frank Hurley, under an article entitled "Forgotten Mountains".

But the work was far from over, and not until 1953 were 3360 hectares finally proclaimed as the Warrumbungle National Park, with a further 2300 hectares of adjoining Crown Land being reserved as a buffer zone to protect the natural vegetation. Since then, the size of the park has been increased several times and today it covers an area of over 18 000 hectares, which includes all of the major, and many of the minor, volcanic peaks. A prominent man-made landmark, the Siding Spring Observatory built in the late 1960s, contains one of the world's largest telescopes. □

Bulky hills and jagged rocky outcrops . . .

1. The Breadknife, from the Grand High Tops
2. Wonga wonga vine (*Pandorea pandorana*) on a sandstone pillar near Bluff Mountain
3. Crater Bluff (centre) and Tonduron Spire
4. View south from Mt Wambelong to the plains
5. Blackboys (*Xanthorrhoea sp.*), Mt Wambelong
6. Pink orchids (*Glossodia major*)
7. Golden orchids (*Diuris aurea*)
8. Belougery Spire

1

8

6

7

5

118

2

3

4

Gardens of coral
THE GREAT BARRIER REEF

Spiky *Acropora* and rounded *Favites* coral species at Eagle Cay, north of Cooktown

T HE Great Barrier Reef, which stretches some 2000 kilometres along the Queensland coast, is the most remarkable coral reef system in the world. Built by myriad tiny
animals known as coral polyps, its mighty ramparts spread out
over an area approximately twice the size of England. For its
full length, it is a tropical paradise of jewel-like islands,
turquoise seas and magnificent coral gardens.

The Barrier Reef is the showcase of the sea—an underwater
wonderland decorated by brightly-coloured corals of fantastically intricate design. Among these beautiful structures live
brilliantly patterned fish and other aquatic creatures, their variety and numbers astonishing, for the Reef is the home of more
animal life per square kilometre than any other region on
Earth. Above the water, the many islands—crested with emerald green vegetation and encircled by white sandy beaches—
highlight a superb seascape of crystal clear blue.

The Barrier Reef is not a single reef, but a series of some
2500 individual reefs of varying shapes and sizes. These reefs
are of several distinct types: outer or barrier reefs, platform
reefs, and fringing reefs. Together they form a formidable
blockade which protects the Queensland coast from the onslaught of the Pacific Ocean.

The Outer Reefs are the true barriers which bear the full
brunt of the ocean's waves. Long and comparatively narrow,
they lie roughly parallel to the coast, often on the very edge
of the continental shelf so that their seaward side slopes down
very steeply to the dark depths of the ocean. They are best
developed in the regions north of Cairns, where for several
hundred kilometres they form an almost continuous wall
marked by thundering, foaming white breakers. To the south
they are intermittent, often merging with islands and broader
reefs.

The Outer Reefs form the seaward border of an area called
the Great Lagoon, which runs parallel with the coast and contains countless other reefs known collectively as the Inner
Reefs. These are primarily the platform or patch reefs and they
vary from small crescent shapes to very large circular, oval or
irregular expanses covering many square kilometres. Often
they support cays, or "low islands", which consist of sand and
broken coral that has built up, usually on the protected leeward
sides of the reefs. The cays always cover only a very small
portion of the underlying reef and seldom reach more than
a metre or two above the high tide mark. They range in size
from tiny patches to quite large islands and are usually vegetated by plants which have been carried there as seeds by the
wind, the sea or birds.

Generally, less than 50 plant species colonise the cays.
Among the most common vegetation are the pretty coastal she-
oak *(Casuarina equisetifolia)*, several mangroves, the palm-like
pandanus *(Pandanus tectorius)* and the unusual pisonia tree
(Pisonia grandis). The pisonia is often referred to as the "bird-
catching" or "bird-killing" tree because of the nature of its seed

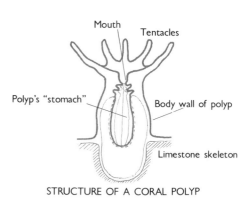

Mouth Tentacles

Polyp's "stomach" Body wall of polyp

Limestone skeleton

STRUCTURE OF A CORAL POLYP

1

vessels, which have a sticky surface that adheres to the feathers and limbs of white-capped noddies *(Anous minutus)* which nest in very large colonies among its branches. This glutinous substance ensures that seeds are carried elsewhere when the birds leave the tree at the end of the breeding season. Unfortunately, smaller and weaker birds are occasionally so covered with seeds that they become stuck to the tree or their wings become entangled, and they die.

Not all the 250 or so islands of the Great Barrier Reef are cays. A great many are continental or "high" islands, which are the hilltops of former coastal ranges that have been submerged by a rise in sea level, perhaps combined with a subsidence of the coastline. These islands are large by comparison with the cays and usually rise steeply from the water to heights of 100 metres or more above sea level, sometimes reaching over 1000 metres. They are generally surrounded by a thin border of coral—the "fringing" reefs. The plants on these islands are similar to those found on the adjacent mainland. In the north, there are luxuriant rainforests with beautiful orchids, ferns, fig trees, creepers and vines. Notable trees on many islands are the lichen-coated hoop pine *(Araucaria cunninghamii)* and the umbrella tree *(Schefflera actinophylla)* with its circles of slender, drooping leaves. Coconut palms *(Cocos nucifera)* are also abundant on these islands and on cays.

This magnificent system of reefs and islands extends from the Gulf of Papua in New Guinea to Lady Elliott Island south of the Tropic of Capricorn and is by far the largest coral reef structure in the world. It is not uniform throughout, but has distinct northern, central and southern regions.

The majority of the true barrier reefs are found in the region north of Cooktown. It was here that the sighting of the long line of breakers flanking the coral inspired Matthew Flinders

to use the term Great Barrier Reef at the beginning of the last century. Over much of this area the continental shelf terminates only 30-80 kilometres from the coast, although in the extreme north it widens suddenly to almost 200 kilometres. Reefs are abundant and distributed fairly evenly over the shelf, separated from each other by narrow passes, many of which are navigable by large ships. The lagoon waters are generally less than 30 metres deep and dramatic differences in water colour can be seen on the seaward side of the Outer Reefs, which fall away to ocean depths of up to 2000 metres. Of the islands in this region the most interesting are Lizard Island, from the peak of which Captain Cook found the safe Cook's Passage out of the Reef's lagoon in 1770, and the Murray Islands, three island-summits of extinct volcanoes that erupted from the sea in the same manner as the many atolls of the Pacific Ocean and the nearby Coral Sea. One of these islets, Weier, retains a distinct crater shape, part of which is submerged, leaving a crescent-like island with a semi-enclosed lagoon. Hidden perhaps forever in its craggy, jungled slopes are the war drums of the much feared headhunters who once lived on the largest of the three islands, Mer.

In the central region of the Reef, between Cooktown and Mackay, the continental shelf gradually widens and the lagoon waters deepen to between 30 and 60 metres. There are very few reefs on the edge of the shelf; however, the area includes many of the most popular continental islands—Dunk, Hinchinbrook, Magnetic, Hayman, Whitsunday, Lindeman, Brampton, Daydream and South Molle—and the famous cays of Green Island and Low Isles.

Some of the most beautiful reefs are in the region south of Mackay, where water depths often exceed 60 metres and the

2

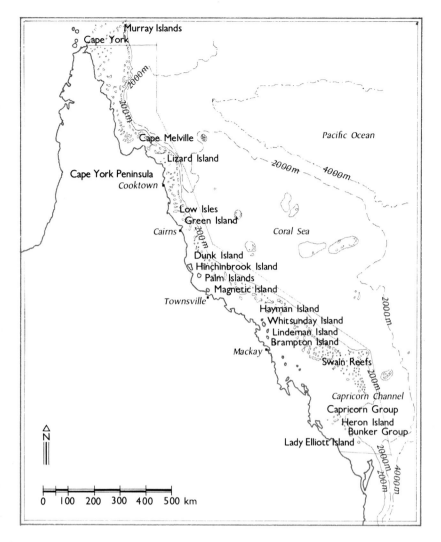

The Great Barrier Reef

retracts during the day safe from foraging predators, emerging only at night to feed. When the polyp dies, its skeleton remains firmly encrusted with countless others to form a layer of limestone. The build-up of generation after generation of coral skeletons slowly creates the massive reefs.

The living portion of any coral reef is always just a thin veneer on the stony surface of accumulated skeletons. The polyps have little tolerance to exposure to air, and for this reason the level of the sea at low tide limits the height of the reef and influences outward growth. To cater for the symbiotic algae's requirements of light for photosynthesis, the stony corals are found only in clear, shallow waters, whereas other corals live in deeper waters.

Some environmental factors can destroy the corals. An excess of silt or the dilution of the sea waters by too much fresh water, for example, will kill the polyps, hence gaps in reefs are often opposite river mouths.

Due to their sedentary life, coral polyps look very much like marine flowers. Although several Greek philosophers recognised them as "zoophytes" (animals that look like plants) as far back as the third century BC, they were not generally accepted as animals until the eighteenth century. Even today much remains unknown about their life processes.

The growth rates of the reefs vary considerably according to conditions and the type of coral, with upward growth appearing to average only a few millimetres per year. Polyp reproduction is either sexual or asexual. In the sexual process a polyp releases sperms which, if they drift into a polyp containing eggs, will fertilise them. Free-swimming larvae develop from the egg, but they must soon settle to form a colony or they will die. To reproduce asexually, the polyp buds off a new individual which remains joined to it.

Living corals display a kaleidoscope of colour and countless intricate designs. The variety is endless, ranging from branching purple and green staghorn corals (*Acropora spp.*) to patterned green domes of brain coral (*Lobophyllia spp.*) and brilliant clumps of orange coral (*Dendrophyllia spp.*). These vivid colours, however, come either from pigments in the living polyps or from the algae, and when these organisms die only the white skeleton remains. On the Barrier Reef a few "soft corals" (which usually have a soft, flexible skeleton and are not true reef-builders) have a hard coat and retain their colour after the polyps have decayed. Notable among these species are the red organ pipe coral (*Tubipora musica*), which has long tubes, and the fine-tubed blue coral (*Heliopora coerulea*).

Other aquatic creatures of the Great Barrier Reef rival the coral in beauty and in diversity of colour, pattern, shape and size. The waters are simply teeming with life. About 10 per cent of the world's saltwater fish are thought to inhabit the region. Over 1500 species of fish are known, but perhaps more than 2000 species are present. In addition there are about 10 000 species of sponge, over 4000 species of mollusc and

edge of the continental shelf is more than 250 kilometres from the shore. The Outer Reefs occur intermittently, sometimes around 30 kilometres within the shelf's edge. The Inner Reefs are very well developed, although they tend to occur in isolated groups such as the widely known Capricorn Group, the Bunker Group and the Swain Reefs. Heron Island, a thickly wooded islet in the Capricorn Group, and Green Island, near Cairns, are the only permanently inhabited coral cays on the Reef.

In geological terms the Barrier Reef is young, having begun to form only 15 000 years ago when sea levels rose at the end of the last ice age. The area was formerly dry land, and it is thought that the incoming sea carried the coral polyps and other marine life to the area from the Pacific region.

There are about 400 species of reef-building coral polyps on the Reef. Although simple organisms, the way in which they function is complex and varies in detail from species to species.

Coral polyps live in almost all oceanic waters, but reef-building types are found only in warm, shallow waters with fairly high salinity. These are the "stony" corals. Many species are tiny (some only the size of a pinhead), but they generally gather in large colonies, connected to one another by living tissue. Only a few, such as the giant 25-centimetre-wide mushroom corals (*Fungia actiniformis* and *F. echinata*), live individually.

The polyps are small, soft-bodied animals shaped like a bag or sac, with a circle of tentacles at the top. Voracious feeders, they use the tentacles, which are equipped with stinging cells, to harpoon copious quantities of microscopic organisms such as zooplankton. The sac is basically a "stomach", through which the food is taken and waste eliminated.

Reef-building is an intriguing process. The polyps have a symbiotic relationship (beneficial to both) with microscopic algae which live in their tissues. For the algae, the body of the polyp provides protection and its waste matter supplies nutrition. In return, the algae play an essential role in building the reef by helping the polyp to secrete a protective underlying limestone coat (or skeleton) into which the coral animal

123

some 150 species of echinoderm (starfish, sea urchins, etc.).

This extraordinary variety of marine life is dazzling. Fish of almost every colour and pattern imaginable dart among the coral gardens, while others such as the beautiful butterfly fish *(Chaetodon spp.)* move slowly and gracefully like exotic butterflies. However, some reef dwellers are less easily seen, for example, the strange cream and brown lizard fish *(Synodus engelmani)* which lives on the bottom and relies on immobility and camouflage to catch unsuspecting prey.

Shellfish, too, have glorious patterns and colourings that complement their coral environment. For example, the bright blue shell of the reef crab *(Metopograpsus spp.)* is like opal, being beautifully mottled with lighter hues.

The bodily forms of some creatures are even more fascinating than their colourings and markings. Among the most delightful in appearance are the seahorses and the radially symmetrical starfish and sea urchins. Others, notably the stonefish *(Synanceia spp.)*, are bizarre and grotesque. This ugly dark fish with wart-like lumps looks like stone and lives camouflaged among coral. It is the most venomous fish known and its sting can kill anyone unlucky enough to walk on it.

The stonefish is not the only marine animal that poses a threat to humans. Other venomous animals whose sting will cause death are the sea wasp *(Chironex fleckeri)* and the blue-ringed octopus *(Hapalochlaena maculosa)*, while stings from some sea snakes, sea urchins and cones have also been known to be fatal. Several shark species will attack and kill, as will the saltwater crocodile *(Crocodylus porosus)* which is sometimes found in muddy regions of both the coast and the continental islands in the north of the Barrier Reef. Serious wounds may also be inflicted by moray eels, gropers and barracudas, but they are usually not deadly. Two rather fearsome-looking animals which are often thought to be dangerous are the giant clam *(Tridacna gigas)*, said to use its shell as a "man trap", and the huge manta ray *(Manta biostris)*. In fact, both animals are harmless plankton feeders.

Despite its dangers, the Reef offers a plentiful bounty to man. Although many fish species are poisonous to eat, numerous others provide an abundant food source.

Aborigines have probably lived in the region for longer than the Reef itself has been there, and Macassans and other traders from Asia were attracted to its northern shores centuries before the white man came. Favourite marine foods of the Aborigines included turtles and the strange sea-cow, the dugong *(Halicore dugong)*, which grazes on aquatic plants and has a red flesh that tastes much like steak. For the Asians, the prize of the sea was the *bêche-de-mer* or trepang *(Thelenota ananas)*, a succulent sea-cucumber regarded as a delicacy in China.

Coins, cannons, anchors and other relics recovered from the Barrier Reef indicate that galleons from Spain, Portugal and possibly other European nations brought the first white men to the waters of the Barrier Reef. However, the first fully documented voyage in the area is that of James Cook, who sailed along the full length of the Reef in 1770 and gave many of the islands and coastal features the names by which they are known today. His journey nearly ended in tragedy when his ship HM BARK *Endeavour* struck the Endeavour Reef, near present-day Cooktown, incurring considerable damage. But the brilliant navigator managed to beach the boat for repairs and later continued his journey safely. Understandably, he was more concerned about the dangers of the "innumerable banks and shoals lying along the coast in every direction" than with the incredible beauty of the Reef. The botanists, Joseph Banks and Daniel Solander, however, took the opportunity to investigate the area while the ship was being repaired.

The next known voyager to the area, William Bligh, was in an even worse predicament. He passed through the Torres Strait section of the Reef in an open longboat in 1789, having been cast adrift with 18 others after the mutiny on the HMS *Bounty*. Ironically, two years later, four of the *Bounty* mutineers (who had been captured) drowned in this area when HMS *Pandora* hit a reef and sank. In that same year, escaped convicts William and Mary Bryant, their two young children, and seven other convicts, made an epic journey in a stolen cutter from Sydney, through the Reef to Timor, only to be exposed to the authorities there by survivors from the *Pandora*.

Such were the beginnings of the white man's association with the Great Barrier Reef. In the years that followed, men like Matthew Flinders in HMS *Investigator* in 1802, Phillip Parker

1. Aerial stilt roots of mangroves
(*Rhizophora sp.*), Lizard Island lagoon
2. A clump of pandanus (*Pandanus
tectorius*) on Rocky Island, north
of Cooktown

King in the cutter *Mermaid* in 1819 and Captain Francis Price Blackwood in HMS *Fly* in 1843 made extensive surveys of the area, and naturalists (particularly Joseph Beete Jukes of the *Fly*) collected the first extensive scientific data.

Although many shipwrecks and other tragedies, often involving violent conflict with the Aborigines, occurred on the Reef throughout the nineteenth century, settlements were established at various points along the coast and a range of industries soon operated from the area. Fishing, especially for Spanish mackerel, cod, coral trout and shellfish, found an early market and still operates on a large scale. Mother-of-pearl and trochus shells were gathered for making buttons until superseded by plastics, and pearling, too, once had a heyday, though it is now almost entirely confined to cultured pearl farms. For some time the *bêche-de-mer* were gathered extensively and dried for Asian markets, and the now-protected green turtle *(Chelonia mydas)*—from which the famous turtle soup is made—was hunted and processed at canning factories on islands of the Capricorn Group. The collection of guano for phosphates and the slaughtering of the dugong for oil and hides have also periodically been profitable in the past.

Today the biggest industry on the Great Barrier Reef is tourism. Associated with this is a considerable demand for corals and shells; however, the taking of these items, and also of small exotic tropical fish for aquariums, is controlled by law.

The beauty of the Barrier Reef was brought to world attention by the publication in 1908 of *The Confessions of a Beachcomber*, the first of four books by the legendary Edmund James (Ted) Banfield. Better known simply as "The Beachcomber", Banfield leased Dunk Island in 1897 and lived there with his wife until his death in 1923. Through his books he has left not only a lasting account of the romance of his idyllic island home, but also a valuable record of natural history and of Aboriginal lifestyles in the Reef region.

Since Banfield's days, numerous scientific explorations of the Great Barrier Reef have been undertaken and permanent research establishments have been set up on the mainland and on some of the Reef islands. Probably the most important investigations in recent years are those dealing with the invasion of parts of the Reef by the crown-of-thorns starfish *(Acanthaster planci)*. This spiny dark starfish is one of the few predators of the reef-building coral polyps. Once rare on the Barrier Reef, its numbers increased to plague proportions in the 1960s and extensive areas of coral, especially the staghorn species, were destroyed. The problem, which is now under control, appears to have been caused by a temporary imbalance of nature, possibly precipitated by overfishing of the waters by man. However, some scientists fear that future mass attacks by the starfish are imminent and research is continuing.

Studies of the Barrier Reef are not confined to the marine life, but also cover other aspects of the ecology. Naturalists are attracted, for example, to many of the islands and cays because

of their significance as nesting sites for six species of turtle and for a vast array of seabirds including herons, gulls, gannets, muttonbirds and sea eagles.

Tourist resorts have also been established on many islands of the Reef, and other islands have been set aside as national parks. More than a quarter of a million people visit the Reef each year, mostly during the Dry season, from May to December, avoiding the Wet summer months when cyclones are brought by monsoons. With the increasing growth in tourism, it is becoming essential to introduce control measures to protect the natural environment: walking heedlessly over coral reefs, for example, has been likened to looking at a garden by walking through the flower beds and results in breakage of both corals and shells.

However, several other activities are presenting more serious threats to the fragile ecology of the Reef. Astoundingly, proposals have been put forward to drill areas of the region for oil and to mine for limestone and other minerals including gold, silver and several rare earths. Pollutants such as pesticides, fertilisers and effluents from the mainland are being released into Reef waters, and coastal rainforests, which help regulate siltation, are being logged. Further problems include illegal and indiscriminate fishing (especially by people who remove large portions of the Reef itself) and overuse of the waters by large vessels such as tankers which risk damaging the Reef by collision or oil spillage.

The preservation of the Great Barrier Reef is one of the most important conservation concerns in Australia today. Work is currently under way to have almost the entire reef system declared as the Great Barrier Reef Marine Park. So far, only a small percentage of the region has been reserved, but it is hoped that other areas will soon follow. □

The variety of corals is endless . .

1. Plate and purple staghorn corals (*Acropora spp.*), at Bird Island in the Lizard Island group
2. Staghorn coral (*Acropora formosa*), Bird Island
3. A bright blue starfish (*Linckia laevigata*) hides beneath the folds of a "soft" leathery coral (*Sarcophyton sp.*) and rests on a "hard" coral (*Pocillipora eydouxi*)

1

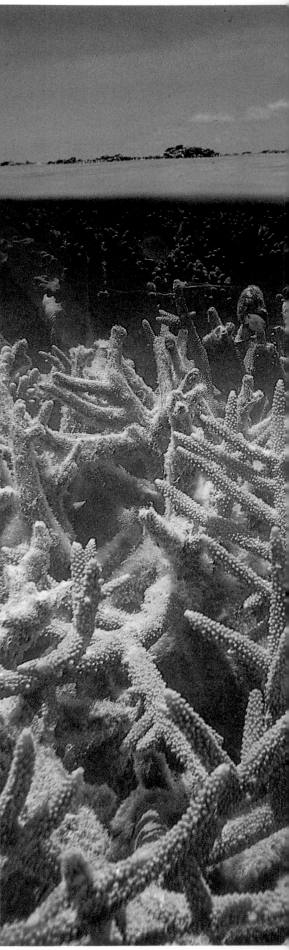

2

3

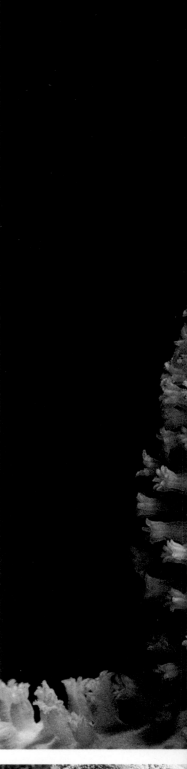

1

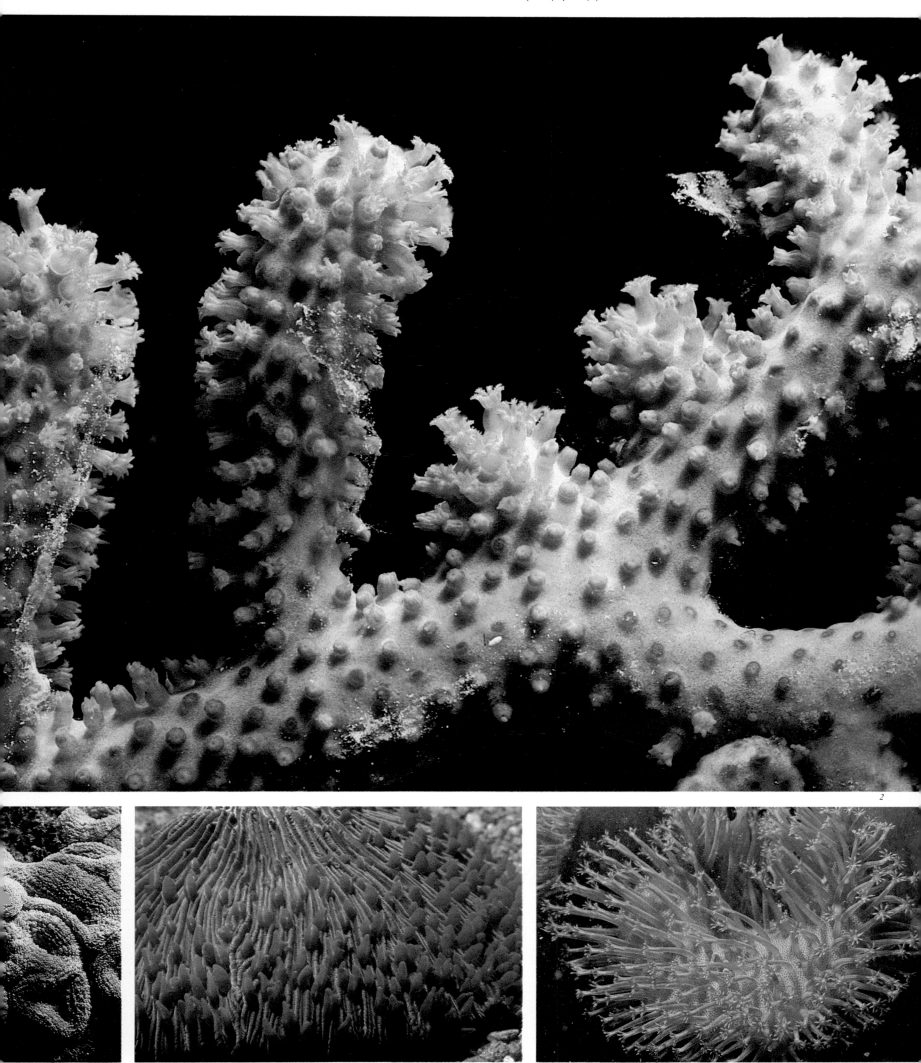

1. Polyps of *Goniopora tenuidens*, a "hard" coral
that feeds during the day rather than at night
2. A horny fan coral (*Subergorgia sp.*), draped with
a mucous discharge common to fan and hard corals
3. A brain coral (*Lobophyllia hemprichii*)
4. A giant mushroom coral (*Fungia fungites*)
5. A "soft" coral (*Sarcophyton sp.*)

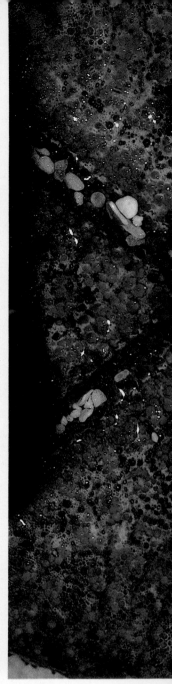

Other aquatic creatures rival the corals in beauty and diversity . . .

1. A gaudy nudibranch (*Notodoris gardineri*) slithers over the base of a giant "hard" coral polyp (*Catalophyllia plicata*)
2. Pincushion starfish (*Culcita novaeguineae*)
3. Sea cucumber (*Pseudocolochirus violaceus*)
4. Sea anemone (*Stoicactis kenti*)
5. Tube or fan worm (*Hypsicomus sp.*)
6. Blue starfish (*Linckia laevigata*)

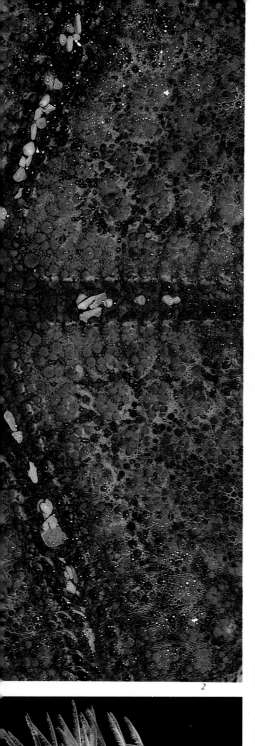

2

6

3

Galleries of natural art

CARNARVON GORGE

Livistona palms highlighted by the white cliffs

CARNARVON Gorge has long been famed for its magnificent Aboriginal art sites, but its beauty is not confined to these ancient works of man. With groves of straight-trunked palms and eucalypts set against a superb backdrop of towering white cliffs, the stately main corridor is but the hallway to numerous smaller side gorges, each displaying its own special character and charm.

Located about 600 kilometres north-west of Brisbane, Carnarvon Gorge is a lush, well-watered haven surrounded by extremely dry and rugged terrain. The main gorge, which is entered from the east, is approximately 30 kilometres long and is formed where Carnarvon Creek winds through the Carnarvon Range, a spur of the Great Dividing Range.

Part of a large belt of soft sandstone known as the Consuelo Tableland, Carnarvon Range was formed 200-230 million years ago, then uplifted, and later capped by a layer of basalt during a period of further uplift and volcanic activity some 25 million years ago. Extensive erosion has occurred since

then, with Carnarvon Creek and other streams sinking courses along vertical joints in the sandstone, resulting in the many deep, sheer-sided gorges of today.

The sandstone is an important intake aquifer for the Great Artesian Basin. The water that filters through the rocks is held by an impermeable layer of shale beneath the sandstone and then finds its way southward through rivers and creeks of the Channel Country and the Darling River system, and eastward to the Burdekin River. In places where the aquifer is cut, the surface rocks in the gorge are constantly saturated, providing a habitat for mosses, ferns and other moisture-loving plants. The aquifer also ensures that there is always water in the creeks of Carnarvon, despite the hot and generally dry climate of the area.

At its entrance, Carnarvon Gorge is about 400 metres wide and like a canyon, but it soon narrows and in some places it is only 50 metres across. The creek is usually 10-20 metres wide and fairly shallow but occasionally, after heavy rains, flash floods swell the stream into a wide, raging torrent.

The grand white cliffs, reaching as high as 200 metres, are easily the most impressive feature of the gorge. In some places the walls are smooth-cut, elsewhere they are contoured by weathering. But for the most part the clifftops are of uniform level. The colour of the cliffs varies subtly throughout the day, being tinted grey in the shade and creamy-yellow in the sun. Their picturesqueness is enhanced by tall eucalypts that line the clifftops for almost the full length of the gorge and also grow in rows on craggy ledges lower down the cliff face.

Due to the height of the cliffs, the gorge is often in shadow, giving shelter as well as water for many plant and animal species that could not survive on the open range.

River she-oaks (*Casuarina cunninghamiana*), bottle brush (*Callistemon viminalis*) and native cherry (*Acumena australis*) grow along the creek. Black-trunked palms (*Livistona sp.*) and tall white flooded gums (*Eucalyptus grandis*) flourish above the creek bank and there are also good stands of pink and yellow flowering hibiscus (*Hibiscus splendens* and *H. heterophylla*) and several figs (*Ficus spp.*). On thinner soils these trees give way to eucalypts such as spotted gum (*Eucalyptus maculata*) and to primitive cycads (*Macrozamia moorei*) and grass-trees (*Xanthorrhoea spp.*). Numerous smaller plants such as blady grasses, bracken, ferns, mosses, orchids, native violets and other wildflowers also grow throughout the gorge.

Carnarvon is always teeming with birdlife, from small robins, honeyeaters and wrens to colourful lorikeets and elegant waterbirds. There are numerous goannas and snakes, at least a dozen species of frog, fish such as eels and catfish, countless insects, several unusual spiders and a wide variety of marsupials including kangaroos, wallabies, bandicoots and the carnivorous satanellus or "northern quoll" (*Dasyurus hallucatus*), a brown native-cat with white spots.

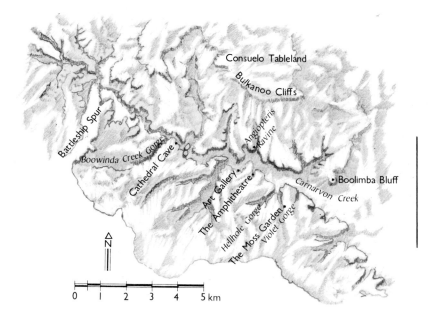

Many of the most beautiful places at Carnarvon are in the smaller gorges that branch off from both sides of the main corridor. These gorges are usually twisting, very narrow and dimly lit. Most of them climb very steeply and contain lovely waterfalls and icy pools.

At the Moss Garden in Violet Gorge, an exquisite waterfall cascades from a large rock overhang to a clear pool partly framed by a wall dripping with water and supporting a rich green hanging forest of velvety mosses, ferns, lichens, liverworts and hornworts. Further along the main gorge, beyond a beautiful waterfall named Aljon Falls, the peaceful Angiopteris Ravine harbours a dense growth of rainforest species including the rare dark green king fern (*Angiopteris evecta*), which is found only here and at Fraser Island and the Blackall Range near the coast. A superb plant, the *Angiopteris* fern has a thick, bulbous base and huge fronds extending as much as 5 metres across. Only 20-30 of these extraordinary plants survive at Carnarvon and they are shaded by the canopy of tall rough tree-ferns (*Cyathea australis*) which grow more than 8 metres high.

Other tributary gorges at Carnarvon have a starker beauty, such as Boowinda Creek Gorge which leads to Battleship Spur, one of the region's best lookout points. Deep, narrow and winding, this gorge is very sculptural, with undercut walls, a boulder-strewn cobbled floor and little vegetation.

But the most intriguing part of Carnarvon Gorge is the still and tranquil Amphitheatre, hidden deep within the southern cliff of the main gorge. A large, oval-shaped cleft created by water erosion, it is almost completely enclosed and can be reached only by climbing 15 metres up a ladder on the sheer rockface and then walking about 40-50 metres along a narrow crevice. Its walls, which soar more than 100 metres high, have been hollowed out and form an almost conical shape, with the base of the cleft being wider than the opening at the top. There are a few cave-like fissures and a permanent pool, and when it rains several waterfalls form. However, sunlight seldom reaches the bottom of the cleft and, apart from ferns and a few mosses, the Amphitheatre is quite bare.

Several isolated rock formations are also prominent features of Carnarvon Gorge, including Wongalinda Arch, a natural bridge spanning a side gorge cut by Kamoloo Creek, and a group of fantastic square-cut monoliths as tall as the cliffs in an area known as Parrabooya.

Aboriginal people lived in or visited Carnarvon Gorge at least 4000-5000 years ago, and were probably there more than 20 000 years ago. Unfortunately, very little is known about these people or their culture, for a century has passed since they left the area—shot, poisoned, infected by disease or driven away by white settlers. The only physical evidence of their long occupancy of the land is at rock art sites in the cliff walls and at burial grounds in caves and on rock ledges.

The main art sites in the gorge are the Art Gallery and the Cathedral, where paintings have been dated as being about 3500 years old. However, several sites in the range nearby include works more than 18 000 years old.

The rock art at Carnarvon is of three styles—stencil painting, freehand painting, and engraving—and often paintings are superimposed over older works.

The most numerous paintings are of the stencil type, whereby dampened pulverised ochres were blown from the mouth over a hand or an object such as a tool or a weapon held against the rock surface. When the hand or object was lifted, a clear silhouette remained on the rock. In the freehand style, ochre and other pigments were applied to the rock with the finger or with a simple implement such as a brush made from a chewed twig. Subjects usually depicted in this style were animals, especially goannas, but there were also many "net" patterns and occasionally human figures.

Two types of engraving are found at Carnarvon: rough-surfaced designs executed by pecking the rock, and smooth-surfaced designs made by scraping it. Sometimes both techniques were used for a single design, giving a very elaborate effect. The implements used to fashion these engravings are not known, but they were probably made of bone or stone. Common motifs include animal and human tracks, oval depressions, geometric lines and parts of the human body.

The first Europeans to visit Carnarvon Gorge were probably cattle graziers who established runs in the region during the 1860s. The range itself, however, was sighted as far back as 1844 by the explorer Ludwig Leichhardt, who traversed part of its eastern fringe, about 100 kilometres from the gorge. Two years later the explorer and surveyor Thomas Livingstone Mitchell passed the western side of the uplands and named the area Carnarvon Range because the scenery reminded him of the mountainous Carnarvon County in Wales.

Grazing leases continued to be held in the region for several decades. But the roughness and isolation of the country, plus its lack of exploitable minerals, prevented further settlement, and eventually even the graziers were discouraged. In 1931, when the leaseholder failed to pay the rent on the land, the Queensland Commissioner for Lands recommended that because the area was extremely beautiful but of little commercial use, it should be declared a national park.

The following year the gorge and a large area of surrounding plateau country totalling almost 30 000 hectares were set aside as the Carnarvon National Park. At that time the region was not readily accessible, but since then various tracks have gradually been improved and in 1964 an unsealed road was built to the entrance of the gorge.

Still as vibrant and untouched as it was throughout the centuries that Aboriginal people lived there, Carnarvon Gorge will remain one of the most magnificent natural environments in Australia, provided that it is not subjected to overuse or vandalism by modern man. □

. . . Covered with velvety mosses and rich green ferns

1. Black-trunked *Livistona* palms
2. Rough tree-ferns (*Cyathea australis*) framed by the darker leaves of the rare king fern (*Angiopteris evecta*), in the Angiopteris Ravine
3. Freak twin trunks of a spotted gum (*Eucalyptus maculata*)
4. Yellow hibiscus (*Hibiscus heterophylla*)
5. Redhead cottonbush (*Asclepias curassavica*)
6. The Moss Garden, in Violet Gorge

1

2

3

4

5

The rivers and lagoons are fringed with paperbarks and other trees such as the spreading freshwater mangrove (*Barringtonia acutangula*) which has graceful sprays of crimson flowers that blossom only at night. Where the rivers empty into Van Diemen Gulf or the Arafura Sea, there are treeless tidal flats and swampy estuaries with patches of mangroves (mostly *Rhizophora* and *Avicennia spp.*).

Despite its tropical climate, Arnhem Land today supports little rainforest. In the past, however, much of the area was covered by rainforest species, and in the shelter of some of the gorges and in other niches along the escarpment a few tiny pockets remain. The main trees are tall palms such as *Livistona benthamii* and Carpentaria palm (*Carpentaria acuminata*), with an understorey of mosses, ferns, vines and orchids. Other hardier tropical plants grow on the cliffs, including a stilt-rooted rock "screw palm" (*Pandanus basedowii*) and a strangler fig (*Ficus sp.*).

Wildlife is abundant in Arnhem Land. In the Kakadu area alone, more than 50 species of native mammal, over 270 birds, 75 reptiles, 43 native fish and 22 frogs have been recorded. Some 6000 insect species have also been identified throughout the region and 10 000 species or more may exist.

A haven for birds, Arnhem Land is always ringing with song. As in other parts of the continent, there are numerous parrots, ranging from cockatoos and galahs to rosellas and lorikeets, plus a variety of other widespread species including honeyeaters, warblers, martins, butcher-birds, woodswallows and the flightless emu (*Dromaius novaehollandiae*). However, more conspicuous are the many beautiful waterbirds and waders that make this region their home.

The tall jabiru (*Xenorhynchus asiaticus*), Australia's only stork, forages for fish along the marshy shores of billabongs and lagoons, its long red legs contrasting dramatically with black and white plumage. Grey brolgas and sarus cranes (*Grus rubicunda* and *G. antigone*) perform graceful ballets across the grasslands, and in lily-filled pools chirpy, long-toed lotusbirds (*Jacana gallinacea*) step elegantly across the floating vegetation, as though walking on water.

Smaller birds of the wetlands include darters, cormorants, herons and ibises. But the largest bird population of the region is that of the black and white magpie geese (*Anseranas semipalmata*). In the Wet season huge flocks spread out over the grasslands, then in the Dry they crowd together at watered places known as "goose camps", their presence audible for great distances due to their resonant honking call. Often they are with grass and water whistle-ducks (*Dendrocygna eytoni* and *D. arcuata*), both on the ground and in flight.

The bushlands and rocky areas support marsupials ranging from kangaroos and wallabies to tiny possums. Of particular interest are rare black-furred euros (*Macropus robustus*) living near the headwaters of the Alligator rivers.

Some animals build amazing homes for themselves. In the forests and on savannah grasslands, several species of termite construct long and narrow mounds as high as 6 metres, which can withstand both flood and drought. Another mound-builder, the little scrub fowl (*Megapodius freycinet*), lives in the woodlands, where it makes a huge dome-like mound of soil up to 4.5 metres high and 7 metres in diameter.

Many creatures of Arnhem Land are rare and bizarre, such as the vivid orange and blue spectacular grasshopper (*Petasida ephippigera*) — often known as "Leichhardt's grasshopper" — which looks like a miniature court jester. Feeding only on an aromatic native mint bush (*Pitterodia sp.*), it is believed to live only in Arnhem Land and along the Victoria River, further west. It was first known to Europeans in 1839 when J. E. Dring, chief clerk on the survey vessel HMS *Beagle*,

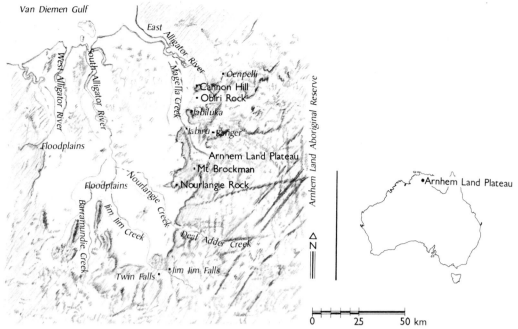

Australia's largest lizard . . .

Perentie (*Varanus giganteus*)

collected specimens along the Victoria River. In 1845 the explorer Ludwig Leichhardt saw "a great number" of the grasshoppers near the headwaters of Deaf Adder Creek in western Arnhem Land and a decade later J. R. Elsey, a surgeon accompanying an expedition led by the explorer Augustus Charles Gregory, also saw specimens near the Victoria River. For more than 100 years, the spectacular grasshopper was not recorded again; however, it was rediscovered in 1971 near Mt Brockman, west of the Arnhem Land escarpment. To date, little is known about this tiny creature, but it seems likely that it often exists only as eggs — a characteristic that would explain the apparent former "disappearance" of the species.

The king of the lowland waterways is the powerful saltwater crocodile (*Crocodylus porosus*). Living in coastal waters, estuaries and murky rivers and lagoons, it grows between 5 and 8 metres long and is Australia's only inland predator of man. Further upstream, the rivers are inhabited by the freshwater Johnston crocodile (*Crocodylus johnstoni*). This fish-eating species normally grows more than 1.5 metres long, sometimes reaching 2.5 metres, but in the upper reaches of the Liverpool River, where the food source is poor, the animals are unusually stunted, seldom being more than a metre or so at maturity. Other river inhabitants include tortoises and the giant perch (*Lates calcarifer*), known locally as barramundi, while in the sea and estuaries there are turtles and the big "sea cow", the dugong (*Halicore dugong*).

The country's largest venomous snake, the deadly taipan (*Oxyuranus scutellatus*), also makes its home in Arnhem Land, though it is seldom seen. The most common snakes are pythons and other non-venomous species, while other reptiles include the giant perentie (*Varanus giganteus*), which grows up to 2 metres, smaller goannas and various lizards.

Aboriginal people have lived in Arnhem Land for at least 30 000 years. Their traditional culture is the most complex of all Aboriginal groups in Australia and it has been enriched by contact over several centuries with people from Indonesia and other parts of Asia.

Like all Australian Aborigines, the most important relationship the Arnhem Land people know is with their land. They believe that before the time of the Dreaming, the land was without form or life. Then the spirit ancestors undertook great journeys, fashioning the landscape and creating everything in it that we know today. Part of the creator remains with each feature of the land and the Aboriginal "owner" or "guardian" takes it as his totem. Many beautiful names of landforms reflect these creation beliefs, such as the rock outliers known as Old Woman Dreaming and Hawk Dreaming, west of the Arnhem escarpment. But the beliefs are also expressed in art, ritual and song. The most important ancestors of the region are the Earth Mother, the symbol of fertility and the original creator of life, and the Rainbow Serpent, symbolising the storms of the Wet season.

For more than 20 000 years, the very hard sandstone of the Arnhem plateau has provided the Aborigines with perfect natural galleries for rock paintings, especially along the western escarpment and on rock outliers near Oenpelli in the Kakadu region.

The paintings, which are the most extensive and significant examples of ancient art in the world, are located at hundreds of sites and are of several styles. The earliest paintings are elegant *Mimi* or *Dynamic* spirit figures portrayed in wonderfully fluid, fine lines of red ochre. Often in friezes of up to 30 or more figures, they mostly depict scenes of movement such as running, dancing, hunting or fighting. The famous *X-ray* paintings, which show the internal parts of human and animal bodies, are also very old. The X-rays are in a variety of colours, consisting of pigments from ochre, clays and charcoal. The subjects drawn depend on the surrounding environment and the artists' lifestyles, with fish, turtles and other aquatic creatures tending to be predominant on art in lowland river areas, whereas marsupials and animals such as the echidna (*Tachyglossus aculeatus*) are more numerous in the plateau country. Other rock art styles include stencil paintings, beeswax figures and petroglyphs (rock carvings), and very often paintings are superimposed on older works.

One of the best-known art sites is Obiri Rock, a large outlier on a beautiful black soil plain west of Oenpelli. The main gallery is a long and narrow array of murals in a rock shelter (or overhang). Mostly depicting X-ray fish and turtles, these exquisite paintings have been dated as being at least 18 000 years old and they are still in excellent condition, with vivid colours and clear detail. Similar art galleries with works more than 20 000 years old are located at Hawk Dreaming, an outlier on the floodplain near Cannon Hill, just north of Obiri. Here, in a rock shelter called Cockatoo Woman Cave, an ancient X-ray painting shows a female with both male and female foetuses inside her body. More recent paintings at both sites testify to the Aborigines' early contacts with Asians and Europeans. Subjects represented include sailing vessels, horses, men with guns, a cat and a steel axe. Other widely known painting sites in the region are Nourlangie Rock and Deaf Adder Gorge, while magnificent petroglyphs are found at Lightning Dreaming in Sawcut Gorge.

As well as their beauty and their spiritual and cultural significance, the paintings of Arnhem Land provide a valuable record of the environment in the past. At Obiri Rock, for example, a painting of a thylacine or "Tasmanian tiger" (*Thylacinus cynocephalus*) indicates that the animal once lived in the region, although no fossil has yet been found. The Fly River turtle (*Carettochelys insculpta*), common in New Guinea, is also featured in rock art and was thought to be extinct until recent years when two specimens were found.

The Aborigines of Arnhem Land are also renowned for their bark paintings. This form of art has probably been best

developed at Yirrkala on the north-eastern tip of the region, where brushes of human hair attached to fish bones were used for centuries to paint designs in pigments of ochre and other local minerals. Fine bark paintings have also been produced by the people of Oenpelli.

Apart from this ancient art, Arnhem Land contains the world's oldest evidence of edge-ground stone axes, dated at about 23 000 years, and it seems probable that the original Aboriginal inhabitants were the first people in the world to grind food and pigments.

Macassan and Malay fishermen are believed to have visited Arnhem Land, which they called *Mariga*, since at least the fifteenth century. They came annually, sailing their *praus* under the power of the north-west monsoons, and they stayed at settlements around the coast for the duration of the Wet season until they could return to Asia with the south-east trade winds. From Arnhem Land they gathered *bêche-de-mer* or trepang (*Thelenota ananas*), turtleshell, pearlshell and other items prized in their homelands. At the same time they brought to the Aborigines such implements as steel axes, metal spearheads and fish hooks, and taught them to make dugout canoes and to smoke tobacco in pipes. Asian influence is evident, too, in the design of many weapons and utensils, and was almost certainly responsible for the development of the famous didgeridoo, a large pipe-like instrument traditionally played only in Arnhem Land. Several plant species along the Arnhem coast were also introduced by the Macassans and Malays, notably the tamarind tree (*Tamarindus indica*), which bears an edible pulpy fruit.

Arnhem Land was first known to European navigators in 1623 when the Dutch ship *Arnhem*, commanded by Willem van Coolsteerdt, was blown towards its eastern shore after parting company with its consort, the *Pera*, during an expedition led by Jan Cartensz. Another Dutchman, Pieter Pieterszoon, sailed about 150 kilometres along the northern coast in 1636 and, thinking that the region was an island, named it Van Diemen's Land after the Governor-General of the Dutch East Indies, Anthony van Diemen. In time, however, the name of Coolsteerdt's vessel survived and Pieterszoon's voyage was commemorated by the naming of Van Diemen Gulf.

Several famous navigators later sailed along the Arnhem coast, including Abel Janszoon Tasman in 1644, Matthew Flinders in 1803 and Phillip Parker King in 1819.

Fearful of the possibility of French colonisation, the British made two abortive attempts to establish military and trading post settlements on the Cobourg Peninsula at the north-western edge of Arnhem Land. The first, Raffles Bay at the eastern end of the peninsula, lasted only two years, from June 1827 to August 1829. But the second, Victoria, founded in 1838 deep inside Port Essington at the western end of the peninsula, struggled on for 11 years until 1849 when it, too, was abandoned, largely because the settlers were unable to cope with the climate and with tropical diseases. A few brick chimneys still mark the location of the settlement.

Yet despite the failure of the Port Essington settlement, the presence of the white man on the northern coast for just those few years led to serious environmental consequences in Arnhem Land. In 1838 a herd of 18 head of Asian buffalo (*Bubalus bubalus*) was imported and in 1843 a further 49 head were brought in. When the settlers left the area, the buffalo were turned loose and, although they have been hunted for hides and meat since the 1880s, they today number about 150 000 head. By wallowing in waterholes and making them murky, the buffaloes often destroy the habitats of fish and other aquatic creatures. They also eat waterlilies and chop up mats of floating vegetation that once provided nesting grounds for crocodiles. On the plains they trample over and destroy grasses and sedges that were nesting sites for birds. With their great weight, they churn up the black soil, break the banks of rivers and create gutters that drain freshwater swamps or allow the entry of salt water. As a result, the sun dries out the ground and, in the Dry season, large parts of the plains that were formerly vegetated are now bare expanses of spongy cracked mud.

While it functioned, the settlement at Port Essington provided a valuable base for explorers and naturalists. Captain J. C. Wickham and his successor J. Lort Stokes visited the region in HMS *Beagle* in 1839 and John Gilbert, explorer and zoological assistant to the ornithologist John Gould, spent 8 months there in 1840-1. Gilbert planned to return to Port Essington in 1845 as a member of an expedition led by Ludwig Leichhardt, which travelled 4800 kilometres overland from the Darling Downs in Queensland, but tragically he was killed during the journey by Aborigines of Cape York Peninsula. Leichhardt and the rest of the party made their way through Arnhem Land to Port Essington as quickly as possible, spending little time in exploring the region. They did, however, discover the Roper River, which Leichhardt named after a member of the party, John Roper. Following the river from east to west, then heading north, they also discovered several streams that issue from the western escarpment.

Other visitors to the area last century included the eminent

*For more than 20 000 years, the
hard sandstone of Arnhem Land
has provided the canvas for
Aboriginal art . . .*

1. X-ray long-necked tortoise, Obiri Rock
2. X-ray painting showing twin foetuses,
at Hawk Dreaming near Cannon Hill
3. X-ray spirit figures, Nourlangie Rock
4. Spirit figures decorate the roof of a
cave shelter, near Obiri Rock

English biologist Thomas Huxley, who called at Port Essington in 1848 aboard HMS *Rattlesnake*, and several explorers, notably Augustus Charles Gregory in 1855-6 and David Lindsay in 1883. But none of these men penetrated far beyond the edges of the Arnhem plateau and even today the vast heart of the region is still largely unknown to white people.

Earlier this century the whole "top end" of the Northern Territory, from the Roper River to the Victoria River, was known as Arnhem Land. However, later the name was applied only to the region eastward of the Alligator rivers' floodplains.

In 1931 an area of approximately 96 000 square kilometres, including several offshore islands, was declared as the Arnhem Land Aboriginal Reserve — the last major stronghold Australian Aboriginal people have from European civilisation. Nevertheless, several Christian missions that had been established around the edge of the region since 1908 still remain and pastoral leases also operate on the western and southern margins of the plateau, adjoining the reserve.

Other land on the edge of the Arnhem plateau has been utilised for mining ventures. Small deposits of uranium were taken from El Sharana in the South Alligator River valley in western Arnhem Land during the late 1950s and early 1960s, and construction work for large bauxite mining operations at Gove Peninsula on the eastern Arnhem coast began in 1969, with a town called Nhulunbuy being built to house workers. Then in the 1970s, the town of Jabiru was constructed in the East Alligator River area, south-west of Oenpelli, to provide for workers connected with large-scale uranium mining projects at Ranger, Jabiluka and Koongarra.

With the passing of the *Land Rights (Northern Territory) Act* by Federal parliament in 1976, ownership of reserves and certain other tracts of land in the Northern Territory became vested in the Aboriginal people themselves, instead of in the Crown. Among the areas for which land rights claims have been recognised are the floodplains of the Alligator rivers, adjacent to the Arnhem Land Aboriginal Reserve.

In November 1978 the Aboriginal owners leased more than 6000 square kilometres of this land to the Director of the Australian National Parks and Wildlife Service to be managed as a national park for all Australians. The following year the Kakadu National Park — named after the vanishing Kakadu or Gagudju people, who traditionally lived in part of the area — was declared, encompassing many beautiful features such as Obiri Rock, Cannon Hill, Nourlangie Rock, Jim Jim Gorge and Deaf Adder Gorge. Plans have been drawn up to enlarge the park, and eventually it will cover some 12 500 square kilometres. In addition, Aboriginal land rights have been acknowledged for the Cobourg Peninsula, which was formerly a wildlife sanctuary but is now being managed as the Cobourg Peninsula National Park.

Today, only the Aboriginal reserve is officially known as Arnhem Land, but the name is still popularly applied to the Kakadu and other surrounding lowland areas, as well. Many major tribal groups inhabit the region, the best known being the Gungwinggu people in the west and the Murngin people in the north-east.

The encroachment of modern civilisation is a serious potential threat to the lifestyle and environment of these people, especially in the Kakadu area. Apart from the pressures that would be brought simply by the presence of the several thousand people expected to populate Jabiru, there is a grave possibility that the ecology of the billabongs and streams may be drastically altered by increased siltation, by the effects of nutrients released from sewage systems or by heavy metal contaminants in run-off waters from the mine area. Furthermore, although cats and dogs are prohibited at Jabiru, the policing of such restrictions is very difficult and it seems likely that an increased number of feral animals and alien plants would be introduced to the region. Vandalism — intentional or unintentional — is also a risk, particularly in connection with rock paintings and sacred sites. Already, at least one precious work of art more than 9000 years old has been damaged by a mining marker placed in the centre of it and other art has been used as targets for rifle shooting.

The importance of retaining the Kakadu area — indeed, all of Arnhem Land — in a wilderness state is incalculable. Relatively little botanical and biological research has to date been carried out in the area, but the great wealth of plant and animal species is evident. Magella Creek, for example, on which the township of Jabiru stands, is the home of at least 28 native freshwater fish species, compared with only 27 in the entire Murray–Darling river system. And the value of the beautiful ancient Aboriginal rock art, much of it well in excess of 20 000 years old, is immeasurable by modern man. □

4

*. . . Beautiful waterlilies, clumps of pandanus
and graceful sprays of crimson flowers that
blossom only at night*

1. The delicate night flowers of the freshwater mangrove
(*Barringtonia acutangula*), at Old Woman Dreaming
2. Red lotus (*Nelumbo nucifera*), near Cannon Hill
3. Residual mat of floating vegetation stranded in the trees
after the annual summer flood, near Nourlangie Creek
4. Forest of "screw palms" (*Pandanus spiralis*) on the
floodplain of the South Alligator River
OVERLEAF: Flight of magpie geese (*Anseranas semipalmata*)
and grass whistle-ducks (*Dendrocygna eytoni*)

Corridor of stone

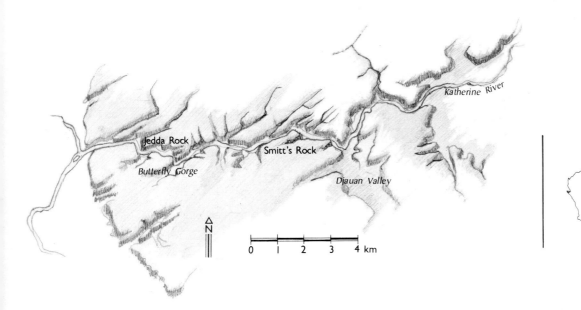

The river fills the gorge from wall to wall . . .

1. The fourth section of the gorge
2–3. The fifth section of the gorge
4. A delicate *Livistona inermis* palm
5. An ancient cycad (*Cycas calcicola*)

POURING down from the Arnhem Land plateau, the flood-waters of centuries have slowly carved the spectacular steep-walled Katherine Gorge along the course taken by the Katherine River as it forges its way to the lowland plains.

About 15 kilometres long, this gorge is like a huge stone corridor. It has a remarkably zigzag course, with 13 straight sections joined at sharp right-angled turns. The walls of the gorge tower 60-90 metres high and are generally sheer, although there are many beautiful caves and rock overhangs. The river extends from wall to wall for almost the entire length of the gorge, and it can be viewed only by boat or by walking along the clifftops.

The gorge has two distinct moods. In the winter Dry season, it is a series of placid reaches up to 30 metres deep that give mirror-like reflections of the vivid orange walls. Rock bars between some of these reaches create little foaming rapids and occasionally the wind makes the water elsewhere in the gorge slightly choppy, but for the most part it is tranquil at this time of the year.

By contrast, the monsoonal rains of the summer Wet season turn the river into a raging torrent, carrying vast amounts of debris and sometimes uprooting trees. The water level may rise by as much as 18 metres and the little rapids of the Dry turn into 3-metre waves. The gorge is completely inaccessible during this period and much of the surrounding country is flooded.

The Katherine River began to carve the gorge about 25 million years ago. The rocks through which it cuts are primarily sandstones and conglomerates laid down as sediments on a sea floor 1400-1800 million years ago. Earth movements and folding later compacted and cemented the sediments into a formation some 500 metres thick, which has two main sets of joints running at right angles to each other. The river's path follows one set of joints and then the other, and so on, producing its zigzag pattern. Weathering and erosion along other joints have created numerous side fissures and there are several faults where large blocks on either side of a joint have moved.

Among the most impressive parts of the gorge are Jedda Rock, a smooth vertical cliff face towering 64 metres high from which a major scene of Charles Chauvel's movie *Jedda* was filmed in the 1950s, and Smitt's Rock, a prominent outcrop between the fourth and fifth sections of the gorge.

Vegetation in the gorge is fairly sparse, but in cool alcoves and other places where they can gain a foothold, there are lush tropical rainforest species, including ferns, orchids, lilies, figs (*Ficus spp.*), pandanus, and an exquisite fan palm (*Livistona inermis*) that grows up to about 10 metres and has a slender trunk and delicate weeping leaf fronds. Numerous other trees such as red-barked bloodwood (*Eucalyptus dichromophloia*) and paperbark (*Melaleuca spp.*) are found on the sandstone plateau above and on the river banks at both ends of the gorge. In the stony country there is also an ancient cycad (*Cycas calcicola*) that has smoky-grey, velvety foliage and is found only in this region.

A great many birds inhabit the gorge, particularly cormorants, darters, rainbow birds and pretty little fairy martins (*Petrochelidon ariel*) that build bottle-shaped nests under overhangs high in the cliffs. However, very few waterfowl live in the area, for although there is always water in the gorge, it is too deep to provide the swampy habitat that these birds require.

For other animals, the cool, clear waters of the gorge are an ideal home. More than 35 fish species, including the giant perch or barramundi (*Lates calcarifer*), have been identified, and there are many other aquatic creatures such as the freshwater Johnston crocodile (*Crocodylus johnstoni*) and tortoises. Land animals include kangaroos, wallabies, bats, the emu (*Dromaius novaehollandiae*), the Gould's sand goanna (*Varanus gouldii*) and thousands of butterflies that congregate in Butterfly Gorge, a subsidiary crevice leading off from the second section of the main gorge.

For some 18 000 years, Katherine Gorge was the territory of the Djauan Aboriginal people. Today, the remaining members of this tribe live mostly in towns or on stations, but their traditional relationship with the gorge is evident through rock paintings on the cliffs. Unlike most Aboriginal rock art, the work of the Djauans is not always under shelters or in caves, but often on open walls that are protected from the sun, the wind and the rain. Subjects depicted are principally spirit ancestors from the Dreamtime and local animals.

The first European to discover the gorge is not known, but it was probably a bushman and explorer named Alfred Giles, who managed the nearby Springvale Station in the 1880s. The river, which rises in western Arnhem Land and flows southwest for 322 kilometres until it joins the Daly River, was discovered some 20 years earlier, in July 1862, by the explorer John McDouall Stuart, who crossed it about 50 kilometres upstream from the gorge and named it the Katherine River after the daughter of one of his supporters, James Chambers.

By the turn of the century several cattle stations had been established in the Katherine area. In 1914 a town named Emungalan was surveyed on the northern bank of the river, about 30 kilometres downstream from the gorge, but it was replaced in 1926 by a town called Katherine on the southern bank. Today Katherine is an important commercial centre. The main industries are beef cattle, mining, and the growing of fruit and vegetables on CSIRO experimental farms.

The magnificent gorge has in the past been described as an ideal site for a dam to harness the floodwaters of the Wet for irrigation, but fortunately it has not been touched. Instead, in June 1963, the entire gorge and part of the surrounding country were set aside as the 22 700-hectare Katherine Gorge National Park. □

1

2

3

4

5

The giant tors
THE DEVIL'S MARBLES

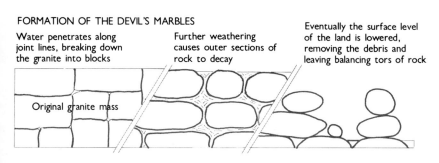

Water penetrates along joint lines, breaking down the granite into blocks

Further weathering causes outer sections of rock to decay

Eventually the surface level of the land is lowered, removing the debris and leaving balancing tors of rock

Original granite mass

As though strewn across a spinifex playground, the Devil's Marbles create a bold and unexpected landscape. Located on a gently undulating plain of quartz gravel, 100 kilometres south of the Northern Territory town of Tennant Creek, they are giant granite tors, some standing isolated, others balancing precariously one on top of the other. They are the only distinctive natural landmark for hundreds of square kilometres.

The Marbles vary from less than a metre to as much as 6 metres in diameter. They are derived from a single mass of granite which crystallised more than 1500 million years ago. This granite had three sets of joint planes at right angles to each other and over millennia weathering along the joints broke down the original mass into blocks 3-7 metres square. Continued weathering—which was greatest at the corners, where rainwater and wind attacked from three directions—gradually rounded the contours of the blocks, and eventually the softer surrounding rocks were eroded away, leaving the Marbles exposed in fantastic piles.

Although the contours of the Marbles are smooth, the texture of the granite is rough and contains quite large grains of feldspar, quartz and other minerals, giving the rock a mottled appearance. When unexposed, the rock colour is whitish-grey with a scattering of small dark patches. However, the erosive action of water and atmospheric gases, which causes the surface of the rock to expand and peel off in small flakes, also produces iron oxides that have given the rock a predominantly orangey-red colour mixed with specks of black and white.

Like many rocks in Australia, the Marbles often appear to change colour depending on factors such as distance, aspect, weather conditions and time of day. They are particularly spectacular in the early morning and late afternoon, when the rising or setting sun illuminates them to an intense, glowing red—an effect that has helped to earn them their name.

To the Aboriginal people in this part of Australia, the Devil's Marbles are believed to be giant eggs laid by the sacred rainbow serpent, an important ancestor of the Dreamtime.

Many early European explorers and travellers chose to rest in the shade of the giant Marbles, among them the Reverend John Flynn, founder of the famous Royal Flying Doctor Service. When he died in 1951, his grave at the foot of Mt Gillen near Alice Springs was sealed with a huge 8-tonne boulder brought from the Devil's Marbles, some 400 kilometres away.

Today the great tors are the main feature of the 1828-hectare Devil's Marbles Conservation Reserve. There is no permanent water, although pools form in crevices and hollows after rare heavy falls of rain. Nonetheless, there is sufficient moisture to support sparse arid vegetation, and lonely ghost gums (*Eucalyptus papuana*) grow from fissures in the Marbles themselves. The tors also provide refuge for reptiles and birds. The environment, however, is extremely fragile and preservation of these precious habitats depends on minimum disturbance by man. □

. . . Giant eggs of the sacred rainbow serpent

THE MACDONNELL RANGES

Mt Sonder, from the south

IN ALMOST the exact geographical centre of Australia, a series of east-west running parallel ridges stretches nearly 500 kilometres across the desert horizon. Known collectively as the MacDonnell Ranges, it is the largest of several mountain groups in the area, and easily the most imposing.

Although not particularly high, the MacDonnells are spectacular in profile. From the southern side many slopes rise sheer to a crest, without foothills or interruption, and along their full length they are seldom broken by passes. Towards the western end, a handful of higher peaks reach twice the general height of the range and stand in stark relief against the brilliant blue sky. From the north they are more indented, a series of long bastions separated by valley-like openings.

These ranges are most surprising amongst Australia's mountain systems. Sheltering the town of Alice Springs, they provide a shady and watered refuge in the very heart of the Red Centre—a vast region famed for its arid, flat red plains and sandy deserts.

Viewed from the distance the MacDonnells seem deceptively out of place, appearing at first as a ribbon of soft pink and purple hues which contrasts strangely with the fiery red and patchy greens of the plains. On nearing the ranges the colours gradually become defined, the sun firing the bare rocks to a burning red which is relieved only by the dry greens and yellows of a sparse but tenacious vegetation.

Once inside the MacDonnells, their true character emerges. They are the mere remnants of a much larger, ancient range of mountains formed of sediments deposited 1400-2400 million years ago. At least 1000 million years ago, extreme folding elevated the rocks to form the ancestral MacDonnell Ranges (including their extensions, the Chewings and Harts ranges), which reached heights of about 4500 metres. Weathering and erosion over millions of years wore down these ancestral mountains and sediments were deposited in seas that at times lapped

their shores. From about 500 million years ago, these eroded younger sediments were uplifted and folded, forming the various other ranges of the Centre which run south of and parallel to the MacDonnells, such as the George Gill Range, the Krichauff Ranges and the Waterhouse Range.

The last folding movements to affect these mountains and the older MacDonnells, which by this time were much reduced in size, took place some 300 million years ago and since then they have been affected only by minor vertical uplifts. Erosion, however, has removed softer rocks and material, forming lower plains but leaving the harder rocks of the mountains in rows of folded ridges separated by long, flat alluvial valleys and dissected by gorges cut by the ancient Finke River and its tributaries in times when the Centre was better watered than it is now.

Today the plains stand about 600 metres above sea level and the MacDonnells average about another 400-500 metres. The rocks are primarily quartzite, which although normally white has become stained red by iron oxide. Other rock strata include conglomerate, limestone, dolomite, sandstone, siltstone and shale. Of complex structure, the mountains have been weathered and eroded unevenly, producing a variety of sculptured rock patterns. The walls of the long valleys are particularly impressive, ranging from scalloped layers of reds and creams to sharply fractured rust-coloured blocks. The more resistant rocks stand as prominent towering peaks: Mt Liebig and Mt Zeil in the Chewings Range both top 1500 metres and others are only a little lower, including Mt Heughlin (1450 metres), Mt Edward (1418 metres), Mt Sonder (1334 metres) and Mt Hay (1249 metres).

But in this arid land it is not only the high peaks and the rock formations that command our attention, but also the narrow, steep-sided gorges.

There has been little surface water in central Australia for at least 20 000 years, but in the gorges of the MacDonnells and other nearby ranges, numerous little springs, rockholes and occasional larger pools remain as reminders of the former times when the climate was much wetter. These pools lie in the old river and creek beds. Occasionally when it rains heavily in the north, floodwaters sweep down and for a brief period the pools are drowned to form part of a reborn stream.

River red gums (*Eucalyptus camaldulensis*) still line the sandy white watercourses, and in some of the shaded gorges there are rare cycads (*Macrozamia macdonnellii*), an ancient form of plant life which has grown here for perhaps 200 million years. Bloodwood (*Eucalyptus terminalis*), corkbark (*Hakea suberea*) and the willow-like ironwood (*Acacia estrophiolata*) are also common throughout the MacDonnells, but loveliest of all are the white ghost gums (*Eucalyptus papuana*). These slender trees grow luxuriantly on the sand and the grassy flats, and often cling like sentinels to high craggy ledges, their white trunks highlighting the sienna colourings of the rocks.

The most dominant of the low trees and shrubs in the Mac-Donnells are acacias, especially mulgas. Of particular interest is the "witchetty bush" *(Acacia kempeana)*, widely known because the "witchetty grub" found in its root is a traditional Aboriginal food. Spinifex *(Triodia clelandii* and *T. longiceps)* provides the main ground cover, but in spring and after rains the land is decorated by a prolific and colourful wildflower display.

The exquisite landscapes of the MacDonnells are known to most Australians and to many people overseas through the paintings of Albert Namatjira, the great artist who was such a part of this country that he could paint much of the scenery from memory with perfect accuracy to detail.

Namatjira's people, the Aranda, have been living in central Australia for thousands of years. Since the coming of the white man they have been virtually dispossessed of the land, and their life today in the missions and towns is a far cry from the days when they camped in the ranges and needed only the ancient *nardoo* (grinding stones), axes and other simple tools to survive.

Namatjira was born on the Lutheran church's Hermannsburg Aboriginal Mission, located on the Missionary Plain directly south of the western MacDonnells. He rose to fame in the late 1930s through his talent as a watercolourist and was the first of several famous Aboriginal artists of the "Aranda School" to adopt the European style of perspective.

But like so many of his countrymen, Namatjira was caught between two worlds. The imposition of the ways of the white man was at the devastating expense of a rich and harmonious culture of which the newcomer had no understanding.

The Aranda people knew how to live within the dictates of the environment, and their lifestyle, art and mythology were far more meaningful to them than anything the white man could offer. Symbolic rock paintings and stories passed down for generations told of the formation of the land and gave the knowledge needed for survival. The life-giving waterholes, for example, were usually sacred and central to important rituals, and the need to conserve these precious water supplies was emphasised by the belief that most pools were occupied by large watersnakes which would kill and eat anybody who swam in the water or lingered too long near the water's edge. Restrictions were also placed on eating certain plants and animals at particular times of the year, in order to maintain their numbers. To these people the MacDonnells were *Altjira*, "the eternal land".

The first European to intrude upon this ancient world of the MacDonnells was the determined Scot, John McDouall Stuart, who in 1860 took up the challenge to find a route across the centre of the continent, from the south coast to the north coast.

On 12 April of that year Stuart and two companions reached the MacDonnells. "This is the only real range that I have met with since leaving the Flinders range," he wrote in his journal. He named the ranges after the Governor of South Australia, Sir Richard MacDonnell—"as a token of my gratitude for his kindness to me on many occasions"—and passed through the mountains by following gaps formed by the Hugh River, west of the present-day town of Alice Springs.

The rocky gaps were difficult to negotiate, but overall Stuart was impressed by what he saw in the MacDonnells: "The country of the ranges is as fine a pastoral hill-country as a man would wish to possess; grass to the top of the hills, and abundance of water through the whole of the ranges."

Stuart's quest to reach the northern coast failed on that occasion, as did a further attempt commenced later in the year, but in 1862 he tried again and this time succeeded, reaching the coast near where the Adelaide River empties into the sea some 45 kilometres north-east of present-day Darwin.

Stuart passed through the MacDonnells six times during these three journeys, but to him they were just a welcome stopover point. Each time, he followed the Hugh River and its branches, and did not investigate the ranges further.

The settlement of the region by Europeans came about largely through a technological development—the establishment in 1870-2 of the Overland Telegraph line linking Adelaide to Darwin, and ultimately connecting with a transcontinental line to Europe.

The task was a mammoth undertaking requiring the laying down of over 3500 kilometres of line, much of it over country which was practically unknown. In addition, the signals in those days were so weak that nine repeater stations had to be built, one of them in the MacDonnell Ranges.

The basic route to be taken was that of the explorer Stuart, but there would be some deviations. One of the biggest problems was to find a pass through the MacDonnells which would be practicable for laying the line. Two advance exploratory journeys led by the explorer John Ross had failed to find such a pass, and when in March 1871 Ross did find a large gap in the range, he was surprised to meet up with a Telegraph surveyor, William Whitfield Mills, who had beaten him to the discovery.

The pass and a dry riverbed passing through it were named Heavitree Gap and Todd River respectively, after the South Australian Superintendent of Telegraphs and Postmaster-General, Charles Heavitree Todd, who was responsible for the construction of the Overland Telegraph line. But it was the Superintendent's wife Alice who was to achieve greater fame, for a little way along the bed of the Todd River, Mills had found a permanent spring which he "had the honour of naming after Mrs Todd".

There was quite a lot of water in the Alice Spring when Mills found it, but sometimes it is reduced to such an extent that it appears to be little more than a puddle. Nonetheless, it is a constant source of fresh water, and a nearby site on the bank of the Todd was selected for the building of the repeater station for the Overland Telegraph. Located a few kilometres north-east of the present-day town of Alice Springs, the station remained in operation until 1932. Today the main buildings have been restored and opened as a museum.

The existence of the telegraph station encouraged further exploration of the MacDonnell Ranges. Ernest Giles and William Christie Gosse each made journeys to the western end of the ranges in 1872-3, and Peter Egerton Warburton chose the telegraph station as the starting point for his 1873 journey to the west coast of Australia. Then in the 1880s pastoralists moved into the area with sheep and cattle.

The eastern part of the MacDonnells was explored by the surveyor David Lindsay in 1885. Two years later alluvial gold was found near "Paddy's Rockhole", which the Aborigines called *Arltunga*, towards the eastern extremity of the ranges. A shanty town named Arltunga soon grew up nearby and developed into a fully fledged settlement with a police station. Alluvial deposits were mined there for 20 years, and from 1897 reef gold was also mined in the nearby White Range. But since 1912 there has been little mining in the area and all that remains at Arltunga today are the ruins of old stone buildings (including the police station and a government-built cyanide works), two old graveyards, and deserted mines.

Alice Springs, the only town in the MacDonnells today, was originally called Stuart. Located a few kilometres south-west of the telegraph station, it was surveyed in 1888 by David Lindsay and settled the following year as a service centre for the cattle industry. The name change came about when the postal facilities were moved into town from the old telegraph station early in 1932. The more romantic name Alice Springs and its derivatives, "Alice" and "the Alice", were unofficially brought to the new Post Office in Stuart and came into fairly wide usage for the whole town. Because of confusion of mails between Stuart and another town, Stuart's Creek in South Australia, the name was officially changed to Alice Springs in 1933.

Until 1929 there were fewer than 50 white people living in the Alice. But in that year the Central Australian Railway from Adelaide via Port Augusta was connected to the town through an extension from Oodnadatta. The *Ghan*—that famous train named after the Afghan teamsters who originally carried goods to the Alice on their camel trains—stimulated the cattle industry and for a time the town's population rose. Then came the Depression, and it was not until World War II that things picked up again. At this time Alice became a military town and the treacherous old track to Darwin was upgraded to become the Stuart Highway, following much the same route as the explorer took. After the war the town continued to develop, attracting further attention in 1967 when the controversial United States–Australian space facility was established at nearby Pine Gap.

Today Alice Springs is a thriving town with a population of about 15 000. The cattle industry is still the mainstay of the surrounding region, but in Alice itself tourism is a much larger concern. With air services from Australia's capital cities, and good rail and road access, Alice is the base for visitors who come to see Ayers Rock, the Olgas, the MacDonnell Ranges, and other famous landforms of the Centre.

The major attractions of the MacDonnells are the many beautiful gorges. They are usually referred to as those of the West MacDonnells and those of the East MacDonnells, with Alice Springs being the dividing point.

The most impressive gorges are in the West MacDonnells. The best known is Standley Chasm, renowned for the spectacular plays of light on its bright orange quartzite walls. Located on the Jay Creek Aboriginal Settlement about 50 kilometres from Alice, this sharp cleft is only a few metres wide and not very long, but its sheer walls tower more than 70 metres high. It is reached by following a serene, shaded gorge which winds along Jay Creek and is covered with lush vegetation. The chasm itself is cool and airy, with a small pool and little plant life. It has a surprisingly gentle atmosphere and the upper portion of the walls glows when touched by the midday sun. Only occasionally does sunlight reach right to the base of the chasm, flaming the walls to a rich ruby red which contrasts strikingly with the white pebbled floor.

The traditional significance of Standley Chasm to the Aranda people is not known. It is thought to have been found in the 1880s by a local pioneer named Joe Gall, who called it "Gall's Spring" (although it is not a spring). The chasm's whereabouts, however, remained unmapped until it was rediscovered in 1929 by a group of Aboriginal children and brought to the attention of some visiting academics. They named it after the first schoolteacher in Alice Springs, Mrs Ida Standley, who was noted for her work among Aboriginal children.

Ormiston Gorge, about 100 kilometres further west, has a far more severe beauty than that of Standley Chasm. Probably the most colourful of all Australian gorges, it has a complex geological structure. The orange and red quartzite walls have been wildly fractured and the floor of the gorge is strewn with fallen boulders and rocks of every colour and pattern imaginable: deep purples and pinks; rich oranges, reds and yellows; veins of black; and softer creams, greys and browns.

Several kilometres long, the gorge is the gateway to Ormiston Pound, a huge amphitheatre which stretches some 10 kilometres in width. Both the gorge and the pound take their names from Ormiston Creek which drains through them. A tributary of the Finke River, the creek has several permanent waterholes. Together with the waterholes of nearby Glen Helen Gorge, these pools are among the few in the MacDonnells which according to Aboriginal legend are occupied by friendly rather than fierce watersnakes.

Although it has large permanent pools and shattered rock walls, Glen Helen Gorge scenically bears little resemblance to Ormiston. It is entered from the north through a small gap,

A lone ghost gum (*Eucalyptus papuana*) clings to a high craggy ledge, Ormiston Gorge

but whereas Ormiston Gorge is long and narrow, Glen Helen is wide and canyon-like. The rocks are mainly conglomerates and sandstone, with narrower beds of siltstone and limestone. Many of the high orange cliffs slope precipitously and the deeply fractured rocks appear as angular slabs and stone blocks, showing vertical bedding and prominent joint lines. White sand covers the floor of the gorge and there is a richly varied, water-loving vegetation.

Glen Helen Gorge is cut by the Finke River. Most of the waterholes are very broad pools and at one point water completely blocks the passage along the riverbed. To the Aranda people this large main waterhole is known as *Japala* and is believed to be the place where the first shapeless human emerged. Aboriginal names for other waterholes within the gorge include *Rama* and *Arotna*, but unfortunately it is no longer certain to which pools these names apply.

The explorer Ernest Giles reached the southern end of Glen Helen Gorge on 6 September 1872. But the water was too deep and the terrain too rugged to get his horses through, so he did not explore the area, although he did climb a hill on the western flank of the gorge, from the summit of which he was rewarded with fine panoramic views.

Although the term "glen" is typical of Giles, he did not name the gorge, as is so often believed. The Glen Helen referred to in his journal is another gorge which he discovered in February 1874 in the Rawlinson Ranges of Western Australia. It seems that Frederick Raggatt, who took up a pastoral lease in the Mac-Donnells at the turn of the century, named this gorge after a niece called Helen Wakefield.

Other lovely gorges in the West MacDonnells include Ellery Gorge, Serpentine Gorge and Redbank Gorge, the last of which is accessible only to those prepared to swim through the deep, cold pools that stretch from wall to wall at various points along the narrow chasm. Back towards Alice there is also a large and interesting ochre pit, from the walls of which Aboriginal artists selected the ochre for their traditional paintings. The widely known Simpson's Gap, just west of the town, is particularly picturesque with a permanent jade-green pool, a sandy white creek bed, and a large community of rock wallabies living on one of the cliffs.

The most spectacular gorge of the East MacDonnells is Trephina Gorge, about 110 kilometres from Alice. An expansive gap in the ranges, it features a clean white creek bed lined by avenues of pale river red gums. This pretty scenery is set against a brilliantly contrasting background of high quartzite cliffs in tones of orange, red and rust according to the varying amounts of iron oxide staining the rocks. Because of the open and exposed nature of the gorge, pools soon dry up. However, a few kilometres west of Trephina a narrow gorge shades the John Hayes Rock Holes, which remain filled long after rains.

At N'Dhala Gorge, south-east of Trephina Gorge, ancient petroglyphs (rock carvings) decorate the stone walls. Executed at least 20 000 years ago, these geometric engravings remain virtually untouched by time.

To the west of N'Dhala Gorge a small, steep-sided hill of dolomite known as Corroboree Rock recalls more recent Aboriginal times. The rock strata stand vertically with horizontal joint planes, and near the top a joint block has fallen out, leaving a narrow window right through the rock. This hole is thought to have been used in the past by the Aranda people to store their *tjurunga*, or "churinga" (sacred implements).

Back towards Alice Springs are two further well-known gorges of the East MacDonnells, Emily Gap and Jessie Gap. Although now named after the wives of early white surveyors, these two deep cuts in the quartzite were important areas to the Aranda people because of the near-permanent pools found on their shadowy floors.

These pools and the many other waterholes in the gorges of the MacDonnells sustain a large and varied animal population. The most conspicuous wildlife are the numerous bird species. The pied butcher bird (*Cracticus nigrogularis*) and the nankeen kestrel (*Falco cenchroides*) are among the most common birds found in the ranges all year round. Cormorants (*Phalacrocorax spp.*), darters (*Anhinga rufa*) and the white-faced heron (*Ardea novaehollandiae*) frequent most of the pools, but ducks and larger waterbirds are seen only on the big open stretches of water such as those at Ormiston and Glen Helen. The Australian pelican (*Pelecanus conspicillatus*) is among the occasional visitors, and huge flocks of migrating budgerigars (*Melopsittacus undulatus*) often pass across the ranges during spring and summer.

Euros (*Macropus robustus*) and rock wallabies (*Petrogale penicillata*), both of which favour the high rocky terrains, are the largest marsupials, but many smaller nocturnal marsupials and native rodents are also widespread. Reptiles including snakes, goannas, lizards and the huge perentie (*Varanus giganteus*) are also common in the rocky areas, and the pools are alive with fish, tadpoles and other aquatic animals.

Unfortunately, alien animals introduced over the last hundred years pose a great threat to the native wildlife. Feral cats and foxes are predators of many of the native ground animals, while cattle, donkeys and other heavy grazing animals, many of which now run wild, destroy vital habitats and together with rabbits dangerously deplete the available food supplies.

Since the 1960s, all the major gorges—with the exception of Standley Chasm, which is owned and administered by the Jay Creek Aboriginal Settlement—have been removed from pastoral leaseholds and declared as national parks or reserves. They are now controlled by the Territory Parks and Wildlife Commission. Wisely, development of all areas has been limited to basic facilities and the Commission's main efforts have been directed towards the preservation of the fragile natural environment and to the elimination of feral species that do not live in harmony with the land. □

Wildly fractured and strewn with
boulders of every colour . . .

1. Glen Helen Gorge
2. Ellery Gorge
3. The rocky floor of Ormiston Gorge
4. Oxide-stained rocks, Ormiston Gorge
5. The southern wall, Ormiston Gorge

1

2

3

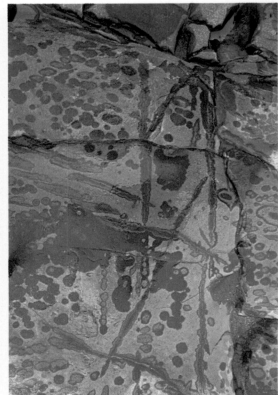

4

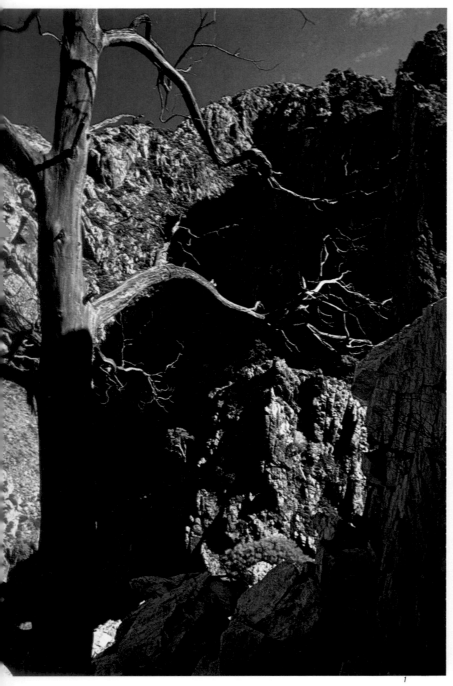

1. The ranges beyond Standley Chasm
2. The northern entrance to Standley Chasm
3. Simpson's Gap
4. The deep cleft of Standley Chasm

164

Impact from outer space

GOSSE'S BLUFF

SELDOM does a landscape give a more powerful testimony of Earth's position in a greater cosmic world than the crater-like mass of Gosse's Bluff in central Australia. Thrown up when a huge but unknown object from outer space hurtled to Earth some 130 million years ago, it measures an impressive 6 kilometres in diameter but is only the central part of a much larger crater which once extended 20-25 kilometres across.

Gosse's Bluff is an extremely rare — perhaps unique — landform on Earth. With most impact craters the whole formation is visible, but here the huge outer crater wall has been eroded away while its former central area, the present-day Gosse's Bluff, has been uncovered and forms a massive circular range of mountains enclosing a pound. Although in other parts of the world there are impact craters of equal or greater size than that of which the Bluff was originally a part, none has such a large and spectacular inner section.

Gosse's Bluff has been known to Europeans for more than a century, but its geological history has been discovered only recently. Following regional mapping of the area in the late 1950s, various geological and geophysical surveys were conducted by the Bureau of Mineral Resources and by petroleum exploration companies. From the data gathered, a number of conflicting theories were put forward to explain the Bluff's origin, including that it could be a fossil mud volcano or that it may be derived from a gigantic volcanic eruption or from the impact of a body from outer space. It was also suggested that there might be a salt dome under the Bluff, and as oil is often found above such domes one of the petroleum companies made some exploratory drillings. Neither salt nor oil was found there, but the drilling provided scientists with valuable rock samples.

In the mid-1960s a team from the Australian National University recognised what is known as a "shatter cone effect" in the rocks: in other words, many of the rocks were found to be deeply fractured with fine conically-radiating fissures, the apexes of which always pointed inwards to a central point. This discovery, and also some photographs of the Bluff taken from the United States' *Gemini 5* spacecraft in 1965, confirmed that the Bluff was part of a crater formed by an explosion, but it was still not known if the explosive force was of terrestrial or extraterrestrial origin. Further mapping and survey work conducted jointly by geologists from the Bureau of Mineral Resources and the United States Geological Survey organisation (the latter being funded by NASA to look for sites for experimental work connected with the United States Moon Programme) produced convincing evidence that both the Bluff and a large disturbed region of rock surrounding it were formed by a "bolide", a general term for a projectile from outer space which hits Earth.

As no fragments of the bolide remain, there is some uncertainty as to exactly what type of structure it was; however, many scientists believe that it was probably a comet, which,

although primarily a solid body consisting of ice and frozen gases such as ammonia, would completely vaporise on explosion. Alternatively, it may have been a huge meteorite, for the heat generated by the explosion could well have been sufficient to vaporise the nickel-iron of which such a structure is composed, and even if any fragments had remained they would have been weathered away during the 130 million years since the impact.

But regardless of whether the bolide was a comet or a meteorite, the studies made at Gosse's Bluff have provided much information on the stages that probably occurred in the formation of the range as we know it today. When the bolide hit the land, the surface was flat and at a somewhat higher level than it is at present. On impact, there would have been a cataclysmic explosion and the bolide would have vaporised, mushrooming up like an atomic cloud thousands of metres into the sky. The detonation must have been massive: scientists estimate that the energy spent would have been in the order of 10^{20} joules, or in layman's terms the equal to that of a bomb with an explosive power at least 200 000 times greater than the one that destroyed Hiroshima. The convulsion from the impact would have been felt over the whole Earth and would have had a devastating effect for thousands of square kilometres.

The size of the Gosse's Bluff bolide is unknown, but to achieve such an impact it must have been travelling at an incredible speed, possibly as much as 70 kilometres per second. The bolide probably penetrated less than 600 metres below the ground surface before it started to vaporise, but its tremendous impact caused a zone of breakage affecting rock strata more than 4 kilometres deep.

The shock wave of the impact caused extraordinary compression of the rocks, followed immediately by a tremendous rebound, which created a huge crater 20-25 kilometres in diameter and brought to the surface a central core of very resistant rock layers (the present-day Bluff) which formerly lay thousands of metres beneath the ground: the rocks forming

FORMATION OF GOSSE'S BLUFF

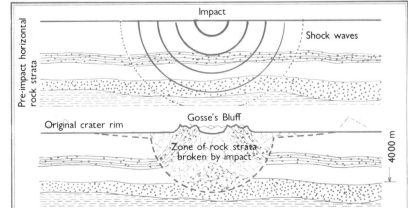

the outer section of the Bluff came from about 2000 metres below the surface, while those in the centre came from 3000 metres or more.

Over millennia, the ceaseless processes of erosion slowly removed the rim of the crater encircling the Bluff and the crater itself became filled with sediments. At that time the whole area appeared as a plain, with the site of the Bluff marked only by several low, isolated sandstone hills. But it was also traversed by a stream. In time further erosion removed the post-impact sediments and the remaining loose debris, leaving only the very resistant rocks which form the spectacular circular range of today.

Located on the pretty Missionary Plain, south of the MacDonnell Ranges, Gosse's Bluff belies its awesome origins. Because of its immense size, the circular shape of the range is not always readily apparent from the plain outside (which perhaps explains the misnomer, "bluff"). The steeply dipping walls, composed primarily of pinkish sandstone, reach 200 metres above the plain and are unusually wide in comparison with the 2.5-kilometre-wide pound that they enclose. Furthermore, the rim of the range is not level all the way around, but dips in places and is often marked by jagged serrations.

The explorer Ernest Giles—who discovered the range in 1872—mapped only the eastern walls, which he depicted as north-south running ridges. Looking for water, he entered the range by riding along "a small creek, lined with gum-trees", which had worn through the north-eastern part of the range. In his journal he makes no mention of having reached the pound, although he does record that the slopes of the range were "...barren and covered with spinifex from turret to basement, wherever sufficient soil can be found among the stones to admit of its growth". He also notes seeing "cypress pines" *(Callitris glauca)* growing on the walls. However, as he found little water in the area, Giles did not explore the range further, preferring to continue westward along the better-watered MacDonnells. He named the range "Gosse's Range" after a friend, Harry Gosse—not after the explorer William Christie Gosse, as is often believed.

The creek bed which today provides the only vehicle access to the pound is probably the same one that Giles followed. The floor of the pound is flat and sparsely vegetated with spinifex and small scrub, and often it is swept by swirling gusts of wind. However, most interest lies in the thick rocky bastion that encircles it. Many caves and overhangs have been etched into the stone walls and in several places the paths of former watercourses are marked by prominent notches high in the range.

Looking at Gosse's Bluff on a star-filled night, one can vividly imagine the terrifying cataclysm that created it. However, comets are seldom visible and although more than 1600 have been recorded orbiting at varying distances from the sun, little is known about them. Meteorites, on the other hand, are often seen. Most of them originate in the Asteroid Belt orbiting between Mars and Jupiter, and are believed to be the debris from a small planet that broke up. While still in space, they are known as meteoroids. Those that enter Earth's atmosphere but are so small they burn up are called meteors. Meteorites, which are bodies large enough to reach Earth's surface, are much rarer. Fortunately, huge comet or meteorite falls such as that of the Gosse's Bluff impact occur only once in many thousands or millions of years. □

The convulsion from the impact would have
been felt over the whole Earth. . .

1. The inner south wall of Gosse's Bluff
2. Looking east across the pound from a cave in the
wall of the Bluff
3. Boulder showing the "shatter cone" fracture pattern
4. Weeping berry (*Pittosporum phylliraeoides*)
5. Gosse's Bluff pound

171

A relict oasis

PALM VALLEY

Travelling across the parched deserts and plains of central Australia, it seems inconceivable that once the environment was wet and lush. Yet just a few million years ago the dry riverbeds were full-flowing and the arid land was clothed in luxuriant tropical vegetation. Crocodiles, brilliantly coloured birds and numerous species of terrestrial animals thrived in the well-watered surroundings. Then, about 20 000 years ago, a major change in climate occurred and aridity set in. With little rainfall the savage sun dried up the surface streams, creating an environment in which the water-loving vegetation could not survive.

Remarkably, in one small mountain area of central Australia, there remain a few pockets of a relict tropical palm, *Livistona mariae*. One of the rarest trees in the world, its continued existence in the heart of the Australian desert is due to microclimates provided along the Finke River Gorge system, which cuts the Krichauff and James ranges.

The Finke River has cut several gorges in the Centre, but this gorge which takes the river's name is the most interesting. Although broad and not particularly deep, it twists and turns through the mountains for more than 150 kilometres to cross an area which on a straight course could be covered in a third of the distance. Here, sheltered from hot winds and shaded so that moisture lingers in the deep sandy riverbed, the *Livistona mariae* palm is able to live much as it always did, regenerating regularly and growing among ferns and other luxuriant plants including the rare and ancient cycad, *Macrozamia macdonnellii*.

The *Livistona mariae* is a tall and graceful tree, with a straight slender trunk and a green canopy of "cabbage palm" leaves. It grows very slowly, reaching a height of 14-20 metres, and has a lifespan of a few hundred years. Only about 3000 trees still exist, all growing near permanent pools or soaks on the riverbed where they can tap water from only a metre or so below.

Standing on the sandy white soil of the riverbed, the larger groves of *Livistona mariae* are in some ways reminiscent of an Arabian oasis. However, their setting within the rich, red walls of the gorge gives them a distinctively Australian character, which is confirmed by the presence nearby of trees such as the river red gum (*Eucalyptus camaldulensis*) and the native "cypress pine" (*Callitris glauca*).

The *Livistona mariae* is related to several palms in Australia, including the taller cabbage-tree palm (*Livistona australis*) which is common along the entire east coast. However its closest relative, *Livistona rigida*, is less well distributed, growing only in north-western Queensland and in places such as the Mataranka Hot Springs in the far north of the Northern Territory. Some scientists believe that the similarities between the *Livistona mariae* and *Livistona rigida* palms are so profound that they are arguably the same species.

In eastern Australia the "palm cabbage" (unexpanded fronds, appearing much like an artichoke) of *Livistona australis* was a popular food amongst the Aboriginal people. However, it seems unlikely that the palm cabbage of the *Livistona mariae* was included in the diet of the Aranda people of central Australia. The removal of the palm cabbage kills the trees, and whilst the coastal variety exists in sufficient numbers to provide an ongoing food source, *Livistona mariae* does not.

The first white man to see the *Livistona mariae* palms was the explorer Ernest Giles, who discovered the southern opening of the long and winding Finke River Gorge in 1872. Giles entered the gorge—or "glen" as he characteristically called it—on 30 August, hoping to pass through to the northern side within a day or two. In fact the journey was to take him seven days, the serpentine gorge proving to be "the longest feature of the kind I ever traversed".

Although the rough and rocky gorge was a very difficult road for the unshod horses—and at times made Giles wish he were back on the arid plains—the grandeur, picturesqueness and variety of the scenery were constant sources of pleasure. Apart from the lovely palms, which he occasionally passed growing in patches on the riverbed, he was delighted by a profusion of beautiful flowers and he deliberated for some time before deciding whether to name the gorge after them or the palms.

"I was literally surrounded by fair flowers of every changing hue," he wrote in his journal on 2 September. "Why Nature should scatter such floral gems upon such a stony sterile region it is difficult to understand, but such a variety of lovely flowers of every kind and colour I had never met with previously . . . . The flowers alone would have induced me to name this Glen Flora; but having found in it also so many of the stately palm trees, I have called it the Glen of Palms. Peculiar indeed, and romantic too, is this new-found watery glen, enclosed by rocky walls, 'Where dial-like, to portion time, the palm tree's shadow falls'."

The section of the Finke River Gorge to which Giles gave the name Glen of Palms includes a permanent waterhole now known ingloriously as Boggy Hole. Several hundred palms grow along the 1-2 kilometre length of the pool, but because it is located about midway along the gorge it is seldom visited.

The area known as Palm Valley is equally luxuriant, and much closer to the northern end of the mountains. Although taking its name from Giles's glen, Palm Valley is not part of the main gorge but a section of a side gorge which branches to the west and is cut by a tributary stream, Palm Creek. Located about 20 kilometres south of Hermannsburg Aboriginal Mission, it can be reached only by following a very rough track along the sandy bed of the Finke River.

After leaving the Finke, the Palm Valley gorge opens into a broad canyon known as the Amphitheatre, then narrows again into a long, winding corridor. The palms grow in patches along this corridor, although at the beginning *Macrozamia* cycads are more populous and hence this part is known as

Krichauff Ranges
Missionary Plain
Palm Creek
Palm Valley
The Amphitheatre
Glen of Palms

"Where dial-like, to portion time,
the palm tree's shadow falls . . ."
ERNEST GILES, 1872

The grand gorge
KING'S CANYON

The north wall

K ING'S Canyon, a great gash in the red sandstone of the George Gill Range, is the Centre's deepest and most striking gorge. In contrast with the almost gentle beauty that characterises other gorges in the region, the Canyon is notable for the severity of its rock formations, especially its massive southern wall which is cut clean as though sliced by a gigantic knife.

Formed where King's Creek issues from the western end of the range, the Canyon is like a huge maze. It has several distinct sections, some of which might easily be missed by visitors who do not have a prior knowledge of the area.

The entrance to the Canyon is wide and valley-like, with thick vegetation and precipitous slopes. After 2-3 kilometres, it turns to the east and straightens into a long, broad gorge with sheer sides towering more than 200 metres high. This

is the location of the spectacular southern wall, its smooth face caused by huge slabs of rock breaking away evenly along vertical joint lines. The northern wall is equally sheer, but the rock breakage is uneven, giving the surface a sculptural appearance.

At the head of the Canyon, these two great walls taper in to form a wide, rounded precipice overlooking an oasis of deep rock pools. When there has been sufficient rain a waterfall flows from a crevice high above, swelling the pools and sometimes causing the creek to flow.

This lovely oasis is the termination of the Canyon, but by no means the end of its interest. Unlike most other gorges in Australia, much of the best scenery is at the top rather than the bottom of the Canyon. Even the great southern wall is seen to its best advantage from the northern rim.

The sheer south wall, from the Garden of Eden

Monument to time

AYERS ROCK

ULURU. *Oo-loo-roo*. The beauty of the mighty monolith which the white man calls Ayers Rock can be truly appreciated by using its Aboriginal name, *Uluru*. As the onomatopoeic qualities of the word suggest, Uluru is mystical and alluring. Far from being simply a "giant pebble", it is a masterpiece of natural art, with beautifully sculptured contours and ever-changing patterns and colours.

Uluru completely dominates the surrounding landscape. An enormous naked dome, it measures 8.8 kilometres in circumference and rises with dramatic suddenness some 348 metres above an extensive plain. Although its sheer towering walls are imposing, they are not harsh. The entire rockface is patterned by gentle ribbing and marked by numerous caves, many of which have been used since ancient times as galleries for Aboriginal art. Even the bare summit is indented by gullies, some of them several metres deep.

Famed as being the largest rock in the world, Uluru is an inselberg—or, literally, an "island-mountain". Its immense size gives a feeling of strength and solidarity. Indeed, Uluru has stood in much its present form for about 40 million years. In all that time there have been no significant changes to its appearance, only minor weathering which has made it a little smaller and its contours slightly more rounded. At times, however, it has been surrounded by water, whereas today it rises from a sea of spinifex and sand.

The sheer height and massive bulk of Uluru—or "the Rock", as it is commonly called—alone make it one of the wonders of the natural world. Yet it has an aura that is even more captivating than its great size. The play of light and shadow on its bare, furrowed walls seems almost magical. No matter how often one looks at it, Uluru never appears to be quite the same.

One of the most notable and justly famous characteristics of the Rock is its colour, which constantly changes according to aspect, distance, weather conditions and time of day. It is necessary to spend a great deal of time at Uluru to see the full range of colours, but even in a single day the changes are memorable.

At daybreak the shadowy surface of the Rock is slowly illuminated to a soft salmon-pink, which contrasts gently with the pale blue background of the early morning sky. The atmosphere is very tranquil and there is no sound, the stillness being interrupted only by an occasional bird flying across the huge face of the Rock. When the sun rises on the horizon, the crest begins to glow, gently at first, but gradually intensifying and spreading until the whole rockface is a golden-red dome. As the sun climbs higher, the beautiful contours become apparent, with caves and crevices falling into deep shadow. By midday the Rock, viewed close-up, blends with the orange-red desert sand, while at a distance it appears bluish-purple. Towards sunset, it takes on richer hues—from an orange that seems to make the Rock glow like an ember, through deep terracotta

Ayers Rock

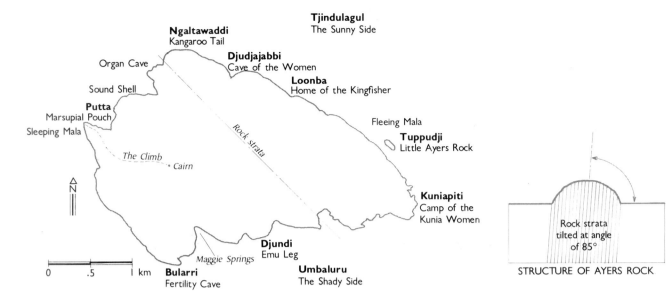

Ngaltawaddi
Kangaroo Tail

Tjindulagul
The Sunny Side

Organ Cave

Djudjajabbi
Cave of the Women

Sound Shell

Loonba
Home of the Kingfisher

Putta
Marsupial Pouch

Sleeping Mala

Fleeing Mala

Tuppudji
Little Ayers Rock

Rock strata

The Climb

Cairn

Kuniapiti
Camp of the
Kunia Women

N

Maggie Springs

Djundi
Emu Leg

0   .5   1 km

Bularri
Fertility Cave

Umbaluru
The Shady Side

Rock strata
tilted at angle
of 85°

STRUCTURE OF AYERS ROCK

red to an intense purple. As the sun disappears, the colour fades until the contours are seen as soft mauve folds. A growing shadow at the base of the Rock gives an illusion that the great monolith is floating, but finally it falls into black silhouette against the deepening night.

How Uluru was formed is one of the marvels of nature. The mineral fragments which make up the rock are thought to have been eroded from an ancient mountainous landmass some 600 million years ago and then deposited in horizontal layers on a sea floor. Eventually these layers were compressed into a highly resistant coarse-grained sandstone known as arkose, which is rich in quartz and feldspar but also contains grains of granite, epidote and clay. About 500 million years ago, earth movements uplifted and folded the arkose above the sea, tilting a large area of rock on an angle of about 85° so that it formed near-vertical strata. Erosion over millions of years subsequently removed the less resistant surrounding rock strata, leaving the vertical strata standing as a steep mountain: Uluru. Unlike most other rock formations, it has few areas of weakness (such as joints, faults or parallel bedding planes) and consequently erosion has not been able to reduce its massive singular form. The fluted sculptural contours are caused by differential weathering of the vertical strata.

Although Uluru has a smooth and rounded outline, almost the entire surface of the rock is flaky. This characteristic is caused by a slow weathering process called "exfoliation" or "spalling", whereby the surface of the rock cracks, forming flakes which then curl up and peel off layer after layer from the main rock mass. Such breakage is caused by expansion and contraction of the rock surface due to the extreme temperature changes which often occur in the desert between day and night, and by expansion due to moisture and air combining chemically with some of the minerals in the rock to produce iron oxides. These iron oxides are also responsible for the rock's rusty colour, for without oxidation it would be a creamy-grey.

The numerous caves of Uluru are formed by extended flaking along susceptible strata of sandstone. Taking many thousands of years to form, they are in a variety of shapes and sizes, ranging from simple hollows and wave-like shapes to fairly complex cavities where new generations of caves have developed in old cave walls. The most spectacular cave is a series of shallow hollows high on the northern face. Known to the white man as the "Brain" and to the Aborigines as *Ngoru* (meaning "ritual chest scars"), it is intricately patterned with grooves that run along the edges of the steeply dipping strata. Other caves are more rounded, and sometimes the overhang becomes top-heavy and breaks off, leaving a pile of tumbled boulders at the foot of the Rock.

Flaking accounts for nearly all the erosion of Uluru. However, another process known as "unloading" is responsible for the formation of a few features, notably a long and narrow vertical

slab of sandstone reaching about 100 metres high which is known to the Aborigines as *Ngaltawaddi* (meaning "sacred digging stick") and to the white man as the "Kangaroo Tail". While buried, this section of rock was subjected to extraordinary compression. When erosion removed (or "unloaded") the overlying rocks, it expanded to create a crack running parallel with the bulk of the Rock. Today it is like a huge handle, joined to the rest of Uluru only at the top and the bottom.

Uluru lies in Australia's arid zone. The area's average annual rainfall of around 200 millimetres is extremely erratic. Sometimes there may be no rain for several years, but on rare occasions there may be a deluge. In 1974, for example, freak rains totalled 926.6 millimetres for the year and at times the Rock was surrounded by water, bringing to mind the times long ago when Uluru was an island. But as the evaporation rate of the area is 2750 millimetres per year, the water soon disappeared.

The appearance of Uluru changes dramatically when it rains, with the huge rockface glistening in a colour of gun-metal grey. The gullies on top of the Rock fill with water to become pools and beautiful waterfalls cascade down many of the fluted ravines.

Usually the water lasts only in a few waterholes around the foot of the Rock. The largest of these pools is Maggie Springs (a natural reservoir, not a spring) located in a deep indentation called Mutjilda Gorge. It is an idyllic place, with cold green waters framed by a semi-circle of beautifully sculptured, steep rock walls. On the near side of the pool a tall white-trunked eucalypt provides a solitary highlight.

The run-off water from the Rock in times of rain has created a narrow fertile belt of land around its base, where a variety of grasses, trees and shrubs flourish. Acacias, especially mulga *(Acacia aneura)* and the larger "spearwood" *(Acacia doratoxylon)*, are the most conspicuous trees. Mosses, sedges and ferns grow around the near-permanent waterholes, and algae mark the courses of the waterfalls, their dark colour giving the impression that the water has left stains.

This environment supports a variety of wildlife, from kangaroos and dingoes to reptiles and birds, but they are seldom seen during the heat of the day. Unfortunately a great many feral animals including cats, rabbits, foxes and camels live in the area too and they pose a severe threat to the native fauna, either as predators or by seriously diminishing the supply of seed and grass.

Several creatures live on top of the Rock, including a remarkable shield shrimp *(Triops australiensis)* which has the ability to lay eggs that can lie dormant for years, hatching only when there is sufficient rain to form pools in the summit gullies. The reproductive cycle of these tiny animals is fascinating. The first hatchlings after rain are always females, and they are able to produce further eggs without having mated with a male. Successive generations of female shrimps are also able to lay

Recalling the times when Uluru was an island . . .

After unusually heavy rains, 1974

eggs without mating, but by the time the pools start to dry out, some males will have been born. The males mature quickly and fertilise the females that are still laying eggs. When all the adult shrimps are dead, the perpetuation of the species is ensured by numerous fertilised eggs, which have a characteristic not shared by eggs laid without mating: they can dry out and survive until the next heavy rains fall.

The plants, animals and life-giving water at Uluru have been significant in making this area very important to the Aboriginal people of the desert. Today two main tribal groups live in the region: the Yankuntjatjara people and the Pitjantjatjara people, who are now interrelated.

For thousands of years the huge stone monument has been a sacred ceremonial site for these people. There are two ritual zones: *Tjindulagul*, the sunny side; and *Umbaluru*, the shady side.

The caves around the base of the Rock are shrines for the Aborigines and hundreds of paintings decorate the walls. In colours of yellow, red, black and white, these works of art have a stark realism that has long guided the people in their thinking and lifestyle.

Numerous legends, many of them known only to the Aboriginal people, tell how Uluru was created in the *Tjukurpa* (Dreamtime), and each precipice, cave, gully and marking on the Rock commemorates the exploits of totemic ancestors. The main creation story concerns the *Windulka* (or mulga-seed men) of the distant Petermann Ranges, and the *Mala* (plains wallabies) and the *Kunia* (carpet snakes) who were camped at Uluru. The Windulka had invited the Mala and the Kunia to a ceremony, but the proposed guests refused to come. The Windulka were so enraged by this discourtesy that they gathered together their allies and took dreadful retribution on the offenders, resulting in much bloodshed and death at Uluru. Only a few ancestors on the western side of the Rock were not involved in the trouble with the Windulka, notably the *Itjaritjari* (marsupial moles) and *Tatiya* (a little lizard).

The first white man to reach Uluru was the South Australian Deputy Surveyor-General William Christie Gosse, who arrived there on 19 July 1873 and, unaware of the existing name, called it Ayers Rock after the Premier of South Australia, Sir Henry Ayers. Gosse, however, was not the first white man to see the Rock. In October of the previous year Ernest Giles had seen it from the north as a blurred range in the distance, but he did not see the great monolith at close quarters until after Gosse had been there.

Gosse, accompanied by an Afghan camel driver named Kamran, made his way to Uluru by following waterholes discovered by Giles in 1872 and then crossing a gently undulating plain to the north-east of the Rock. At first glimpse he thought the "hill", as he then called it, seemed rather peculiar, but when it came clearly into view he was astonished by the immensity and singularity of its form. Like so many people

who have visited the Rock since, one of his first concerns was to climb to the summit. After one unsuccessful attempt, he found the Rock's only accessible slope—at the north-west end—and scrambled up barefooted. On reaching the top, his feet blistered and sore, he found a magnificent panorama ". . . that repaid me for my trouble": indeed, from the crest of the Rock one can see across the vast spinifex plains to the Musgrave, Mann and Petermann ranges in the south, to the George Gill Ranges and the salt expanse of Lake Amadeus in the north, to the nearby Olgas in the west, and on a clear day to far-off Mount Conner in the east. (Today, with the easiest climbing route clearly marked, the Rock is still as formidable to climb as when Gosse was there, the steepest part rising at an angle of 60°.)

But Uluru has far more to offer than simply a challenging climb and Gosse was soon caught by its alluring spell. On departure he recorded that it was ". . . certainly the most wonderful natural feature I have ever seen". When he returned a week later he was convinced: "This rock appears more wonderful every time I look at it, and I might say it is a sight worth riding over eighty-four miles of spinifex sandhills to see."

Located 478 kilometres south-west of Alice Springs, Ayers Rock is today part of the 126 132-hectare Uluru National Park. At present there are motels and camping sites near the Rock, but a new park settlement to cater for increased tourism is being built about 25 kilometres away, which will leave the immediate area of the Rock almost entirely unencumbered by man-made structures. However, the increasing numbers of visitors to the Rock in recent years is sometimes a cause of great anguish to the Aboriginal people, who regard Uluru as sacred. The complete story of the traditions associated with the ancient monolith is known only to these people and, as in other parts of Australia, if this knowledge is not respected and tourists desecrate or intrude upon sacred grounds, the Aborigines will lose their reason for being and inevitably their culture will be destroyed. For this reason, an important ceremonial area of the Rock is cordoned off and not open to the general public. However it should be remembered that, to the traditional owners of the land, the whole of Uluru is holy. □

. . . A masterpiece of natural art

1. The overhanging entrance to a cave on the southern side of the Rock
2. A deep gully above Maggie Springs, shining after rain
3–4. Water sculptures, near the summit
OVERLEAF: Glistening streams linger after rain

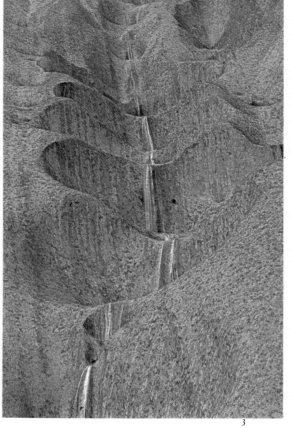

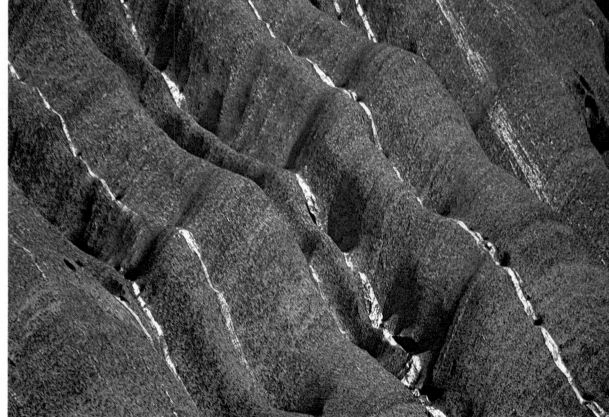

185

1. Maggie Springs after rain
2. Erosion patterns near the summit . . . the tiny white speck near the top right-hand corner is the shirt of a climber
3. View down the ribbed southern flank of the Rock to the road below
4. Water sheen on the summit
5. The Sound Shell, at the foot of the western face
6. Cave of the Women, on the northern side of the Rock

3

4

5

6

Jewels in the dust

THE OLGAS

"THE APPEARANCE of Mount Olga . . . is truly wonderful; it displayed to our astonished eyes rounded minarets, giant cupolas, and monstrous domes. There they have stood as huge memorials of the ancient times on earth, for ages, countless aeons of ages, since its creation first had birth."

These words were written by the explorer Ernest Giles in the narrative of his major expeditions *Australia Twice Traversed*, published in 1889 with the sub-title, "The Romance of Exploration". Despite long and arduous journeys across uncharitable deserts and spinifex plains, Giles was always able to appreciate beauty and the wonder of nature. He loved the grandeur of the lonely desert mountains and ranges, and wrote of them with poetic admiration. But like all true romantics, he was totally captivated by only one—for him it was the Olgas.

Located 32 kilometres west of Ayers Rock, the Olgas are a cluster of more than 30 magnificent dome-shaped monoliths separated by deep ravines. Strange and mysterious giants, their appearance is like no other landscape on Earth. Even Giles, who was well able to express his *feelings* for them, was "baffled" when trying to find an adequate description. He likened them to "several enormous rotund or rather elliptical shapes of rouge mange", to "enormous pink haystacks leaning against one another for support", and to "the backs of several monstrous kneeling pink elephants". To other people they have seemed like giant eggs, or like the ruins of an ancient city. The truth is that no single impression can possibly describe the Olgas: they are a fascinating world of their own.

The Olgas cover an area of 35 square kilometres. Their sheer slopes rise abruptly from the flat desert plain and form a fantastic silhouette against the sky. Without hills or tall trees to give perspective, their great height is not apparent from the distance. The tallest dome is at the western end and towers 546 metres above the ground (considerably higher than Ayers Rock). Several adjacent domes are nearly as tall, but the sizes diminish towards the eastern end.

Some domes of the Olgas are bare on top, others are partly covered with spinifex. All, however, are naked on the sides and, like Ayers Rock, they feature spectacular colour changes according to distance, weather conditions and other related factors. Sometimes they look like shining red jewels, at other times like gaunt mounds of bluish-purple. Occasionally, when the sky is overclouded, they appear in ominous shades of silvery-grey which dance menacingly according to the plays of light and shadow.

This foreboding characteristic of the Olgas is not restricted to the occasional gloomy colours. Howling winds sometimes blow through the rough, rock-strewn ravines (or gorges), making the atmosphere frightening. One area at the north-eastern end of the group is so gusty that it has become known as the Valley of the Winds.

But the winds are not always strong and usually the gorges

The western domes

are pleasant places with just a gentle breeze blowing. Although there are no permanent waterholes in the Olgas, these deep gorges provide sufficient shade to retain water for long periods after rains. A great variety of plants are able to survive in this protected environment, ranging from delicate mosses and ferns to the large river red gum *(Eucalyptus camaldulensis)*. Several plant species are rare; for example, a prickly grass *(Eriachne scleranthoides)*, which grows in clumps, is known only here and at Mount Currie, 40 kilometres to the west.

With this rich vegetation, the Olgas are able to support a large animal population. Birds are the most conspicuous wildlife, but there are also a great many insects, reptiles and marsupials, some of which never venture on to the open plain.

Like Ayers Rock, the materials which form the Olgas were eroded from an ancient mountainous landmass and deposited on a seabed about 600 million years ago. However, whereas the Rock is composed of small fragments, the Olgas are made up of pebbles and boulders of granite, gneiss and volcanic rocks, ranging in diameter from about 50 millimetres to 300-400 millimetres, which were torn away from the mountain by the sea and then rolled smooth before finally being cemented together by a fine sandstone containing epidote. The resulting rock is known as conglomerate—or sometimes as "pudding-stone", because its formation resembles the mixing of a plum pudding.

During earth movements about 500 million years ago, the conglomerate was uplifted above the sea and the strata were tilted about 20° to the horizontal (compared with up to 85° at Ayers Rock). This hard rock withstood the erosion which over millions of years lowered the level of the surrounding plain. However, whilst Ayers Rock retained its oneness of shape, the Olgas did not.

View east towards Ayers Rock, from high in Walpa Gorge at the western end of the Olgas

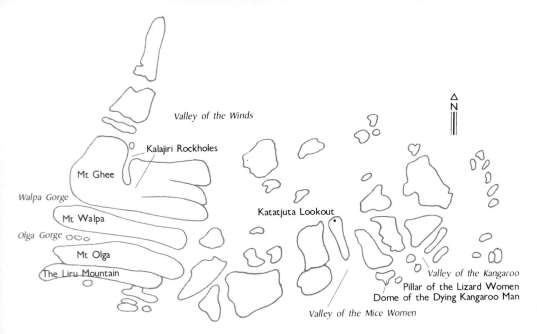

Valley of the Winds

Kalajiri Rockholes

Mt Ghee

Walpa Gorge

Mt Walpa

Olga Gorge

Mt Olga

The Liru Mountain

Katatjuta Lookout

Valley of the Kangaroo
Pillar of the Lizard Women
Dome of the Dying Kangaroo Man
Valley of the Mice Women

N

• The Olgas

0   1   2 km

Ominous shades of silvery-grey dance menacingly . . .

A winter thunderstorm closes in. . .
OVERLEAF: Lightning strikes the domes of *Katatjuta*

The conglomerate of the Olgas is characterised by two sets of vertical joint planes at right angles to one another. The individual joints are widely spaced and in past ages the processes of weathering and erosion etched along them, dividing the rock into huge blocks and sculpturing the rounded contours. The main weathering agent was the process of "unloading", whereby rocks which have been formed under pressure beneath the ground expand when erosion removes (or "unloads") the overlying rock. This expansion creates great cracks that cause large slabs of rock to break away from the main mass. The slabs eventually fall to the ground, and at the Olgas their removal resulted in the formation of the spectacular series of steep-sided domes separated by rocky gorges and valleys. Since then, weathering has been extremely slow. In the words of Giles: "Time, the old, the dim magician, has ineffectually laboured here, although with all the powers of oceans at his command; Mount Olga has remained as it was born."

As the various rocks that form the conglomerate are of a similar hardness, the surface of the Olgas has been worn evenly and in places resembles an intricate mosaic. On shaded walls, different coloured lichens also create interesting patterns, while dark algae emphasise the recesses along which rainwater flows.

Because of their proximity to each other, the Olgas and the more famous Ayers Rock are often compared. Although there are certain similarities between the two landforms, such as pronounced colour change, there are profound differences in character. This scenic comparison has never been more succinctly expressed than by Giles: "Mount Olga is the more wonderful and grotesque; Mount Ayers the more ancient and sublime."

Without realising it, Giles—who usually showed little empathy with Aboriginal culture—had in those words explained the basic differentiation which the Yankuntjatjara and Pitjantjatjara people make between the two great rock mountains. To the Aborigines, the Olgas are known as *Katatjuta*, "the place of many heads". Numerous legends are associated with Katatjuta, but most of these stories are secret knowledge belonging only to the Aboriginal people.

Some legends, however, are widely known. The one most frequently told concerns a pillar-like dome near the eastern end of the Olgas, which has a smaller rock leaning against it. The pillar is the transformed body of a kangaroo man who died in the arms of his sister after being attacked by dingoes. An eroded cavity in the pillar marks his wound and a rock mound at the base represents the part of his body that was torn away.

The large domes on the western side of the Olgas have an equally gruesome story to tell, being the transformed bodies of fearsome Pungalunga men, who were giant cannibals and lived on a diet solely of Aborigines. A huge *Wanambi* serpent is believed to live in the largest dome and to vent his anger at misdemeanours by breathing hard and sending howling gusts of wind through the adjacent gorge.

Unlike the arkose of Ayers Rock, the coarse conglomerate of the Olgas is not suitable for rock paintings and consequently this art form is found at only one small site. There are, however, a number of ancient petroglyphs (rock carvings) and several sites where stones have been arranged in geometrical designs. The age of these works of art is unknown, but they must be extremely old. The present-day Aborigines believe them to be the work of their Dreamtime ancestors.

White Australians have known of the Olgas for only a little over a hundred years. They were first sighted by Ernest Giles in 1872 from the northern shores of Lake Amadeus (about 100 kilometres north), but he was barred from reaching them by the lake's treacherous surface of mud and salt. Giles wanted to name both the lake and the mountains after his patron, Baron Ferdinand von Mueller, but the famous botanist had recently been honoured with the Spanish Order of St Isabella and insisted that the lake be named Lake Amadeus after Amadeo, the King of Spain, and that the mountain domes be named Mt Olga after another member of European royalty, the Grand Duchess Olga Constantinova of Russia, wife of King George I of the Hellenes (Greece). Today the term Mt Olga is applied only to the tallest dome, while the plural form, the Olgas, has been adopted for the whole group. As the word Olgas has a "rounded hardness" that accurately portrays the mountain's physical characteristics, the poetic Giles in hindsight would no doubt have been grateful to Mueller for requesting the change. Nonetheless, the mystical qualities of the domes seem best reflected in the rhythmical Aboriginal name, Katatjuta.

Ernest Giles did not reach the Olgas until September 1873, almost a year after he had first seen them. When he arrived he was mortified to find camel and dray tracks which he knew to be those of his rival, William Christie Gosse. By following Giles's route of the previous year, and then skirting the eastern side of Lake Amadeus, Deputy Surveyor-General Gosse of South Australia had a few weeks earlier become the first white man to set foot in Giles's precious Olgas.

Gosse, however, never formed a strong attachment to the Olgas. To Giles they were always to remain the finest geographical feature he had ever seen. His emotions were at a peak when he departed from them on his final visit in June 1874: "I rode completely round the mass of this wonderful feature; its extraordinary appearance will never be out of my remembrance . . . . Could I be buried at Mount Olga, I should certainly borrow Sir Christopher Wren's epitaph, *Circumspice si monumentum requiris.*"

Actually the inscription to Sir Christopher Wren at St Paul's Cathedral in London reads *Lector, si monumentum requiris, circumspice.* But the meaning applies equally well in this part of the Australian desert: "If you seek a monument, look around."

Strange and lonely giants . . .

1. View west to the main domes, from Katatjuta Lookout
2. A narrow gorge near the Valley of the Mice Women
3. The eastern approach to Mt Walpa (left) and Mt Ghee
4. Lengthening afternoon shadows silhouette a lone tree on the naked wall of Mt Walpa
5. View across the eastern domes of the Olgas to Ayers Rock
6. The setting sun lights Mt Olga and adjacent domes

Remnant of an ancient plateau

CHAMBERS PILLAR

Chambers Pillar

O N A FLAT plain bordering the red sand dunes of the Simpson Desert, a strange group of sculptured sandstone monoliths creates a striking landscape. Resembling "nothing so much as a number of old castles in ruins" (as the explorer John McDouall Stuart described them), they are dominated by an imposing natural monument known as Chambers Pillar.

These withered stone formations are the last vestiges of an ancient plateau—the hardest rocks which have been able to resist erosion and weathering while the surrounding land has been lowered to a flat and featureless plain. Located 175 kilometres south of Alice Springs, they now stand as breakaways from the nearby Charlotte Range. With the red dunes of the Simpson rolling in like waves breaking at their feet, they bear a remarkable resemblance to ocean stacks such as the Twelve Apostles at Port Campbell.

Chambers Pillar, rising 34 metres above the plain, is like an old carved column standing on a huge pedestal. Known as a butte, it is the remnant of a mesa (table-topped mountain) and is in the final stages of decay. The gently sloping mound of the pedestal is partially covered by loose sandstone talus that has fallen from above, and in the centre of this debris the column towers determinedly, its sheer vertical sides leached white for most of its height but capped with a twin-peak of burning red. Despite its friable texture the column is still solid, being about 6 metres wide for the whole of its height.

The sediments making up the sandstone of the pillar, the nearby castle-like formations and part of the Charlotte Range were laid down as horizontal layers in an ancient seabed about 400 million years ago. In the course of time, the sandstone was raised as a plateau, but it has never been tilted.

Chambers Pillar has been in its present form for thousands of years. It was first recorded by John McDouall Stuart in April 1860. Stuart likened it to "a locomotive engine with its funnel" and named it after his friend James Chambers who had helped to finance all of his expeditions. To the Aborigines of the desert it was known as *Itakaura*. A Dreamtime legend tells that Itakaura was a spirit ancestor who took a woman from a forbidden totemic group. The couple were exiled and he became the pillar while she turned into the largest of the castle-like hills.

Stuart's discovery of the pillar (and of the nearby Finke River) was important to later explorers. Ernest Giles selected the prominent towering landmark as the starting point for his 1872 journey of exploration, in which he discovered many of the Centre's most remarkable features. As always, Giles was able to appreciate the pillar's finest qualities. "There it stands," he wrote, "a vast monument to the geological periods that must have elapsed since the mountain ridge of which it was formerly a part, was washed by the action of old Ocean's waves into mere sandhills at its feet . . . . We turned our backs upon this peculiar monument, and left it in its loneliness and its grandeur—'clothed in white sandstone, mystic, wonderful!' "

2

Today Chambers Pillar is the focal point of a 340-hectare scenic reserve, declared in 1970. With its setting amid weeping casuarina trees and green grassy flats, backed by red desert dunes, it provides some of Australia's most contrasting scenery. The dramatic character is enhanced by the prevailing weather conditions. On clear days the vibrant colours of the land are stark against the bright blue sky, but if the day is grey and overcast the atmosphere is sombre. At night the pillar seems peaceful and perhaps a little melancholy, but when there has been sufficient rain the scenery is softened by the pleasant colours and patterns of myriad wildflowers which carpet the land. Yet always there is the overwhelming wonder and beauty of the craggy stone battlements that have weathered the storm of time. □

1. With the Simpson Desert already deep in shadow, the setting sun lingers only on the monumental western face of Chambers Pillar
2. Chambers Pillar, from the north-west

In its loneliness and its grandeur . . .

1. The weathered northern face of Chambers Pillar
2. The pillar from the south
3. The pillar towering above its talus pedestal

"Resembling nothing so much as a number of old castles in ruins . . ."
JOHN McDOUALL STUART, 1860

1–2. Castle Rock, flanked to the south by a red sand dune that encircles a small claypan green with new growth after rain
3. Castle Rock, from the east
4. Chambers Pillar at dawn
5. Castle Rock (background) and an outlier, at dusk
6. Chambers Pillar during a stormy dawn

1

2

3

4

5

WHEN European explorers ventured into the vast interior of Australia in the middle of the last century, they reported finding harsh and hideous desert wastelands. In scorching heat and with little or no water, many lost their lives. The stories of Ludwig Leichhardt, Burke and Wills, and Gibson are well known, their tragedies having earned them a secure niche in the realms of Australian history. But the lonely and austere conditions under which the explorers travelled were a far cry from those of today. With modern transport and equipment, and greater knowledge, the deserts—while still places to be respected—are no longer death-traps to be feared.

Covering almost half the continent, the deserts of Australia have great beauty and fascination. They are extremely diverse in appearance, ranging from huge rolling red sand dunes to glimmering stony expanses of flat gibber plains. Few areas are entirely barren. For the most part the land is lightly clothed with spinifex and tussocky grasses, mulga, mallee and small scrub. Across these vegetated areas, the deserts are decorated with hard-surfaced red claypans and sinuous white arteries of ancient watercourses and salt lakes. Only occasionally is there a spring, rockhole or life-giving soak.

The deserts are powerful landscapes. The seemingly endless red dunes appear like the swells and flows of huge waves in a treacherous sea of sand. On the plains, a dead tree or a bleached bush shows the masterful strength of the blazing sun. In the steaming gibber country, the shattered hot rocks are devoid of vegetation, making the area seem lifeless.

But all is not still. As the hot air rises from the burning ground, it lifts thin spirals of red dust to form spinning willy willies that dance across the plains. Winds push the crests of the drifting dunes, and in the gentle light of morning, fluted symmetrical patterns can be seen streaming over the sand. Sometimes tortuous winds stir up violent dust storms of such strength that eventually small quantities of red sand might be carried as far as Mount Kosciusko, or across the Tasman Sea to New Zealand.

During the summer monsoonal months, the northern deserts are frequently hit by electrical storms. Almost every afternoon, huge thunderheads gather in a sinister brownish-grey wall, usually rising from a pool of red dust. The thunderheads do not move very fast, nor do they always precipitate rain. But when they do break, the terrifying roars of thunder are accompanied by spectacular displays of lightning which crack the dark sky. The tremendous flashes highlight a variety of colours, from the deep purples and slate blues of the clouds to the reds and goldy-yellows of the approaching sunset. Where the lightning hits the highly inflammable spinifex-clothed ground there is a high probability of starting a grass fire, which might burn for days. But usually the storm soon passes and peace reigns over the land.

There is a poignant simplicity about these desert landscapes.

For thousands of square kilometres there is no intervention by man. In the calm of twilight one is overwhelmingly aware of only the empty sky and the lonely earth. The circular line of the horizon all around makes the sky seem close and dome-like. At nightfall the stars twinkle reassuringly, and every so often a stray meteor skips across the sky. The elements and the land are all that matter.

The great deserts swirl around the mountain ranges in the heart of the Australian continent, reaching into all mainland States except Victoria. They are divided into two main areas: the Western Desert, which incorporates the Great Sandy, Gibson and Great Victoria deserts; and the Arunta Desert, comprising the Simpson and Sturt's Stony deserts. Two further deserts, the Tanami (an Aboriginal word meaning "rock holes") and the Channel Country, complete the gigantic circle.

The largest sand dunes occur in the Simpson Desert. Running in a roughly north-south direction, they extend up to 300 kilometres in length and reach as much as 40 metres in height. They are usually parallel, separated by corridors ranging from about 100 metres to more than a kilometre wide, but sometimes they converge in a "Y" shape. With an annual average rainfall of less than 125 millimetres, the area is one of the driest parts of the continent.

Smaller dunes and sandy undulations occur in most of the other deserts, although according to wind patterns they sometimes trend east-west rather than north-south. One of the most interesting areas is the Great Sandy Desert where the red sands extend almost to the coast, finally giving way to the unbroken white sand expanse of the Eighty Mile Beach in Western Australia. Formed several thousand years ago when sea levels were lower, this remarkably flat beach is washed by big tides which rise and fall up to 8.5 metres. When the tide is in, the beach looks just like any other white sand beach, but when the tide goes out the whole area is transformed into a vast, shining patterned plain with the water only just visible as a band on the horizon.

The main expanse of gibber land is Sturt's Stony Desert, though gibbers occur in smaller patches throughout the arid region. The term "gibber" is an Aboriginal word meaning "stone". Predominantly quartzite and ironstone, most of the rocks have been sand-blasted and rolled smooth, although some fragments have retained angular shapes. This rocky terrain appears to be very hard, but the ground beneath the gibbers is actually soft and spongy, and after rain it becomes extremely muddy. The glistening surface of the rocks which is always apparent—the "desert varnish"—results from a thin coating of iron oxide, polished by incessant dust-laden desert breezes.

Directly north of Sturt's Stony Desert is the most unusual of Australia's great desert areas, the Channel Country. Known as a "riverine desert", this region is a complex lacework of interconnecting channel-like rivers and creeks. Extraordinarily flat, it forms a vast floodplain extending over approximately

The eastern edge of the Simpson Desert

5 per cent of the continent. The watercourses, which include the Barcoo and the Diamantina rivers and the famous Cooper's Creek, are fed by the northern summer rains. There is seldom enough water to flow to the southernmost reaches, but on rare occasions sufficient rains fall for the streams to empty into Lake Eyre. Further north, permanent billabongs fill a number of channels, but the remainder of the region is either swampy or dry for most of the year. The vegetation, headed by the famous coolibah *(Eucalyptus microtheca)*, is highly specialised for it must withstand both drought and flood.

The formation of the great deserts of Australia varies. As the salt lakes and the dry watercourses indicate, the sandy deserts are ancient drainage areas. They were formed about 20 000 years ago when increased aridity and a probable build-up of salt inhibited plant growth and caused the prevailing winds to heap up vast amounts of unconsolidated alluvial quartz sediments into long dunes and sandplains. In most areas the sand grains have been stained red by a thin film of iron oxide, but near watercourses they are clean and white. Some of the plains, however, originate from the breakdown of granite and other crystalline rocks.

The stony gibbers are the remains of the hard crusts of former plateaux. Over millennia, the agents of weathering and erosion etched away the underlying softer rocks, undermining the hard crusts and causing them to break up into small fragments which then rolled to lower levels. With the removal of softer surrounding materials, the hard rocks became concentrated in flat pebbly pavements which protect the underlying softer ground from further erosion.

Although not as arid as they once were, the Australian deserts today receive less than 250 millimetres of rain per year and have an evaporation rate significantly greater than the precipitation. The rain, however, is extremely fickle, so many years may pass without a drop of rain and then several hundred millimetres may fall in a single year. When this happens, a dramatic change comes over the landscape, with the red sands being covered by a carpet of verdant green patterned with countless colourful wildflowers.

The temperature in the deserts is more reliable than the rainfall, with very hot days and cool to warm nights in summer, and warm days and very cold nights in winter. In this climate, rivers and streams cannot live. Their parched beds disappear wearily into the sand, rejuvenated only by rare downpours of rain. The lakes into which they once emptied are generally dry and encrusted with salt.

Drinkable water is scarce in all Australian deserts. In some places artesian waters supplement the few springs, rockholes and soaks, but usually they are too saline for human consumption. Some relief, however, is brought after good rains when the numerous claypans act as tiny reservoirs. The fine clay has been baked so hard that it is virtually waterproof. Wherever there is a depression, a shallow pool will gather, but in the hot sun the water will not last long. For a brief time after the claypans dry out, their surfaces are covered with intricate natural ceramic designs, but these are soon destroyed by the wind.

Despite the high temperatures and the lack of water, abundant plant and animal species have adapted to survive in the desert lands.

The plants are generally divided into two basic types: the drought resisters and the drought evaders. The resisters are perennials such as grasses, succulents, and hardy trees and shrubs, which cling to life. They have various means of obtaining water, some storing reserves in their tissues, others having both shallow roots to collect rainwater and long taproots to soak up deep groundwater or reach a water table below. Most species, however, reduce water loss by means such as the shedding of leaves in times of drought. Of necessity, they restrict regeneration to times when there is sufficient water, and consequently there is no regular period of growth.

The drought evaders are ephemeral plants such as flowering peas and daisies which grow only when conditions are favourable and otherwise exist solely as seeds. The majority of these species complete their life cycles extremely quickly. The seeds are able to remain dormant for years, having inbuilt chemical indicators which inhibit germination until sufficient rain has fallen to allow them to sprout, flower and produce new seeds before drought sets in again. These drought-evading plants are largely responsible for the remarkable visual transformation that takes place after rain, when the usual reds and greens of the desert become merely the backdrop to a kaleidoscope of colour.

Among the loveliest desert plants are the tall desert oak *(Casuarina decaisneana)* and the ephemeral Sturt's desert pea *(Clianthus formosus)*. The desert oak grows to about 10 metres and is one of the most interesting desert plants. As a young tree it is long and slender with its foliage tapered like that of a pine, but when it matures the foliage spreads out into a graceful willowy canopy. Sturt's desert pea is seen only after rain, when it grows as a trailing plant with magnificent scarlet flowers.

In times of drought the desert regions are usually still and quiet, as though inhabited by few or no animal species. Only termite mounds on the vegetated plains give obvious signs of life. This impression, however, is deceptive, for all Australian deserts support a rich and varied animal population. Apart from insects, birds, reptiles and conspicuous large mammals such as the euro and the dingo, there are numerous other animals which are seldom seen, including native rodents, tiny marsupials, the echidna *(Tachyglossus aculeatus)*, and frogs.

Like plants, the animals of the desert have developed various ways of coping with the harsh environment. Many animals such as rodents, bandicoots and marsupial mice avoid the heat of the day, being either nocturnal or active only in the twilight.

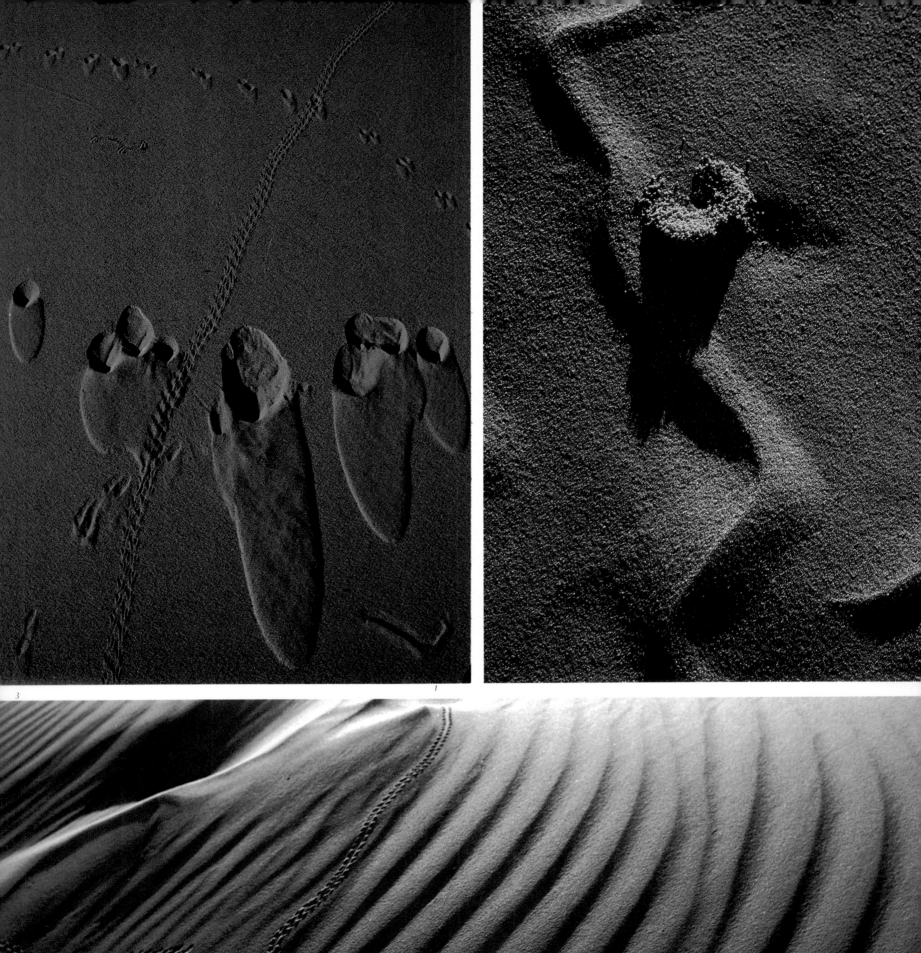

1

3

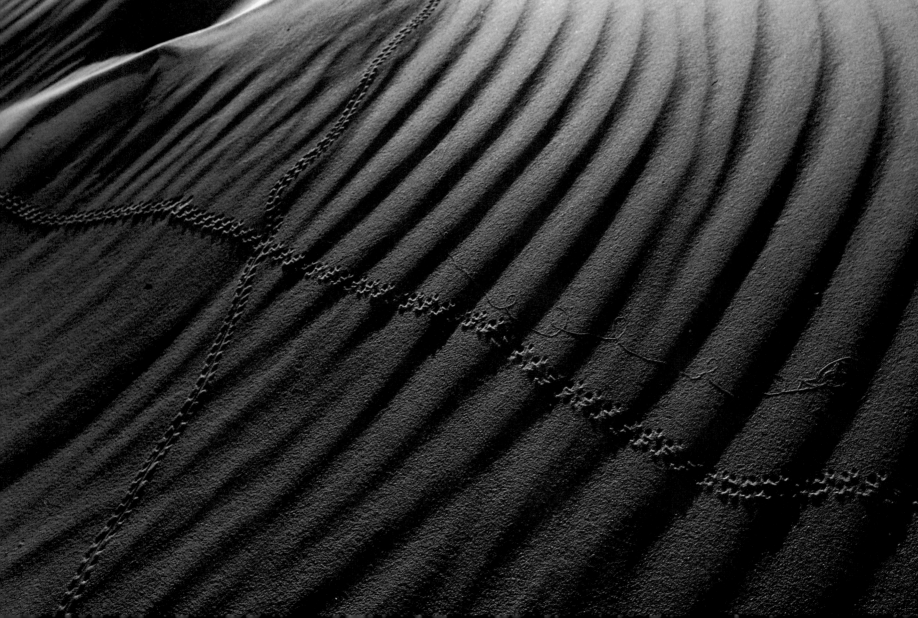

1. A miniature landslide triggered
by foraging rabbits
2. An ant burrow and a wind ripple
on the crest of a dune
3. Sharply defined beetle tracks
held by dew-moistened sand

Some find sufficient shelter under scrub or rocks, others dig burrows to protect themselves from extremes of temperature. Their presence is apparent only in the early morning, when networks of tracks give mute testimony of the encounters of the night.

In times of drought some burrowing species, for example, the carnivorous little marsupial known as mulgara *(Dasycercus cristicauda)*, are virtually undetectable as they further conserve their energy by storing food in their bodies and aestivating, that is, spending long hot periods in a torpor in much the same way as hibernating animals do in colder climates. Like many other desert dwellers, these animals require little water or moisture. Others such as frogs store water in their bodies and bury themselves in the sand.

Only when it rains are the animals of the desert really active. For many this is the only time during which they can mate and thereby ensure the perpetuation of their species. Birds, many of them migratory, are particularly noticeable, their bright colours and melodic songs filling the air. Budgerigars, cockatoos, other parrots, finches, chats—all are engaged in a frenzy of activity. But soon the sun will dry out the land and all will be quiet again.

Although human survival is difficult in the desert environment, the Aboriginal people of Australia have even here been able to live in harmony with the land. With their intimate knowledge of plant and animal life they have been able to eke out the available food and water supplies for long periods under conditions in which the white man would quickly perish. Additional water reserves were stored in small, man-made reservoirs and natural supplies were often covered to protect them from the evaporating effects of the sun. In particularly hard times, various methods were used to stave off hunger and thirst: the leaves of the native "tobacco" or pituri bush *(Duboisia hopwoodii)*, for example, were treated and chewed for their narcotic properties. Had the white explorers of the last century understood more about the desert Aborigines' way of life, their journeys would not have been so perilous.

The European colonists' quest to discover what lay in the vast interior of Australia began in 1839-40 when the explorer Edward John Eyre penetrated the country north and west of Adelaide. Eyre, however, was disillusioned by what he saw and turned his attention towards crossing the continent from east to west. In 1845 Charles Sturt took up the challenge to explore the Centre and crossed the Stony Desert that now carries his name. He reached the southern dunes of the Simpson, but was so disappointed by the country that he did not give the desert a name. The South Australian government surveyor Augustus Poeppel visited the region in 1879-80 and again in 1884, planting his famous Poeppel's Peg at Poeppel's Corner, which marks the border between South Australia, Queensland and the Northern Territory. But not until 1929 when Dr C. T. Madigan studied the area for the South Australian branch of the Royal Geographical Society of Australasia did the desert receive its present name, honouring the then President of the South Australian branch of the Society, A. A. Simpson.

Meanwhile, the deserts had claimed several lives. Leichhardt and his party disappeared without trace, probably in the Simpson, in 1848. Burke and Wills—and a third member of their party, Gray—died near Cooper's Creek in 1861 on their return after crossing the continent from south to north. Ironically, the Cooper country was quite well-watered and temperatures cool, but they were too weak to avail themselves of the sustenance the land had to offer. A fourth member of the expedition, John King, survived only because Aborigines, who had been helping the party from time to time, took pity on him and gave him food, water and pituri. On the other side of the continent, Ernest Giles's companion Alfred Gibson was not so lucky. In 1873 he became the first white man to lose his life in the desert which now bears his name.

Giles, Warburton, John and Alexander Forrest, and Augustus Gregory are just some of the other explorers who crossed the true desert regions, but none had much of promise to report.

In light of the explorers' experiences, few colonists were encouraged to settle in the arid regions. Towards the end of the nineteenth century, however, graziers recognised the area's potential for cattle and sheep. "The Cattle King" Sidney Kidman, for example, established a large station in the Channel Country. In 1882 the famous Birdsville Track stock route was pioneered from the Channel lands across Sturt's Stony Desert to Adelaide, and in 1907 the Canning Stock Route was surveyed by A. W. Canning across the Great Sandy Desert in Western Australia. Although this industry proved to be an economic success, the cattle and sheep and other introduced animals including camels, brumbies, cats, foxes and rabbits pose serious threats to the native wildlife by depleting or destroying the finely balanced habitats and natural food supplies.

Until recent years the great central deserts have held little attraction for the mining industry. Gold was mined on the Tanami Desert for a brief period in 1909 and again in the Depression years of the 1930s when several hundred hopefuls made their way to gold mines at the Granites, along a route which became known as "Tragedy Track". Gold was certainly to be found there, but the miners were beaten by the heat and the lack of water. The only other mining in the region was on a much smaller scale.

Today geologists are prospecting in the deserts for minerals other than gold—uranium, oil, natural gas and other substances required for the technological developments of the cities. In some deserts, however, such as the Simpson and the Tanami, large tracts of land have been set aside as national parks and wildlife reserves. Areas such as these are of the utmost importance if the fragile ecology of Australia's unique desert wildernesses is to be protected from the effects of interference by modern man. □

In times of drought, the deserts are quiet and still . . .

1. Gibber plain on the northern edge of the Simpson Desert
2. A sandy plain near the low Black Hill Range in the western Simpson Desert
3. Claypan on the floodplain of the Diamantina River, in the Channel Country south of Birdsville

. . . A poignant simplicity

1. Gibber plain, west of Lake Eyre
2–4. Dune patterns near the southern end of the Simpson Desert

When huge thunderheads gather . . .

Summer monsoonal storms in the Tanami Desert

Sea of salt

LAKE EYRE

For several decades early last century, many European explorers believed that in the centre of the Australian continent they would find a huge inland sea. But, as they were eventually to learn, Australia's "inland sea" lies far beneath the ground in artesian basins. Traces of its life above the surface are found only in a few springs and in a series of salt lakes, the largest and most impressive of which is Lake Eyre in the remote desert lands of South Australia.

Lake Eyre covers approximately 9300 square kilometres and spreads across the horizon like a vast, desolate white plain. It is the lowest part of the Australian continent, having sunk to between 12 and 17 metres below sea level, and it is divided into two parts, Lake Eyre North and the smaller Lake Eyre South, which are joined by a narrow neck of salt called the Goyder Channel. Only four salt lakes in the world are larger.

Nearly one-third of Lake Eyre is covered by a hard salt crust about half a metre thick. Most of this crust lies in the southern part of the lake, where it overlies a silty bed of gypsum-rich mud up to 6 metres deep. In the north, a treacherous area known as the "slush zone" has only a very thin covering of salt over liquidy mud that never dries out.

Almost nothing lives on the lake, except primitive micro-organisms and a few tiny animals. Notable among these are the mud-dwelling salt-lake louse (*Haloniscus searlei*) and the brine shrimp (*Artemia salina*), both of which are less than a centimetre long, and the camouflaged Lake Eyre dragon lizard (*Amphibolurus maculosus*), which is whitish to pale grey in colour. A few small, inconspicuous plants also survive around the shoreline, such as samphire (*Sarcocornia quinqueflora*).

The formation of Lake Eyre began some 200 million years ago when a large area of the Australian landmass, from the Gulf of Carpentaria to the region now occupied by the great salt lakes of South Australia, began a steady downward movement. About 100 million years ago, this whole area became inundated by the sea. Some 20-30 million years later, earth movements and other factors caused the sea to withdraw, leaving dry land cut by several big rivers that probably flowed to the southern coastline. Then, about a million years ago, further earth movements tilted the land and caused faulting, which blocked the passage of these streams and formed a huge freshwater lake that geologists have named Lake Dieri, after an Aboriginal tribe that lived east of Lake Eyre.

Just 35 000 years ago, Lake Dieri was about three times more extensive than today's Lake Eyre and averaged at least 17 metres in depth. Conditions were much moister than they are now and lush vegetation surrounded the lake. Among the animals inhabiting this environment was the herbivorous *Diprotodon*, the size of a hippopotamus and the largest marsupial ever to exist. But about 20 000 years ago, the climate started to change and aridity set in. The surface streams dried up and Lake Dieri shrank in size, leaving only the various salt lakes of today. The salt on most of these great lakes is primarily

common salt (sodium chloride). Most of the salt has been leached from the ancient marine sediments that underlie the entire catchment and, as there is no outlet to the sea, it has been deposited in the lowest areas.

With an average annual rainfall of less than 125 millimetres, Lake Eyre is one of the driest parts of the continent. Ironically, it is also one of the largest inland drainage basins in the world, its catchment area covering some 1.3 million square kilometres. The rivers of the catchment include the Finke and the Todd, which rise in the mountains of central Australia, and the Warburton and Cooper's Creek (really a river), which have headwaters in north-eastern Queensland, where they are fed annually by heavy rains brought by the summer monsoons. But from there they cross the dry deserts of the interior and their waters are usually lost in the sands or evaporated by the heat of the sun. Rarely is the rainfall in the north heavy enough to give the rivers sufficient volume to reach Lake Eyre, a journey taking some 5 months.

Lake Eyre has filled with water only twice this century, first in 1950, and again in 1974. This second flooding is believed to have been the greatest inundation in 500 years, the average depth of the water being almost 4 metres, with some places reaching more than 5 metres.

When it is flooded, Lake Eyre fulfils the explorers' dreams of an inland sea. It becomes by far Australia's largest lake and the whole character of the region changes. Pelicans, waterfowl, white cockatoos, emus and other birds flock to the area, ground animals such as kangaroos become prolific, and people arrive with swimming gear, fishing tackle and boats.

Studies made during the 1974 flooding found that when the lake was first filled, the water was mostly fresh, with two brine layers. Eventually these layers mixed with the fresh water, causing the lake to become a little saltier than normal sea water. The many freshwater fish that had been carried downstream by the flooding rivers began to die and by mid-1975 the lake began to dry up. Before long, the lake bed turned into a vast quagmire of black mud that was too thick and slushy to walk on or to navigate a boat through. It looked as though a huge tide had gone out, but in fact the water had evaporated in the hot desert air. Then the slush disappeared, leaving only briny pools. But they, too, soon dried out and within 4 years of the first water reaching the lake, the salt crust set once more.

Traditionally, Lake Eyre was in the territory of the Arabana, Tirari and Kujani Aboriginal tribes. However, these people feared the lake, which they called *Katitanda*, and never went near it, for it offered neither drinking water nor food.

Several legends relate to the lake. The main one, telling of its formation, concerns a large kangaroo that was chased and speared by a young boy named *Wilkuda* in the *Tjukurpa* or Dreamtime. Wilkuda put the kangaroo on a fire to cook, but the animal was not dead and managed to escape. The boy pursued

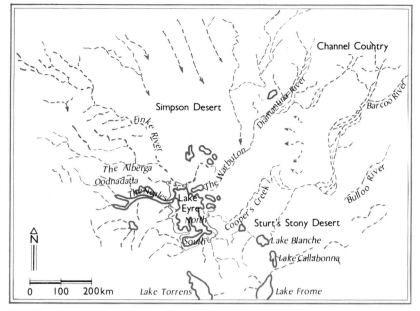

the kangaroo for several days, but eventually it was killed by an old man with the help of his dog. The old man gave the skin of the kangaroo to Wilkuda. Twice a bird warned the boy not to throw the skin away, but finally he was so tired of carrying it that he threw it down. The skin became Lake Eyre and Wilkuda turned into a stone near its shore.

The first white man to see Lake Eyre was the explorer Edward John Eyre, after whom the lake is named. In 1840 he led a party to the southern shore of Lake Eyre South and also saw parts of lakes Torrens, Frome, Blanche and Callabonna, but he thought they formed a single horseshoe-shaped lake.

For some years after Eyre's journey, most explorers thought that the region was an impenetrable barrier. Then in 1858 Augustus Charles Gregory found a route between lakes Blanche and Callabonna, and during the next two years further exploration was carried out by men such as Benjamin Babbage, Peter Warburton, John McDouall Stuart and George Goyder.

But to the explorers, the country around Lake Eyre was considered useless in every sense—a godforsaken place that threatened them with imminent death.

The first person to like Lake Eyre was the geologist and explorer Cecil Thomas Madigan, who visited it in 1929. Madigan had been a member of the Australasian Antarctic Expedition of 1911-14, led by Douglas Mawson, and he was struck by the likeness of the pinky-white salt crust to the polar regions he had seen. He found the lake "fascinating" and "tantalising" and returned to it many times, describing its effect upon him as "the spell of Lake Eyre". The explorer Eyre before him had described the salt country as "glittering and brilliant beyond conception", but he had felt uneasy there, calling it a "region of magic" where "all was uncertainty and conjecture".

Indeed, many things about the lake are strange and alluring. The sandy beaches, headlands and spits of the shoreline seem out of place without water, and the arctic appearance of the saltpan is completely incongruous with the oppressive heat. There are hideous dangers, too. In summer the region is so hot that one can die quickly of thirst or heat exhaustion, while on the rare occasions that wild torrents of water flow from the rivers into the lake, the possibility of drowning is a serious threat. And at any time of the year it is possible to become lost if travelling on the trackless salt crust without a compass.

Although a monochrome landscape, Lake Eyre has a surprising variety of scenery. The southern shoreline resembles a stony gibber plain frosted in white, while much of the saltpan, as Madigan noted, appears to consist of pack ice and snow. In some places the saltpan is smooth and unbroken, but elsewhere the arctic impression is emphasised by a frothy foam that exudes from the salt crust, giving a feeling of water movement below.

This foam always rises near delicate salt crystal formations that occur in an extraordinary variety of designs, ranging from coin-like shapes to intricate flowerettes and shell-like patterns. Often there are hundreds of individual formations of a single design, repeated with complete accuracy of symmetry and detail. Scientists are still baffled as to how they are formed.

Apart from these decorations, the salt has coated pieces of driftwood and other debris, creating some very sculptural ornaments, and on the southern fringe of Lake Eyre South the high ground is composed almost exclusively of gypsum that lies in glittering shards like broken, semi-transparent glass.

The saltpan also varies in mood. In the daytime it is a blinding sheet of white that contrasts starkly with the metallic blue sky. The area is extremely hot, for the effects of the sun are increased considerably by reflection and glare, and shimmering mirages constantly mock the visitor. But at dawn and dusk the scenery is softer, with the salt glowing pink at sunrise and seeming opalescent at sunset. At night it is haunting, with howling winds and sometimes, when it is especially hot, a midnight mirage.

Today, part of Lake Eyre has been reserved as the Elliot Price Conservation Park. But in the past, there have been several moves to completely change the character of the region.

Since as early as the 1880s, proposals have been put forward to utilise Lake Eyre to irrigate Australia's arid interior. Several people have suggested that if the lake were permanently filled with water it might induce a higher rainfall and they have recommended that a canal could be dug from Spencer Gulf to fill it with sea water. However, meteorologists have pointed out that such a scheme would rely on wind circulation patterns and that it would be unlikely to work because the water evaporated from large water surfaces is usually carried for considerable distances before falling as rain. The dry Nullarbor Plain bordering the Southern Ocean lends weight to this argument.

Other people have expounded theories based on building dams to harness the heavy monsoonal rains of northern Queensland and then diverting the waters by pipeline to the drier lands of the Lake Eyre catchment. One such plan even involved damming the gorges of the MacDonnell Ranges and other mountain systems in central Australia; however, it and similar schemes were found to be impracticable.

A purpose for which the lake proved eminently suitable was the famous land speed record attempt made there in 1964 by the British racing car driver Donald Campbell, when his Proteus *Bluebird II* reached 692 kilometres per hour.

The desert country that surrounds Lake Eyre is not as entirely useless to the white man as the early explorers supposed. With a sparse covering of saltbush, spinifex and acacias, it is used for grazing. Bores have been sunk to take advantage of the artesian water, which, although too saline for human consumption, is suitable for cattle and sheep and for some domestic purposes on the few lonely stations in the area. But in the immediate vicinity of the great lake, all remains quiet and parched. □

221

224

Mountains of mystery

THE FLINDERS RANGES

WHEN THE landscape artist Sir Hans Heysen first visited the Flinders Ranges in the late 1920s, he felt that a new world had opened up to him. He loved the purple mountains and the twisted river red gums that line the creek beds, and he was fascinated by the deep blue skies, the intense quality of the light, and the dominating hues of red, ochre and brown on the exposed rockfaces. For at least a third of his long career, the ranges provided him with much of his subject material and it is largely due to his paintings that the region has achieved widespread fame.

The Flinders Ranges are a series of long parallel ridges separated by narrow valleys and broad alluvial plains. Forming South Australia's most extensive mountain chain, they rise near Port Pirie on Spencer Gulf and stretch northward for some 430 kilometres, descending into the desert country south-east of Lake Eyre. The ranges are not high, seldom reaching more than 1000 metres above sea level, but their primitive colours and contours have a compelling beauty and mystique. In the south the scenery is gentle, with rows of interfolded hills rolling in regular succession, their softly rounded slopes clothed in pale golden grasses. But in the north, the ranges are wild and stark. Spectacular jagged peaks and scalloped ridges form a dramatic backdrop to sweeping grasslands, boulder-strewn foothills, stately forests of native "cypress pine" (*Callitris columellaris*) and giant old river red gums (*Eucalyptus camaldulensis*).

Heysen called the Flinders "the 'bones of Nature' laid bare". In the north, particularly, huge expanses of naked rock dominate the landscape, their domed, shattered and tilted forms illustrating like textbook diagrams the processes of nature that must have taken place in their creation. It is this quality—and the presence of a wide variety of minerals, gemstones and rare fossils—that has attracted numerous scientists to the area, including the famous Antarctic explorer and geologist, Sir Douglas Mawson, who first studied the mountains in about 1910 and maintained his interest in them for almost half a century.

The Flinders Ranges are primarily composed of ancient quartzites, limestones, sandstones and shales that began to accumulate as sediments on a shallow seabed more than 1000 million years ago. However, in the extreme north there are granites and other crystalline rocks more than 1650 million years old.

As the seabed was subsiding for several hundred million years, the sediments built up and consolidated into an enormous mass, in some places as much as 16 kilometres thick. About 600 million years ago a period of mountain-building began, with the rock strata being thrust up and squeezed into huge, complex folds. The greatest pressure came from the east and the west, resulting in the formation of very high north-south running ranges. But strong pressure also came from the north and the south, warping the mountains and creating dome-like rises and pound-like basins. Igneous intrusions at

this time left numerous mineral deposits, notably of copper and uranium, and in the north there was faulting, too.

By about 200 million years ago, weathering and erosion had reduced these ancestral mountains to low ranges. For several million years, plant debris accumulated in freshwater swamps, forming coal seams, and these were covered by further sedimentary deposits.

Some 60 million years ago, the former ranges had been worn down to an almost flat plain. But then minor earth movements gradually uplifted and rejuvenated the landscape, forming a vast plateau. Weathering and erosion, especially during periods of high rainfall, have since removed the softer rocks, leaving the more resistant folded strata of quartzites and other hard rocks standing as the magnificently sculptured ridges of today.

For thousands of years, the Flinders Ranges supported a large Aboriginal population belonging to several tribal groups. Some of the most beautiful place names in the region, such as those of the tourist settlements of Arkaroola and Wilpena, originate from these people. But other names commemorate Europeans who have been associated with the mountains during the last 200 years, notably the navigator Matthew Flinders, who sighted them from the head of the Spencer Gulf in 1802, and the explorer Edward John Eyre, who led two expeditions along the western edge of the ranges in 1839-40. Eyre described the country he saw as sterile and useless, but within 20 years others were to view the region in a more favourable light.

The Flinders Ranges are dotted with homestead ruins and ghost towns, for they have been the hope and the heartbreak of many European settlers.

The white infiltration of the ranges began when graziers—among them, the explorer John McKinlay—established sheep and cattle runs there in the 1840s and 1850s. John McDouall Stuart was also in the area at this time, having been sent to survey holdings taken up by his employers, James Chambers and William Finke.

1. Wilpena Pound, from the south-east
2. Edeowie Gorge, draining the north-western end of Wilpena Pound
3. Cuesta formation, ABC Range

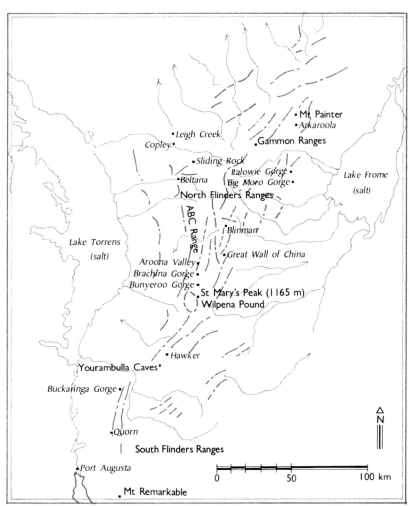

Before long, copper mines were established in the ranges, too, and flourishing towns grew up at places such as Blinman. It is estimated that in 1862 the combined pastoral and mining population of the Flinders was about 6000, whereas less than half that number of people live in the region today.

For the graziers, life in the Flinders was a lonely existence beset by troubles. Paramount among these was the fact that the Aboriginal people objected to the invasion of their lands and fought hard to turn the newcomer away. They stole, killed or disabled stock, burnt dwellings, and occasionally attacked the settlers.

Ultimately, the Aborigines could not win. Although less than a dozen white people were killed by them, the settlers' retaliation (with superior weapons and "gifts" of poisoned food), together with the introduction of European diseases, amounted to the near-extermination of these original owners of the land. Today, very few Aboriginal people live in the area and much of the traditional knowledge of the ranges has been lost forever. However, many legends and several rock painting and carving sites still survive.

But conflicts with the Aborigines were not the only problems facing the early graziers. Almost the entire Flinders Ranges lie in arid and semi-arid country with an average but very erratic rainfall of less than 350 millimetres. A lack of understanding of the land led to heavy overgrazing, and consequently when a great drought came in 1864-6 many pastoralists were ruined. Numerous mines also closed down, defeated by the isolation, the difficulty of extracting the minerals and the high cost of transport.

During the drought, the then Surveyor-General of South Australia, George Woodroffe Goyder, was instructed by the government to determine ". . . the line of demarcation between that portion of the country where rainfall has extended, and that where drought prevails". Known as "Goyder's Line", it classified as drought country all the land north of Mt Remarkable, near the southern edge of the Flinders. Nevertheless, by 1870 wheat farmers had begun to press northward and within the decade the population of the Flinders Ranges was booming again.

An unusual run of good seasons produced several excellent harvests and for a time the region became known as the "Golden North". In 1878 construction began on a railway running from Port Augusta through Pichi Richi Pass in the southern Flinders and then north, in an attempt to further open up the country. Numerous towns including Quorn and Hawker soon appeared, and more mines—most of them copper—were opened.

But a spate of drought years in the 1880s and 1890s saw scores of wheat farms abandoned and caused grave environmental problems in the region. Unlike the graziers, who had a vested interest in maintaining the native groundcover of saltbush (*Atriplex spp.*) and bluebush (*Kochia spp.*) to feed

their stock, the wheat men had removed it to plant their own crops. So whenever drought was followed by flash floods, as often happens in semi-arid parts of Australia, vast areas of soil were severely eroded. The wild hops (*Rumex vesicarius*) and the Salvation Jane (*Echium plantagineum*) that grow in the Flinders today and are renowned for their springtime blankets of crimson and purple flowers are both introduced plants.

Agriculture and grazing continue on a fairly small scale in the Flinders today and there is also some mining, notably for coal at Leigh Creek. Although numerous other mineral deposits exist in the ranges, few are large enough to make exploitation economically viable and almost all of the 120 or so copper mines that once operated in the area have long been closed down. Most of the old towns are in ruins or decline, too, and even the railway that once ran through the heart of the ranges now takes an easier route across the plains to the west.

However, several areas have been set aside as reserves, including the Flinders Ranges, Mt Remarkable and Gammon Ranges national parks and the privately owned Arkaroola–Mt Painter Sanctuary. Unfortunately, the native animal population has dwindled in numbers, having been pushed out by sheep, cattle and feral animals such as rabbits, goats, cats and foxes, but it is hoped that it will slowly recover.

Probably the best known part of the Flinders Ranges is Wilpena Pound, a picturesque oval-shaped valley enclosed by a wall of precipitous peaks and entered only via a winding gorge cut by Wilpena Creek. Approximately 18 kilometres long by 8 kilometres wide, it was an important Aboriginal ceremonial site until the middle of the last century when it was taken over by Europeans for grazing stock and growing wheat. The Aboriginal word *Wilpena* means "place of bent fingers" and is thought to relate to the pound's resemblance to a cupped hand. About a kilometre inside the pound, the ruins of a sandstone homestead built in 1904 by a pioneering family named Hill, and abandoned 10 years later after a severe flood, still stands.

St Mary's Peak (1190 metres), which forms part of the wall surrounding Wilpena Pound, is the highest point in the Flinders and looks out over one of the region's prettiest mountain ridges, the ABC Range—said to have as many peaks as there are letters in the alphabet. Called a "cuesta" formation, its scalloped pro-

Springtime blankets of flowers . . .

1. Purple Salvation Jane (*Echium plantagineum*), known on the east coast of the continent as Paterson's Curse, in the southern Flinders Ranges
2. Big red kangaroos (*Megaleia rufa*), east of Wilpena
3. A "cypress pine" (*Callitris columellaris*), Edeowie Gorge

file was described by Hans Heysen as having ". . . the appearance of arrested waves on the verge of breaking". It is cut by several beautiful gorges, including Bunyeroo Gorge and Brachina Gorge, and forms a superb backdrop to the sprawling Aroona Valley.

The "Great Wall of China", a low stone structure that winds for several kilometres over the ridges just east of this valley, is one of the most mysterious landmarks in the Flinders. Built without mortar, it is obviously very old but its origin is unknown.

But for many people the most intriguing part of the Flinders Ranges is the bold and dramatic Arkaroola-Mt Painter area in the remote north. Fascinating geological features are found in this region and there are also numerous minerals and gemstones including gold, sapphire, amethyst and garnet.

To the Aborigines, *Arkaroola* means "the place of *Arkaroo*", a Dreamtime serpent who drank Lake Frome and Lake Callabonna dry, creating saltpans, and then dragged his way through the mountains, cutting the sinuous course of Arkaroola Creek and several deep gorges before finally coming to rest in the Gammon Ranges. Arkaroo has been asleep ever since, but the great amount of salty water that he drank gave him a terrible stomach ache and his indigestion is said to be the cause of loud rumblings often heard in the area today. A more prosaic explanation of the noises is that they are caused by minor earth tremors along fault lines—a characteristic typical of relatively stable parts of the Earth's crust that are still readjusting after uplift.

Also located on a fault line are the Paralana Hot Springs, just north of Arkaroola, where near-boiling waters bubbling with carbon dioxide, hydrogen, helium and radio-active gases escape from deep within the Earth's crust. These springs were extremely sacred to the Aboriginal people, who believed that they were formed as a result of a tragic duel between two young men who loved the same woman. They are reputed to have remarkable curative properties and in the 1920s an Adelaide business syndicate set up a health resort there, complete with a medical staff headed by a Dr Clyde Fenton. But the remoteness and ruggedness of the area, together with the terrible food and accommodation that were provided, soon brought an end to the venture.

Other places of interest nearby include the ancient granite peak of Mt Painter, where uranium deposits were worked briefly for atomic purposes during World War II, the unique Mt Gee, composed of crystal quartz, and Bararranna Gorge, where ripple marks on a cliff face date back more than 1000 million years to a time when this region was a continental shelf washed by the waves of the ancestral Pacific Ocean.

Although the geological secrets of these and many other landforms in the Flinders Ranges are gradually being unravelled, the distinctive character and beauty of the rolling purple mountains always retain a compelling air of mystery. ☐

A hidden world

THE NULLARBOR

THE VAST wasteland of the Nullarbor Plain has often been described as one of the most monotonous landscapes on Earth. Flat, barren and virtually uninhabited, it is so devoid of landmarks that a compass is necessary for even the slightest diversion from the few well-defined tracks.

But beneath this desolate surface, the Nullarbor conceals some of the most fascinating scenery in the world. Its entire southern section is honeycombed with extraordinary limestone caves and for much of its length it falls away abruptly in sheer cliffs that tower up to 100 metres above the Southern Ocean.

The Nullarbor is an ancient seabed composed of limestones embedded with many varieties of shells and other marine organisms. Up to 300 metres thick, it began to be laid down about 20 million years ago. From about 3 million years ago it was gradually and gently raised, forming a huge tableland with fracturing occurring only on the coastal margins.

Covering an area of 200 000 square kilometres, the Nullarbor is one of the largest single slabs of limestone in the world. It curves around the Great Australian Bight, from the arid salt lake region of Western Australia to the parched ridges and plains of South Australia, and stretches northwards until it merges with the Great Victoria Desert. Its borders are not strictly defined, although the region is generally taken as being about 700 kilometres long and extending up to 300 kilometres inland from the coast. About one-third of this area is in South Australia and the remaining two-thirds in Western Australia. The entire surface of the plain appears extremely flat, although it dips imperceptibly from 200-300 metres above sea level in the north to 40-120 metres above the sea near the coast.

The name "Nullarbor"— derived from the Latin *nullus* (meaning "no") and *arbor* (meaning "tree") – was conferred on the region in 1866 by the South Australian surveyor Alfred Delisser and originally applied only to one area of treeless land in the centre of the plain. Today, however, the term is used for the whole limestone region and is something of a misnomer since most parts are sparsely vegetated with bluebush (*Maireana* and *Bassia spp.*), saltbush (*Atriplex spp.*), mallee (*Eucalyptus spp.*) and various stunted eucalypts. (By a curious coincidence, the word *nulla* means "none" or "not any" in some Aboriginal languages. This fact has in the past led to much debate about the origin of the name, however its Latin derivation has been established as the correct one.)

The Nullarbor has three distinct divisions: a large main plateau (the Bunda Plateau); a long southern scarp known in different places as Wylie Scarp, Baxter Cliffs, Hampton Range and Bunda Cliffs; and two coastal plains, the Roe Plains and the Israelite Plains, both of which are backed by the scarp and are partly covered by sand dunes.

The cliffs of the coastline occur in two breathtaking, unbroken stretches: the Baxter Cliffs in the west, rising 60-100 metres above the sea; and the Bunda Cliffs in the east, which are 40-75 metres high. Each of these sections of cliff extends about 200 kilometres and is beautifully coloured with brown hues on the upper parts, fading to chalky-white lower down. Although the cliffs are lashed by giant waves and blustering southerly winds, the horizontal rock strata and vertical jointing are extremely regular and there are no weaker areas to be carved into coastal gorges or valleys. As a result the undercut cliffs break off in straight slabs, creating a remarkably uniform coastline, with the plateau dropping vertically to the sea. Where the cliffs retreat inland behind the Roe and Israelite plains, they retain their sheer edges, having also been lapped by the ocean during past phases of higher sea level.

Beyond the cliffs, in the southern part of the Bunda Plateau, the Nullarbor contains Australia's largest area of "karst" or cave landforms. During past periods of heavy rainfall, great volumes of water seeped down through microscopic cracks in the hard surface limestone and over millennia etched out massive cave systems in the softer rock below.

The caves are of two basic types: small, shallow caves less than 25 metres below the ground; and large, deep caves as much as 120 metres below the ground. Many of these larger caves reach the water table (which almost certainly underlies the whole plain) and have beautiful clear lakes and complex networks of underwater passages.

The entrances to the caves are difficult to locate on the featureless surface of the plain. About 50 caves, particularly the deeper ones, are accessible via passages leading from huge sinkholes known as dolines. Formed by the collapse of a cave roof, these great gaping holes are generally circular or oval in shape and range from a few metres to more than 200 metres in width. They may be very shallow depressions or holes as much as 40 metres deep. Many caves, however, can be entered only through blowholes, which are narrow, vertical shafts up to 10 metres deep. There are thousands of them on the plain, although not all lead to caves. A great many are known as "breathing holes" because sometimes air rushes up from them with tremendous violence and at other times it is sucked down into them. This curious phenomenon is thought to be caused by the fluctuation of air pressure due to changes in the weather: when the air in underground channels below the blowholes becomes heated it expands and is blown out, but during cooler periods air flows in again.

The deeper caves are easily the most spectacular landforms of the Nullarbor. The chambers are immense, often reaching several hundred metres in length. Usually they have a huge domed ceiling and a flat floor strewn with enormous piles of fallen rock. The atmosphere is extremely cool, still and dark, totally contrasting with the hot, bright plain above.

Many of the caves are of great archaeological and geological importance. There are several ancient Aboriginal art and artefact sites, and numerous fossils including some of extinct animal species such as the Tasmanian tiger (*Thylacinus cynocephalus*). In addition, rare mineral "speleothems" (cave

1. The main chamber, Weebubbie Cave
2. The orchard inside the Koonalda sinkhole
3. A blowhole near Weebubbie Cave

decorations) of halite and gypsum are found in many of the caves, and in some places delicate crystals have been deposited around the margins of the underground lakes. However, today the lack of rainfall and vegetation to provide carbon dioxide prevents the formation of the more common cave decorations such as stalactites and stalagmites. The only examples of this type of decoration are found in a few shallow caves on the eastern edge of the plain and in the Lynch Caves near Loongana, but almost all have long been dried out. Cave formation is also virtually at a standstill, although rockfalls still occur.

Probably the best known of the Nullarbor caves is Koonalda Cave in South Australia. It is entered via an awesome sinkhole, 85 metres across and 30 metres deep. The entire lip of the sinkhole is level with the plain and the sides are sheer or undercut for about the first 20 metres. From there, a steep-angled slope leads down to the gigantic main chamber, which is more than 70 metres below the plain. Measuring some 90 metres long and 60 metres wide, and with a domed ceiling about 45 metres high, this chamber opens into two further passages, one of which leads to three lakes.

Archaeological evidence shows that Aborigines quarried flint from Koonalda Cave at least 20 000 years ago and intriguing markings on the walls of the main passage have also been dated as being the same age. In more recent times water has been pumped from one of the cave's lakes for sheep and, incredibly, the protected environment of the enormous sinkhole has been utilised as an orchard, with a variety of fruit trees and fodder plants such as clover having been planted.

Most of the other major caves of the Nullarbor are on the Western Australian side of the border.

Weebubbie Cave, near Eucla, is one of the prettiest caves in the region. Entered from a sinkhole about the same size as that of Koonalda, the main chamber is reached by following a wide, boulder-strewn tunnel that slopes gently down to a large and extremely beautiful lake. The water here, and in a smaller adjacent pool, is so clear that it is hard to tell where it starts. But even more impressive is the sculpturing of the chamber, for the pure white walls are perfectly smooth and the ceiling is remarkably flat.

Abrakurrie Cave, a little west of Weebubbie, contains the largest and most imposing single cavern on the Nullarbor. Some 180 metres long and 45 metres wide, this extraordinary chamber is like a cathedral. The ceiling, which is about 40 metres high, is arched for the full length of the cavern and the walls at both ends are vertical. The entire rock surface is smoothly sculptured and pure white, while the flat floor is covered with soft, dark sand. Huge white fallen boulders are strewn throughout the chamber, but unlike other large caves on the Nullarbor, Abrakurrie does not reach the water table and there is no lake. The entrance also differs from most large caves in that it can simply be walked into from a shallow sinkhole and does not involve any vertical climbing. Instead, a narrow slit from the sinkhole opens onto a steep talus slope that leads down about 70 metres below the plain and then turns sharply into the main cavern.

Other notable caves on the Nullarbor include Mullamullang Cave and Cocklebiddy Cave, both of which lie further west. Extending 4.8 kilometres, Mullamullang is the largest cave network known in Australia and also contains an exquisite chamber of mineral formations known as the Salt Cellars. Cocklebiddy, on the other hand, has the longest underwater cave passage known in the world: more than 2 kilometres have so far been explored but the limits have yet to be reached.

The caves hidden in the depths of the Nullarbor are a world removed from the parched desert lands of the plain above.

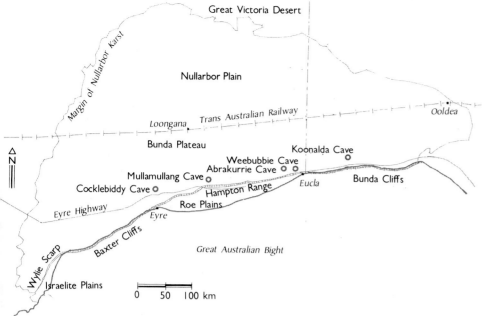

Today there are no surface streams on the Nullarbor. The average annual rainfall is less than 250 millimetres, and the little water that does not evaporate in the hot sun sinks straight through the porous limestone to the lakes and rivers in the caverns below. Some of this groundwater seeps south, where it emerges as springs at the foot of the coastal cliffs or forms soaks in the sandhills. Sometimes it is still fresh, but often it becomes saline.

The only other natural sources of fresh water on the Nullarbor are impermanent. On hard areas of limestone where there are no cracks, small rockholes hold water for a week or two after rain. In the northern part of the region similar waterholes form in shallow, tree-filled depressions known as dongas. Up to 800 metres across and 2-3 metres deep, dongas have a hard clay surface and sufficient shade to retain rainwater for some time after it falls.

Apart from the dongas and the coastal dunes, the Nullarbor has only very thin soil cover and this, coupled with the unavailability of groundwater within the reach of plant roots, limits vegetation to the hardiest desert species. These plants have developed specialised means of coping with their harsh environment. The prolific saltbush and bluebush, for example, survive by absorbing atmospheric moisture through their leaves.

As with other desert regions in Australia, there is an abundance of wildlife on the Nullarbor. Many types of ground animal, ranging from lizards and snakes to kangaroos, wombats and the occasional dingo can be seen on the plain itself, especially congregating around the sinkholes. Birds, too, find an ideal habitat on the lonely plain, and emus (*Dromaius novaehollandiae*), little black crows (*Corvus bennetti*), and vivid green budgerigars (*Melopsittacus undulatus*) are common sights. But the most interesting fauna of the region live deep within the caves. Small, furry bats with high-pitched voices cling to the ceilings and high walls of many large chambers and a variety of tiny and unusual invertebrate creatures inhabit the lower levels.

Aboriginal people have lived in the Nullarbor region for at least 20 000 years. The earliest inhabitants visited the dark depths of some of the larger caves, where they made finger markings and etchings on the walls, and left a few simple artefacts. Almost nothing is known about these ancient people or their motives for making the difficult underground journeys, but it seems that they ceased to visit the caves several thousand years ago.

In recent centuries the Nullarbor was the territory of the Mirning tribe, which had over 20 local groups. These people lived near the coastal margins and seldom penetrated far onto the plain. They did not enter the deeper caves, which they believed to be the home of a fearsome water serpent, *Jeedara*, who was once chased by *Yugarilya* (the Pleiades constellation) and in his flight pushed up the cliffs of the Bight and slithered into

the caves to hide. Jeedara's breathing could be heard and felt coming up through the many blowholes in the ground, and it was said that he would seize anyone trespassing on his land. The Mirning people, however, did visit many of the shallower caves, and examples of their art can be seen on the walls.

To Europeans, the Nullarbor has always presented a hostile front. The earliest known European sighting of the coast was made in 1627 by the Dutch navigator Frans Thijssen who, as commander of the *Gulden Zeepaard* ("Golden Seahorse"), led an expedition to examine the coastline of New Holland for the Dutch East India Company. With a view to finding riches for trade, Thijssen sailed 1500 kilometres east from Cape Leeuwin across the whole of the Great Australian Bight, naming the

The Bunda Cliffs

Nullarbor "Pieter Nuyts Land" in honour of his distinguished "supercargo" (superintendent of cargo), Pieter Nuyts. Seeing nothing but high, unapproachable cliffs and desolate land, Thijssen turned back about 300 kilometres west of Spencer Gulf where he would have found fertile land. His abandonment of the search discouraged further Dutch exploration of the continent's southern coast and it was not until 165 years later that another European sighted the magnificent cliffs of the Bight.

In December 1792, the Frenchman Bruni D'Entrecasteaux, on an assignment to enquire into the disappearance of an expedition led by the Comte de la Pérouse, sailed along the full length of the Nullarbor coast on his way to eastern Australia, where La Pérouse had last been seen.

Ten years later, in 1802, the British navigator Matthew Flinders sailed HMS *Investigator* along the same course at the beginning of his famous circumnavigation of the Australian continent. Flinders made detailed and accurate charts of the region, paying great attention to his geographical description of the stupendous cliffs. For the ship's artist, William Westall, these great edifices provided a dramatic subject to sketch, and his work later accompanied the published edition of Flinders' journal, *A Voyage to Terra Australis*.

One of the most avid readers of this account was the explorer Edward John Eyre. In 1841, having failed in an attempt to reach the centre of the continent, Eyre determined to find a route across the Nullarbor (at that time still unnamed) and hence provide a land link, and possibly a stock route, between the eastern colonies and the Swan River Colony (now Perth) in the west.

His journey was an epic of human endurance. Friends and other explorers tried to dissuade him from attempting the expedition and Aborigines warned him of the desolate, harsh terrain and lack of water. Nonetheless, Eyre set off from Fowler's Bay on 25 February 1841 with a small party consisting of his faithful companion and overseer John Baxter and three Aboriginal boys—Wylie, from Albany in Western Australia, and Joey and Yarry from New South Wales. Horses were taken to carry the supplies, but the men themselves were to walk.

The destination was Wylie's birthplace, Albany, some 1500 kilometres away on King George Sound. Right from the beginning of the long journey, the party was tormented by the weather, the constantly blowing sand, and the flies.

By 10 March they were desperately short of water. But the first set of cliffs (the Bunda Cliffs) still stretched as far as the eye could see and there was no sign of the sandhills in which they had been told by Aborigines that they would find freshwater soaks. Yet despite thirst and fatigue, Eyre—the first white man to stand on the superb Nullarbor cliffs—was able to appreciate the beauty of the wild coastline.

"Distressing and fatal as the continuance of these cliffs might prove to us," he wrote in his journal, "there was a grandeur and sublimity in their appearance that was most imposing, and which struck me with admiration. Stretching out before us in lofty unbroken outline, they presented the singular and romantic appearance of massy battlements of masonry, supported by huge buttresses, and glittering in the morning sun which had now risen upon them, and made the scene beautiful even amidst the dangers and anxieties of our situation. It was indeed a rich and gorgeous view for a painter, and I never felt so much regret at my inability to sketch as I did at this moment."

Two days later, their water gone, they staggered up to the great white sandhills where Eucla was later built and found an abundance of water. The next soaks (now known as Eyre's Sandpatch) were about 300 kilometres away on the western side of the Roe Plain and by the time they reached them they were again without water.

At this stage of the journey, Baxter was convinced that the party's only hope for survival lay in returning to Fowler's Bay, but he dutifully acquiesced to Eyre, who insisted they continue west. It was a fateful decision for Baxter, for one night shortly after reaching the second set of cliffs he was killed by two of the Aboriginal boys, Joey and Yarry, who had decided to plunder the stores and leave the expedition.

The death of his friend left Eyre in the appalling position of being alone in the desert, save for the company of Wylie whose loyalty was uncertain as he had almost certainly been in allegiance with Joey and Yarry until frightened by the killing of Baxter. Albany was still 800 kilometres away and the food supply had been reduced to 18 kilograms of flour, a little tea and sugar, and less than 20 litres of water.

Sadly, Eyre broke camp early the following morning. It was impossible to dig a grave in the hard limestone plain, so he was compelled to leave Baxter's body carefully wrapped in a blanket behind the cliffs that now bear the murdered man's name.

For almost three weeks Eyre and Wylie staggered on, tired, sick, hungry and thirsty. Finally on 17 May they passed from the Nullarbor to the adjacent granite country of Western Australia. Winter was now coming on and, as if to mock them after their drought-stricken months on the plain, it was cold and occasionally rainy.

On 2 June, still 500 kilometres from Albany, they headed towards a long bay, around the headland of which they planned to stop at a little inlet which Flinders had named Lucky Bay because it had provided a sheltered anchorage for the *Investigator* when in danger in 1802. Unable to believe their eyes, they saw a boat sailing in the bay. Before they had time to gain the attention of those on board, the boat had passed out of sight, but mercifully it reappeared about half an hour later, in company with another boat. Eyre and Wylie signalled frantically, and within an hour they were aboard the *Mississippi*, a French whaling boat commanded by an Englishman named Captain Rossiter. The two travellers, who had come so close to death, rested aboard ship for two weeks before continuing their journey on foot to Albany, well-stocked with warm clothing, food and six bottles of wine.

Eyre arrived in Albany on 7 July 1841, some 4½ months after leaving Fowler's Bay. The gruelling journey had proved that there was no stock route across the Nullarbor, but it had also shown that some day—albeit difficult—communication links could be established across the vast plain.

For the time being, however, there was no rush to follow Eyre across the Nullarbor. A few bushmen and surveyors—including Delisser, who named the region—explored the eastern fringes of the plain over the next 30 years, but not until 1870 was another crossing attempted.

This expedition was led by John Forrest, who later became the first Premier of Western Australia. With him were his brother, Alexander, two other white men and two Aborigines. Setting out from Perth, they travelled overland to Esperance Bay and from there followed much the same route as that taken by Eyre, only in the opposite direction. But their journey was far less traumatic than Eyre's, for Forrest had carefully studied his predecessor's journal and had arranged for a 30-tonne schooner, *Adur*, to rendezvous with them at Esperance Bay, Israelite Bay and Eucla.

Forrest shared Eyre's opinion that the Nullarbor cliffs were grand in the extreme, but he found their height terrible to gaze from. "After looking very cautiously over the precipice," he wrote, "we all ran back quite terror-stricken by the dreadful view." Of the country behind, he reported that it would make excellent grazing land if water could be obtained by sinking wells, but he was doubtful about the likelihood of this as he had seen nothing to indicate that the water table might be within easy reach of the surface.

Nonetheless, during the next few years several scattered sheep stations were established on the Nullarbor, and by 1890 the presence of caves and underground lakes was known. Although the lack of fresh water did prove to be a problem, it was not insurmountable as sheep can tolerate fairly saline artesian waters. But the isolation of the region was a big drawback.

Things, however, were soon to change. For business and security reasons, colonists on both the eastern and western sides of the continent saw advantages in establishing a faster means of communication than that available via the sea routes.

In 1877 the South Australian and Western Australian governments jointly erected an overland telegraph from Port Augusta, across the Nullarbor to Albany, with the two terminals transmitting to Adelaide and Perth respectively. The original telegraph followed Eyre's route, and the eastern and western sections of the line joined at Eucla, where the main repeater station for relaying messages was established. Smaller stations were also erected at regular intervals, including two on the Nullarbor: one at Eyre, near Eyre's Sandpatch on the lonely Roe Plains, and the other at Israelite Bay (although after 20 years this station was closed and the line was redirected inland to Perth).

Eucla was a bustling little settlement with a thriving port. The town layout was a rectangle of four streets, and at its peak the population was 90, consisting mostly of postal employees and their families.

The telegraph station was operated by staff from both South Australia and Western Australia. But there was no unity in the codes, equipment and procedures used, and originally those from each colony worked on opposite sides of a partition, which acted like a border and divided the building in two. Messages from the east would be received by the South Australian operator, who would then pass them through a small porthole to a Western Australian operator, who in turn would transmit the message through to Perth. With the advent of Federation in 1901, Morse code was introduced for the whole country and the partition was removed and replaced by an extremely long table, with the operators from each State sitting on their respective sides of the new "half border".

The facilities brought by the telegraph line enabled the few lonely sheep stations on the Nullarbor to consolidate into permanent establishments. Afghans with camel trains soon began to take supplies to the homesteads, and in the 1890s they expanded their services to cater for the needs of diggers on the rich goldfields around Kalgoorlie and Coolgardie in the west. But by the 1920s the days of both the telegraph and the Afghans were nearing an end.

As an inducement to Western Australia to join Federation, an undertaking was given to construct a railway across the

Nullarbor. This became a reality in 1917 when the Trans-Australian Railway between Port Augusta and Kalgoorlie was opened, having taken five years to build. Located about 160 kilometres from the coast, it is famed as having the longest straight stretch of railroad in the world — a section extending some 478 kilometres. The railway was constructed on standard gauge measurements, but as the connecting lines on either side were of narrow gauge, passengers travelling between capital cities had to change trains at Kalgoorlie and Port Augusta. Not until 1970 did a through service, the *Indian-Pacific*, become available between Perth and Sydney.

The railway quickly superseded the camel trains as the main means of transport across the Nullarbor, and it also brought tiny settlements of railway gangers and fettlers to the region. Today these settlements still dot the plain. Most shopping needs of the inhabitants are catered for by a weekly visit from a legendary supply train called the *Tea and Sugar* which sells fresh meat, fruit, vegetables, dairy foods, groceries and other goods, and also offers various welfare services.

Many of the 50 or so sidings along the Trans-Australian route are named after Australian Prime Ministers, but others have Aboriginal names or honour people who have been associated with the track. One such siding is Bates, named after the famous Irishwoman, Daisy Bates, who spent more than 40 years living with Aboriginal people in various parts of Western Australia and South Australia. Known to the Aborigines as *Kabbarli* (meaning "grandmother"), she first came to the Nullarbor in 1912 and spent two years living near Eucla, before moving to Fowler's Bay where she stayed for four years. But in 1919, after a brief period of ill-health in Adelaide, she returned to the Nullarbor, setting up camp near the Ooldea railway siding, on the eastern side of the plain, where she remained for 16 years.

Ooldea, an Aboriginal word meaning "meeting place where water is available", was the site of a valuable freshwater soak and had been visited for centuries by tribes from the north, east and west. In her book *The Passing of the Aborigines*, Daisy Bates relates the effect that the railway had on these people, many of whom were cannibals and had not previously come in contact with the white man. Particularly poignant is the fact that the railwaymen took over the soak and installed pumps and piping, forcing the Aborigines to obtain their water from taps at the siding. But within a few years, bores were pierced through the blue clay bed that formed the natural reservoir of the soak and the waters turned brackish. Except for one small well, the soak which for generations had provided the Aboriginal people with abundant water was ruined.

The overland telegraph along the southern coast was another casualty of the railway. From the time it was erected, the telegraph line had been continually hindered by corrosion caused by the salty sea air and finally in 1927 it was replaced by a new inland line following the railway track. Eucla, which had

been in decline since the automation of the telegraph station in 1909, became a ghost town. Today its ruins are almost buried in drifts of stark white sand, for earlier in the century plagues of rabbits removed the vegetation from the coastal dunes and without stabilisation the great sandhills began to be blown inland, moving at a rate of about 25 metres a year. Only the tops of a few beautiful old stone buildings can still be seen on the original site, although several other buildings have been relocated in a new settlement, also called Eucla, on the high ground of the Hampton Tableland. A similar fate caused by sand drifts has befallen the telegraph station at Eyre.

Road access across the Nullarbor is a relatively recent innovation. A coastal dirt track, which had been established over the years by motorists following the old camel train route, was upgraded in 1941 as a World War II military measure to become part of the 1680-kilometre Eyre Highway, extending from Port Augusta to Norseman. However, it was not completely sealed until 1976.

Running parallel with the Bight for more than 1000 kilometres, the highway is only slightly north of the route taken by the explorer after whom it is named. A number of small settlements are dotted along its length, and side roads lead to both the cliffs and the caves. The road is also the route taken by a highly sophisticated "microwave radio" telephone hook-up which came into service in 1970. (The original telephone circuit, opened in 1930, follows the railway.)

Although today a great many people commute from east to west across the Nullarbor, few spend much time there, and as water is still a major problem the permanent population of the region is less than 800. But the lack of people does not lessen the compelling attraction of the beautiful cliffs, the immense caverns and the quiet emptiness of the vast plain.

Nor does the fact that the Nullarbor is considered by many to be a "wasteland" protect it from interference by man. Graffiti, vandalism and dumping of rubbish are evident in many areas. Overgrazing and driving too close to cave sinkholes has led to serious erosion and consequently to pollution of cave waters. And two of the most beautiful caves, Koonalda and Weebubbie, are scarred by pipes and pumping equipment, a disfiguration which is totally unnecessary as water of acceptable quality can be reached by boring directly into the limestone aquifer. Furthermore, a very large area on the South Australian side of the Nullarbor was appropriated in the 1950s as a testing ground for atomic weapons. Known as Maralinga (derived from an Aboriginal word meaning "thunder"), it contains an "atomic ghost town" and entry to the area is prohibited as the testing range is still radioactive.

At present only a very small area of the Nullarbor has been declared a reserve—the Nuytsland Wildlife Reserve in Western Australia. However, there are plans to proclaim other areas as national parks. ☐

*And concealed beneath its desolate surface
. . . a honeycomb of caves*

1. The Bunda Cliffs
2. The sinkhole entrance to Koonalda Cave
3. The Abrakurrie sinkhole
OVERLEAF: The main cavern, Abrakurrie Cave

Petrified in stone

WAVE ROCK

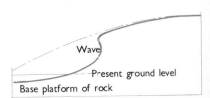

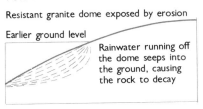

FORMATION OF WAVE ROCK

Resistant granite dome exposed by erosion

Earlier ground level

Rainwater running off the dome seeps into the ground, causing the rock to decay

Wave

Present ground level

Base platform of rock

WAVE formations are not uncommon on rocks of central and southern Australia. Prominent examples occur on the Eyre Peninsula and on sections of both Ayers Rock and the Olgas. But nowhere is the sculptural form of the wave so exquisite as at Wave Rock in the heart of the Western Australian wheatbelt.

The Wave is not a separate rock, but an overhanging wall more than 100 metres long on the northern side of a large granite outcrop known as Hyden Rock. About 2 kilometres long and nearly a kilometre wide, this outcrop rises to about 55 metres above the surrounding plain. It has three hill-like elevations, separated by shallow gullies. Wave-like formations occur on the sides of all three elevations, but they are small and unimpressive compared with the celebrated northern section.

Wave Rock rises 15 metres above the ground like a huge wave about to break. For its full length it is streaked with vertical bands of rusty red, ochre and sandy grey which give a feeling of the rolling movement of the sea. These beautiful bands of colour are caused by run-off waters, charged with carbonates and iron hydroxide derived from the rock, trickling down the curved slope. When the water evaporates, the minerals are deposited on the slope and often algae and lichens gain a foothold, their various colours increasing the banded appearance of the rockface. The perfect lines of the streaking are interrupted only at one place, where a whitish-cream intrusion vein strikes out across the Wave at a 30° angle. This prominent scar is a dyke of finer-grained granite.

Hyden Rock is one of many rock residuals found in a large area of southern Western Australia which geologists call Yilgarnia. This area is one of the oldest land surfaces on Earth, its granite rock having crystallised at least 2700 million years ago.

The Wave was formed largely by a sub-surface process known as "scarp foot weathering" and later uncovered by erosion. Originally the whole of Hyden Rock lay buried beneath the ground. Over millions of years erosion gradually removed layer after layer of the surrounding land, exposing the resistant granite in a low, somewhat domed shape. As the granite is impervious, rainwater falling on the dome ran down the sides and seeped into the surrounding soil and scree, causing the rock just below the surface to decay. With continued erosion, the ground level was steadily lowered and the broken rock was washed away, revealing a smooth curve in the newly exposed rock wall. Further erosion exposed a slightly sloping platform of rock which continues away from the base of the wall for up to 10 metres, emphasising the wave-like shape.

The Aboriginal people of the area seem to have avoided Wave Rock, possibly because of mythological traditions but more likely for practical reasons such as lack of water or, as some anthropologists have suggested, to avoid contact with tribes living in nearby lands to the east who practised circumcision rites. They did, however, visit an area to the north, where valuable water supplies were found in flagon-shaped natural catchments in the granite, known as *gnamma* holes.

Nearby, a dislodged boulder at the side of a large rock residual called the Humps has been hollowed out by erosion to form the small but interesting Bates Cave, which can be entered from two sides. The walls of this cave are marked with hand stencil paintings thought to have been executed only 200 years ago. They relate to a legend about a child borne by a young woman who had fallen in love with a man from a forbidden tribe. The child, Mulka, wore the sign of evil—crossed eyes. It was feared that a curse would be cast on anyone at whom he gazed, and consequently he was outcast from the tribe. He went to live in Bates Cave and the paintings on the walls represent imprints of his hands. As he grew up, Mulka developed a taste for brutal murders and cannibalism. One day, after an argument over his behaviour, Mulka killed his mother. He fled from his cave, but the outrage so aroused the tribes of the district that they hunted him down, finally killing him and leaving the ants to devour his carcass. It is not known if this legend is of relatively recent origin or part of traditional mythology, but the story warns of the folly of departing from tribal lore.

The first Europeans to visit the Wave Rock area are thought to have been sandalwooders, who roamed the inland towards the end of the last century in search of the fragrant sandalwood (*Santalum spicatum*) for which there was a lucrative market in Asia. Various rocks in the district bear their names, including Hyden Rock—originally called Hyde's Rock after a young sandalwooder named Hyde who camped there around 1920. When it was documented by the Lands Department in 1921 it somehow appeared as Hyden Rock. This name became firmly entrenched when a nearby township, which developed following settlement of the area by wheat farmers in the 1920s, was gazetted in 1932 and named Hyden after the rock.

With the influx of settlers, plans were drawn up for the harnessing of run-off water from several large rocks—Hyden, King, Graham and the Humps. A catchment dam was constructed at Hyden Rock in 1928-9 to supply water to the nearby town, and enlarged in 1951. The reservoir fills a gully close to the western end of Wave Rock and it is a miracle that the age-old formation has not been damaged. Unfortunately, an unsightly 60-centimetre-high retaining wall to divert water to the reservoir stands on the summit of the rock, just a few metres back from the top of the Wave. Quarrying, probably carried out during the same period, is also evident near the water catchment area.

For many years Wave Rock remained virtually unknown and its beauty unrecognised. Its rise from obscurity began when it appeared on the front cover of *Walkabout* magazine in the 1960s. Today it is the main feature of a nature reserve which also includes several other interesting rock formations. Tragically, some areas, such as the aptly named Hippo's Yawn cavern on Hyden Rock, just a few hundred metres from the Wave, have been desecrated by vandals. □

A trickle of morning dew accentuates the wave-like appearance of the rock

A unique habitat

THE STIRLING RANGE

The Stirling Range, from the northern wheatlands

Rising majestically from the surrounding lowlands, the Stirling Range fills the horizon in a spectacular jagged outline of heathery purple. Although only a few peaks top 1000 metres, there are no foothills to lessen visual impact and the range stands in stark relief above brilliant green and golden plains. Its grandeur is greatest when the mountains are set against the backdrop of a clear blue sky, but for a few hours on most days it seems moody and ethereal with the high peaks disappearing into swirls of white cloud.

The range is the highest part of Western Australia's south-west region. Located 80 kilometres from Albany (the chief town on the southern coastline), it runs in an east-west direction for some 70 kilometres but never exceeds 15 kilometres in width. Nonetheless, it provides a remarkable natural border between the fertile southern agricultural plain and the flat, dry wheatlands that stretch many kilometres to the north.

Unlike most other high areas in the region, which are composed of granite, the Stirlings (as the range is often called) comprise jagged sandstones, quartzites, slates and shales. They were formed more than 1000 million years ago when a shallow sea inundated the area and sediments were deposited on an existing granite lowland. After the sea receded, there was considerable faulting and the area of the range sank. In time the surrounding land was eroded away to the granite beneath. Subsequent earth movements slowly uplifted the range, and today the prominent northern and southern boundaries can be clearly seen to be parallel east-west running faults.

Erosion and weathering over millions of years have worn down the range to its present relief, which is probably only a remnant of its former bulk. There are many magnificent rock

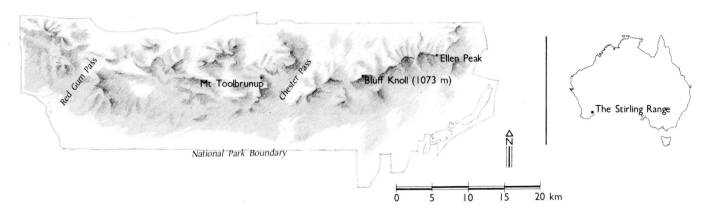

National Park Boundary

The Stirling Range

0 5 10 15 20 km

formations, the most impressive of which are on the craggy higher peaks, where vertical walls, overhanging rocks and intricate tile-like patterns are often shrouded in mist and framed by carpets of wildflowers. Delicate symmetrical ripples formed by an ancient sea are also exposed high on the slopes of Chester Pass and Red Gum Pass, both of which mark the courses of former rivers that flowed through the area in an earlier geological age. Most of the lower slopes are well-rounded and end in U-shaped valleys.

The Stirlings have distinct eastern and western sections, with Chester Pass (the main route through the mountains) acting as the dividing line. On the eastern side, the peaks are part of a long ridge running from Mt Success to Ellen Peak, and including the range's highest point, Bluff Knoll (1073 metres). West of Chester Pass the range is mostly individual mountains, with Mt Toolbrunup (1052 metres) being the highest.

Due to its sudden height and proximity to the sea, the climate of the Stirlings is cooler and moister than that of the surrounding area. Winter tends to be the coldest and wettest period, with regular mist, rain and hail, and occasional snow. However, extremes of weather can be experienced all year round, and in the warmer summer months most of the creeks dry up, leaving little permanent water in the range.

This climate has created an isolated environment for nearly 1000 species of native wildflowers, making the Stirling Range one of the world's most outstanding botanical reserves. More than 100 of these species are unique to the range, and some grow only on specific peaks.

The vegetation of the range fits into two main categories. The lower slopes and valleys are mostly forests of jarrah (*Eucalyptus marginata*), marri (*Eucalyptus calophylla*), wandoo (*Eucalyptus reduuca*) and banksia (*Banksia spp.*), while the higher areas are covered by heaths and dense, prickly scrub. Particularly common is the Stirling Range smokebush (*Conospermum dorrienii*), which is endemic to the area.

The main wildflower period is from spring to early summer. Throughout these months the hills and valleys are decorated by an array of colourful plants, ranging from tiny orchids to flowering eucalypt trees. The most dominant colour is red, coming mostly from the scarlet banksia (*Banksia coccinea*) and the lovely Stirling Range bottlebrush (*Beaufortia heterophylla*), which has spiky, vivid crimson flowers. Among the most beautiful smaller plants are seven unique species of mountain bell (*Darwinia spp.*), some of which are restricted to individual peaks, several species of spider orchid (*Caladenia spp.*), the red kangaroo paw (*Anigozanthos rufa*), and numerous pea flowers.

As most of the surrounding countryside has been cleared of the natural vegetation, the Stirling Range is a significant wildlife sanctuary. A wide variety of birds and insects are attracted to the fragrant nectar-producing flowers, especially honeyeaters and brilliantly patterned beetles. Larger birds include parrots, magpies, currawongs, the wedge-tailed eagle (*Aquila audax*) and the emu (*Dromaius novaehollandiae*). Other animals are also abundant, including kangaroos, wallabies, possums, quokkas, snakes (some of them venomous), geckoes, lizards and goannas. Several smaller species, notably two trapdoor spiders, are unique to the range.

The wild and beautiful Stirlings had important spiritual associations for the Aboriginal people who traditionally inhabited the south-west. They believed that before the range existed, the tribes living to the north and south were enemies. One day the two tribes went to war and many people from both sides were killed. While the survivors were still mourning their dead, a huge cloud settled over the land, like a shroud. Eventually the cloud lifted, and there, lying between the two tribal grounds, was the profile of an old giant Aborigine. Thereafter, whenever a member of either of the two tribes died, part of the mountain giant would be veiled in cloud.

The first European known to have sighted the Stirlings was Matthew Flinders, who in 1802 recorded seeing the mountains from the sea at the start of his historic circumnavigation of the continent. It is possible, however, that they were seen earlier by Dutch navigators. They were not given their current name until 1835 when the surveyor John Septimus Roe explored the area and called them the Stirling Range after Western Australia's first governor, James Stirling.

The range has never been extensively settled by Europeans, although from about the 1850s until early this century, pastoral leases were taken up in the area. Among the early inhabitants was an ex-merchant navy man named Captain Toll who for a time ran cattle in Chester Pass. A track that once ran through the range was called Toll's Pass and it was frequented by sandalwood carters who brought their produce from the plains north of the range to the harbour at Albany, from where it would be shipped to lucrative markets in Asia. Another old sandalwood track, Red Gum Pass, is still in use today. Chester Pass, the main access through the range, was named after a local police constable, George Chester, who last century blazed a trail through the area to shorten his travelling time between Albany and the lands to the north.

Although little evidence of these early pioneers remains in the Stirlings, their activities did have some impact on the environment. The "grass trees" or "blackboys" (*Xanthorrhoea spp.*), for example, were more numerous until cleared by pastoralists, and brumbies, which were once yarded near the south-western end of the range, now run wild. Fortunately, however, plans to prospect for gold in the area during the 1850s did not come to fruition, otherwise some of the most beautiful peaks might now be disfigured. Instead, the entire mountain system was declared a reserve in 1913 and today forms the 115 700-hectare Stirling Range National Park. All flora and fauna are protected and disturbance to the precious natural environment is kept to a minimum. □

Carpeted with wildflowers . . .

1. Catspaw (*Anigozanthos humilis*)
2. Scarlet banksia (*Banksia coccinea*)
3. Trigger plants (*Stylidium sp.*)
4. A bright pink *Isopogon latifolius* shrub
5. Yellow mountain bell (*Darwinia collina*), unique to the summit of Bluff Knoll
6. Red pea (*Chorizema sp.*)
7. Tall white *Sphenotoma drachophylloides*

1. Seabed ripple patterns on the
summit of Mt Toolbrunup
2. Bluff Knoll
3. Showy dryandra (*Dryandra formosa*)

Nature's subterranean palaces

THE LEEUWIN-NATURALISTE CAVES

The Suspended Table, Lake Cave

OF ALL the wonders of nature, few are more opulent than the subterranean palaces of the Leeuwin-Naturaliste caves. Richly ornamented with glistening stalactites and stalagmites and graceful shawls, they also contain many unusual cave decorations, some of which are unequalled anywhere else in the world.

This beautiful underground complex is located on the 100-kilometre-long ridge which juts into the Indian Ocean between Cape Leeuwin and Cape Naturaliste in the south-western corner of Australia. There are more than 300 caves in the system, ranging from small sinkholes to huge chambers, and many of the caverns are linked by an intricate network of passages that has yet to be fully explored.

In geological terms the caves are very young, having developed in a belt of limestone which formed within the last 100 000 years on top of an ancient bed of granite. Sea levels were constantly changing at this time and it is thought that when the waters receded, sediments of sand, shell debris and marine organisms from the exposed sea floor were blown by onshore winds and deposited as dunes on the existing granite coastline. Over thousands of years the dunes slowly compacted and cemented into limestone hills. Later the coast subsided, leaving only a low ridge standing above the sea.

The long processes of erosion soon began to create the beautiful caves. Rivers and creeks forced down through the porous limestone until they reached the impermeable granite. Gradually these waters ate away at the limestone, carving the caverns and finding their way to the ocean where they emerged as coastal springs. In time the roofs and walls of many caverns collapsed, forming chambers of massive size.

At the same time, nature diligently began to decorate the caverns. Drop by drop, rainwater impregnated with minerals from the soil and limestone above has reached the underground openings (as a calcium bicarbonate solution) and there it has deposited tiny amounts of calcite which have slowly built up, being crafted with superb artistry into fantastic designs. Many of these adornments (called "speleothems") are clear white, but some are patterned by tonings of red and brown from iron oxides and other minerals in the water.

The most common cave decorations are the beautiful stalactites, hanging from the ceilings and the underside of ledges. The region is famed for its magnificent "straw" formations, which are extremely thin stalactites measuring only about 5 millimetres in diameter. They are hollow and very fragile, yet some grow several metres in length. The longest straws known in the world are found in the area, the most impressive being a 6.25-metre-long straw in Strong Cave and a 5.9-metre straw in Jewel Cave.

Helictites—fascinating formations about the thickness of straws, but twisting and turning in all directions—are particularly well developed in these caves. Defying gravity, they create delicate patterns reminiscent of blown glass. Many theories have been advanced to explain their growth, but as there is no conclusive explanation, their formation remains a mystery.

Other remarkable decorations include beautiful shawls and flowstone, thick columns, and glittering crystals which grow when the solution creating the speleothems becomes supersaturated with calcium carbonate.

European settlers first became aware of the presence of caves in this district in 1848, following the discovery by a man named J. or G. Turner of two caves just north of the small farming settlement at Augusta, near Cape Leeuwin. As more people moved into the district, further caverns were discovered and by 1892 more than 40 caves were known.

In 1899, a government-commissioned investigation into the tourist potential of the district reported so favourably that a Caves Board was specially set up in 1902 to develop and promote the area. Elaborate advertising campaigns were launched to attract tourists, not only from Western Australia but also from the eastern States and from overseas—a very ambitious project in those days, before the introduction of planes and cars.

The tour organised by the Caves Board operated on a coupon system which was something of a forerunner to today's "package tour". Those game enough to make the journey travelled by train from Perth to Busselton, then transferred to horseback for the remainder of the trip. Many visitors simply camped in the bush, but for those who preferred greater comfort, accommodation was provided in settlers' homes and at State-owned hotels.

At first, tours through the caves were fairly rudimentary, with visitors making their way along roughly defined tracks lit only by candles and dim kerosene lanterns. To point out a feature, the guide would light a magnesium flare which illuminated the cavern for a few seconds. However, the development of several caves proceeded very swiftly. In 1904 an electric lighting system was installed in Yallingup Cave and this was soon followed by the installation of further systems in several other caves. Ladders, stairways and platforms were also fitted to facilitate movement through the caverns.

By the time the Caves Board was disbanded in 1910, thirteen caves were open for tourists. They continued to be managed by the government and in 1914 were placed under the authority of the State Hotels Department. When that department closed in 1960, the caves were handed over to the Lands Department and they are now leased to private concerns which work in affiliation with the local tourist bureau.

Today only four caves are open to tourists: Yallingup Cave near Busselton, Lake Cave and Mammoth Cave near Margaret River, and Jewel Cave near Augusta.

Yallingup Cave has been open to tourists since 1900. The beautifully decorated main chamber is notable for its numerous shawls, ranging from small, daintily-folded white forma-

Australia's living fossils

THE SHARK BAY STROMATOLITES

2

I T IS HARD to imagine a living organism that is so old it doesn't fit into our everyday idea of plant and animal life. This is the marvel of stromatolites, remarkable rock-like structures which live in the intertidal and subtidal waters of Shark Bay in Western Australia. Part living, part fossil, they are remnants of one of the earliest forms of life to have appeared on Earth.

Ranging in height from a few millimetres to more than a metre, the stromatolites create a unique landscape. They vary in shape from simple domes and mushroom forms to complicated columns and cauliflower-like structures, and are usually very dark grey in colour.

Stromatolites are constructed by tiny marine algae which individually are not visible to the naked eye. These algae congregate in colonies called "mats", which trap and bind fine-grained sediments brought in by the tide. As the sediment gathered by each algal mat cements into limestone, a new mat forms above the old. Successive layers of mats build up, one on top of the other, in much the same manner as coral except that they have no skeletal structure. The name "stromatolite", derived from Greek and meaning "stony cushion", is appropriate for these formations because they are slightly spongy to touch.

The earliest evidence of stromatolites are fossils about 3500

1. Foam from an incoming tide swirls around a group of stromatolite domes, creating a misty effect during a twilight time-exposure
2. At low tide the domes are reflected in the still, clear waters

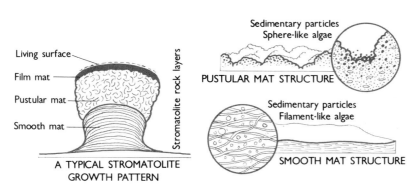

Living surface
Film mat
Pustular mat
Smooth mat
Stromatolite rock layers

A TYPICAL STROMATOLITE GROWTH PATTERN

Sedimentary particles
Sphere-like algae
PUSTULAR MAT STRUCTURE

Sedimentary particles
Filament-like algae
SMOOTH MAT STRUCTURE

Shark Bay

million years old found in the Pilbara district of Western Australia. Other finds in Rhodesia and South Africa, dated at around 3000 million years, are also thought to be stromatolites. They are very common in rocks formed before about 500 million years ago, but from then until the present they have occurred less frequently, probably because of the evolution of grazing organisms, particularly gastropods (molluscs). Today there are only a few places in the world where they are still growing and those at Shark Bay are the most spectacular.

As stromatolitic algae are photosynthetic, requiring light in order to grow, they are active only in shallow waters in which light can penetrate to the bottom. This factor and their need for suitable water currents seem to be the dominant forces in stromatolite growth. All known living stromatolites are restricted to high temperature environments (for example, the hot springs of Yellowstone National Park) or to high salinity environments (such as Shark Bay) where the algae can survive but where grazing by small animals is prevented, or diminished to such a degree that the growth rate of the algae is greater than the rate of consumption. They could conceivably grow in other environments where these conditions are met.

The growth rate of stromatolites is very slow, not exceeding 2 millimetres per year. However, new mats can form on sterile surfaces in as little as 12 hours. The stromatolites at Shark Bay are both the largest and the most diverse living examples in the world. They began to grow about 4500 years ago, when the waters around the area started to become very saline. This was caused by the growth of a seagrass bank across the bay's northern extremity, which limited tidal exchange with the ocean. Today the bank is emerged at low tide and forms a basin known as Hamelin Pool, which has almost permanent waters. As the area has a high evaporation rate, the salinity of the water in Hamelin Pool has become very concentrated: normal sea water has a salinity rate of 35 parts dissolved solids per litre, while the basin waters are currently at 60-65 parts dissolved solids per litre—nearly twice the salinity of normal oceanic waters and a perfect environment for the mats to flourish.

The algae forming the mats are simple organisms, but their requirements for building stromatolites are relatively complex. There are seven types of algal mat: colloform, smooth, pustular, tufted, gelatinous, film and blister. All types are represented at Shark Bay, the most populous being smooth and pustular.

The various mat types are composed of different types of algae and have different building habits, although all conform to the layering system. Each type prefers a particular position in the intertidal or subtidal zones and each has its own style of "fabric-making", requiring differing amounts of sediment.

In smooth mat, for example, the algae are tiny hair-like filaments, mainly *Schizothrix calcicola*, about 10 microns in size (one micron equals one-thousandth of a millimetre), which gather in a smooth layer about a millimetre thick. The mat permeates sedimentary particles brought in by the tide, creating a meshwork of filaments and sediments rather like a carpet. As the filaments are coated with mucilage sheaths, the mat at first has a gelatinous consistency, but then a cement of lime carbonate is precipitated and encases the sediments, finally hardening into solid rock. The algae, however, are motile, so as soon as more sediment is brought in they move up to form another layer and the whole process is repeated.

Pustular mat, on the other hand, is formed by tiny sphere-like algae, mainly *Entophysalis deusta*, which congregate in a rough surface of jelly-like pustules, each about 3 centimetres in diameter and 2 centimetres thick. The sediments brought in by the tide are trapped in the depressions between the pustules. The cementing process is less coherent than in smooth mat and voids (enclosed hollows) form in the resulting rock.

The variation in appearance between stromatolites is due not only to the different types of mat but also to the fact that the mats are intergradational. In other words, a stromatolite that starts out with one type of mat composition may later change to another type, and later to yet another or back to the original mat type.

The smooth mat type, for example, tends to occupy a lower position in the intertidal zone than the pustular mat. A structure, then, which starts with a smooth mat eventually grows to a higher level, where pustular mat may take over, and later when it reaches an even higher level, film mat, say, may continue to build the structure.

Alternatively, the mat type may oscillate according to the speed at which sediment is being gathered. Smooth mat, for example, which builds the biggest structures, likes a good supply of sediment whereas pustular mat does not like too much sediment. So while sediment is being brought in rapidly, smooth mat thrives, but in places where sediment is temporarily not being supplied it may give way to pustular mat. Then when the sediment starts coming in at too fast a rate for pustular mat to cope, smooth mat may take over again, and so on.

As stromatolites are known to have lived just 1000 million years after it is thought the Earth was formed, they are extremely important to scientists studying the origins of our planet. Since the algae can survive only in shallow waters near the coast or in lakes, the presence of fossil stromatolites enables accuracy in delineating ancient shorelines. Living stromatolites, however, have more far-reaching significance, and scientists have come from all over the world to study the Shark Bay community. Usually, in studying ancient rocks one has only the final products and it is necessary to reconstruct the processes that were involved in their formation. Here it is possible not only to see the structures being formed but to observe and even measure the processes as they occur. Such knowledge will lead to a much better understanding of rocks and the prehistory of our planet. □

A labyrinth of gorges

THE HAMERSLEY RANGE

SINCE the Western Australian mining boom of the 1960s, the Hamersley Range has gained recognition both as one of the largest iron ore provinces in the world and as a major economic resource of Australia. To nature lovers, however, the region's great wealth lies in the beauty of its many magnificent gorges.

There are more than 20 major gorges in the Hamersley, ranging from wide clefts with terraced cliffs to narrow gashes with sheer walls plunging down more than 100 metres. They vary greatly in length, some being only a few hundred metres long, while others continue for many kilometres. Tranquil, icy-cold pools lie at the base of most gorges, their green colour highlighting the spectacular banded walls of rich red, brown and bluish-black rock.

The variety of the gorges in the Hamersley is remarkable, with each having its own special character and appeal.

Dales Gorge, which is accessible for only a small part of its total 40 kilometres or more length, is garden-like and set between tall, red, terraced cliffs sculptured by differential erosion of the rocks. At its base are deep pools lined by waterlilies and feathery reeds. A variety of plants grow in profusion on the banks, while lonely ghost gums (*Eucalyptus papuana*) stand like sentinels on the cliff ledges and the low scree slopes. A beautiful waterfall, Fortescue Falls, sprays down into this gorge, and at various places along the floor there are frilled patches of asbestos seams which have been teased out by pebble-laden floodwaters so that they shine like silver lacework.

Weano Gorge, on the other hand, is short, narrow and totally barren. The lower parts of the vertical walls have been deeply sculptured by torrents of water which pass through the gorge in times of rain. High up on the cliff walls the sunlight illuminates the rocks in brilliant streaks of fiery reds, golden yellows and glowing orange-browns, but in the deep shadow at the bottom of the gorge the rocks take on wonderfully purple colours, graduating to indigo and very dark reddish-grey. In the filtered light, the shadowy hues contrast dramatically with the jade green of a crystal clear pool.

Other fascinating gorges in the region include the wide Hamersley Gorge with its folded ribbons of colourful rock, the deep and narrow Red Gorge with its fantastic vertical cliffs and pretty pool, broad and sandy Yampire Gorge with prominent bluish stripes of asbestos, and narrow Joffre Gorge where, when there is sufficient water, the beautiful Joffre Falls cascade over a rounded, sheer cliff.

These gorges, most of which are entered by climbing down into them rather than walking in from the mouth, are the most awe-inspiring of all Australian gorges. At one particularly impressive point, four of the narrowest crevice-like gorges—Red, Joffre, Hancock and Weano—meet, forming a sheer-walled, gaping hole several hundred metres deep.

The Hamersley Range is part of a large tableland lying between the Ashburton and Fortescue rivers in Western Australia's Pilbara region. Trending north-west to south-east, it is more than 320 kilometres long, and is the highest and most extensive upland region of the State, culminating in Mt Meharry (1250 metres) and Mt Bruce (1227 metres).

Both the northern and southern limits of the range are marked by long, prominent escarpments towering up to 300 metres above the adjoining lower land. The northern Hamersley Scarp is much indented, and as most of the rivers draining the Hamersley flow northward, the section of the range beyond the scarp has been deeply dissected and contains the region's major gorges. The southern scarp forms an almost unbroken wall and for most of its length is steeper than the northern one.

The climate in the Hamersley is very hot and usually dry, with an average rainfall of about 300 millimetres. Most of the rain falls in summer and is brought by tropical thunderstorms and cyclones. During these torrential downpours, the rivers are prone to heavy flooding. However, as the evaporation rate is extremely high, the water levels soon recede and for most of the year the only surface water is found in isolated pools.

The most common rocks of the range are conglomerates, quartzites and shales, with thick layers of iron ore and seams of blue asbestos. They were deposited 1800-2400 million years ago in a large sea, and later uplifted and warped by earth movements. A long period of erosion followed, during which time a mature plateau was formed. Then a further uplifting rejuvenated the drainage, causing rivers and streams to gouge through joints, faults and other weak sections of rock, thus forming the superb gorges of the present landscape.

Today the surface of the Hamersley Range is basically broad and flat, relieved only by low residual ridges and hummocky hills. The terrain is very dry and rocky, with a thin covering of hardy grasses, trees and shrubs. Golden-yellow tussocks of spinifex (*Triodia spp.* and *Plectrachne spp.*) are dominant on the ridges and hills, but on the thicker soil of the lower areas there is also a considerable amount of mulga (*Acacia aneura*) and various eucalypt trees. After the summer rains, numerous wildflowers including the scarlet Sturt's desert pea (*Clianthus formosus*) and the pink parakeelya (*Calandrinia polyandra*) transform the landscape into a sheet of vivid colour.

In contrast with the top of the range, many of the cool and sheltered gorges support luxuriant vegetation. Graceful river red gums (*Eucalyptus camaldulensis*), coolibahs (*Eucalyptus microtheca*) and cadjeputs (*Melaleuca leucadendra*) line the watercourses, lush green ferns grow in shady recesses, and a variety of reeds and other water plants thrive around the cool, permanent pools. These protected environments are a haven for abundant species of birds, reptiles and marsupials. An unusual predator of the smaller animals, the ash-grey and white ghost bat (*Macroderma gigas*), also lives in caves and shelters in the cliff faces.

The Hamersley Range has been known to the white man for

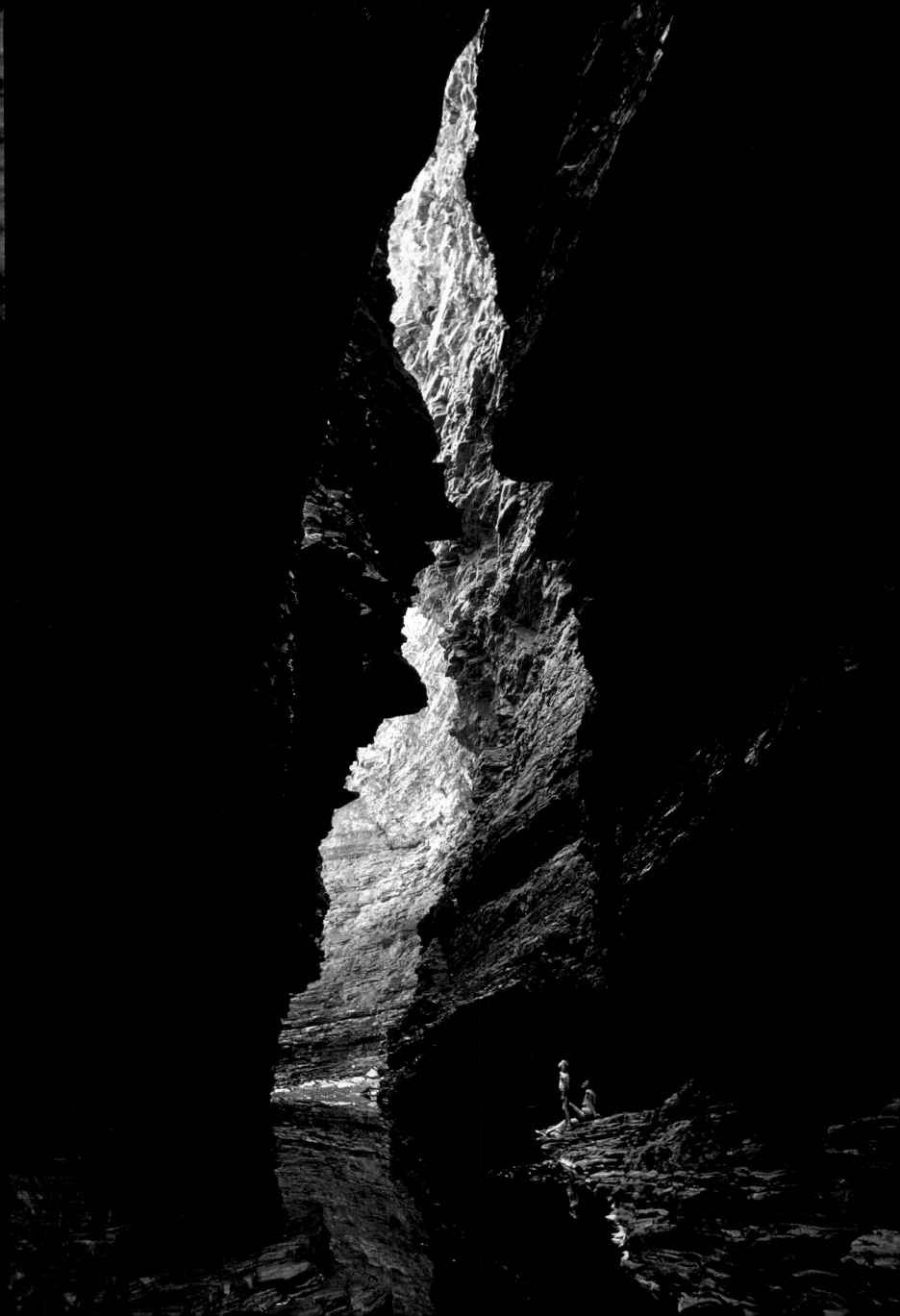

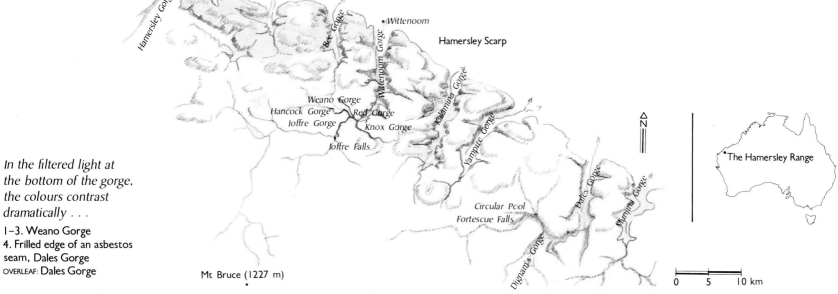

Hamersley Gorge
Bee Gorge
Wittenoom Gorge
•Wittenoom
Hamersley Scarp
Weano Gorge
Hancock Gorge
Joffre Gorge
Red Gorge
Knox Gorge
Kalamina Gorge
Joffre Falls
Yampire Gorge
Dales Gorge
Munjina Gorge
Circular Pool
Fortescue Falls
Dignam's Gorge
N
Mt Bruce (1227 m)
0 5 10 km

The Hamersley Range

In the filtered light at the bottom of the gorge, the colours contrast dramatically . . .

1–3. Weano Gorge
4. Frilled edge of an asbestos seam, Dales Gorge
OVERLEAF: Dales Gorge

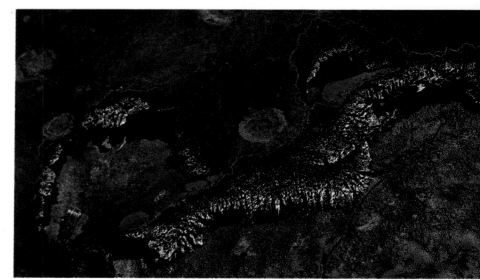

4

120 years, having been discovered in June 1861 by Frank Gregory, who, with a grant of £2000 from the British government, did much valuable exploratory work in Australia's north-west. He named the range in honour of Edward Hamersley, whom he described as "one of the most liberal promoters of the expedition".

Gregory did not traverse the tableland, but his discovery of the range and the surrounding river flats of the Ashburton, Fortescue, De Grey and Oakover rivers soon led to the opening of more than a million hectares of rich grazing land. Within a few years, enterprising pastoralists moved in with cattle and sheep, heralding the birth of agricultural industries which were to remain the economic mainstays of the region until the mining boom of the 1960s.

As convict labour was not allowed in this region of Western Australia, many of the pastoralists soon recruited local Aboriginal people. The relationships between black and white were at times reasonably harmonious, but there were also frequent poisonings and violent massacres. Eventually the Aborigines became dependent on the European lifestyle and, sadly, in the transition to white society their ritual knowledge was lost.

The first mining venture in the Hamersley was for asbestos —not the common white *chrysotile* type, but a long-fibred blue *crocidolite* variety.

A partner in the nearby Mulga Downs Station, Lang Hancock, began mining the asbestos in Yampire Gorge in 1937, but the following year transferred his operation to Wittenoom Gorge. He continued to mine there until 1943, when the business was taken over by the Colonial Sugar Refining company through its newly created subsidiary, Australian Blue Asbestos Pty Limited. Mining of the asbestos continued at a steady pace for the next few years and in 1947 building commenced on the township of Wittenoom, erected at the mouth of the gorge to provide housing and facilities for the mine workers and their families. By the 1960s, however, substantial financial losses were being experienced and in December 1966 the mine was closed. (In recent years, blue asbestos has been found to be highly dangerous and its mining is now banned.)

The closing of the asbestos mine may have seen the end of the Hamersley as a mining centre, had it not been for the discovery of the enormous deposits of iron ore in the Mt Tom Price and Mt Newman areas. Lang Hancock, in particular, was instrumental in turning the region into one of the world's biggest iron ore mining provinces.

While the miners were making their advances, others were concentrating efforts on promoting the Hamersley as a scenic attraction. In particular, a local doctor, Gordon Oxer (after whom a lookout is now named), erected numerous signposts and published the earliest tourist brochure and road map of the area.

Many of the gorges in the Hamersley were discovered and named by Dr Oxer and other local residents, and the nomencla-

ture reveals a special character of its own. Some of the gorges are named after the mining companies that work them, others after famous people, but many are named after the locals themselves.

Two of the early partners in Mulga Downs Station, Frank Wittenoom and George Hancock (father of Lang), have their names immortalised in the Wittenoom and Hancock gorges. Weano Gorge carries the name of an Aboriginal employee of Mulga Downs Station who showed his white bosses the blue asbestos in Yampire Gorge, while Dales Gorge is named after a well-sinker who worked on Mulga Downs Station. Yampire, Munjina and Kalamina gorges are probably all Aboriginal names. Red Gorge is simply descriptive of the rock colour.

The formidable Joffre Gorge was at one time named Bismarck Gorge after the nineteenth-century "Iron Chancellor" of Germany, Otto von Bismarck, but the name was changed towards the end of World War I to Joffre Creek after the Allied Commander-in-Chief on the Western Front. Curiously, the name "Bismark" (without the "c") was transferred to another gorge.

Hamersley Gorge has also had a name change. Originally called Rocky Gorge, its present name probably comes from the Hamersley Iron mining company working the Mt Tom Price deposit, although it may be derived from the name of the range or from the nearby Hamersley Station. Other gorges named after companies are Rio Tinto, after the Conzinc Riotinto company with mining interests at Mt Tom Price, and Colonial Gorge, after the Colonial Sugar Refining company. The origin of the names of the remaining gorges is either unknown or uncertain.

In October 1969 an area of 590 206 hectares of the Hamersley Range, including some of the main gorges, was set aside as the Hamersley Range National Park. Encompassing a variety of habitats and most of the finest scenery in the range, it is a vitally important conservation sanctuary. □

. . . *Dry and rocky, with hardy grasses, trees and shrubs*

1. A flood-scarred river red gum (*Eucalyptus camaldulensis*), Yampire Gorge
2. A small weeping mulla mulla shrub (*Ptilotus sp.*), northern Hamersleys
3. After surviving for decades on the side of a huge boulder in Dales Gorge,
a fig tree (*Ficus sp.*) finally surrenders to a 5-year drought
4. A showy mulla mulla shrub (*Ptilotus sp.*), northern Hamersleys

1

2

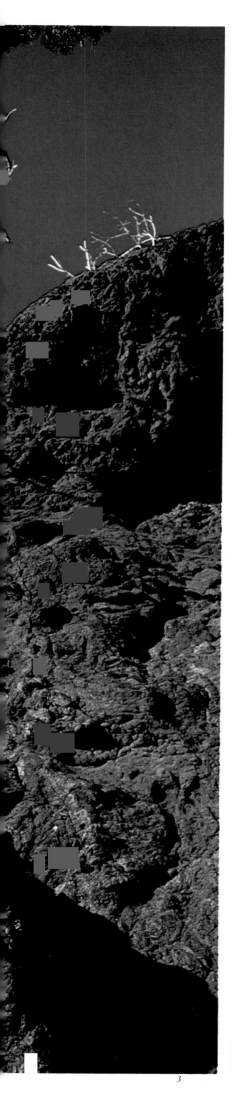

3

4

There is a simple beauty and serenity
about this land . . .

1. Pyramid Hill
2. View south-west from Pyramid Hill
3. Volcanic rock piles, Chichester Range

World of difference

THE KIMBERLEYS

AN ANCIENT barrier reef now raised above the sea, awesome tidal waterfalls rushing furiously between towering cliffs, and a hidden tunnel running right through a mountain range: these are just some of many remarkable natural landforms in the wild Kimberley region of Western Australia.

Covering an area twice the size of Victoria and three times bigger than England, the Kimberley is a fascinating world of its own. Officially called the Kimberley Range, its character is better reflected by the more popularly used plural form, "the Kimberleys". For here is not one mountain range, but an ancient plateau which has been worn down into a series of different ranges separated by deep valleys and wide plains. It is a land of magnificent vistas, where huge rocky ridges and rugged tree-covered slopes are interspersed with sprawling savannah grasslands and fertile river flats. But it is also a land

liberally embellished with beautiful, intimate landscapes—secluded gorges, countless enchanting waterfalls, and a variety of strange and differing rock formations which bear witness to a long and varied past.

Indeed, the Kimberley plateau is one of Earth's most ancient land surfaces. It rose above the sea 1800-2400 million years ago and has never since been submerged. When surrounding landmasses were inundated by water, the Kimberley stood firm. About 600 million years ago it was an island and at several times it has been a peninsula, being bordered some 350 million years ago by a barrier reef which would have rivalled, in both beauty and size, the famous reef along the Queensland coast today. Aeons ago there were periods of glacial and volcanic activity in the Kimberleys, faulting and folding, but for the most part the land has been extremely stable. The last

Boabs (*Adansonia gregorii*), near Derby

major earth movement occurred 3-7 million years ago, when the area was uplifted and tilted to the north-west. This upheaval rejuvenated the rivers and in the millennia that followed they carved with new vigour along lines of weakness to form deep gorges and valleys. Then about 20 000 years ago the melting of the polar ice caps caused a world-wide rise in sea level, which in the Kimberleys drowned the coastal plains and valleys, creating a heavily serrated coastline with numerous inlets and sheer cliffs towering as much as 200 metres above the sea.

The present topography of the Kimberleys is basically a large dome-shaped upland core bounded to the east and south by the lowland arcs of the Ord and Fitzroy rivers. The region is not very high—the tallest peak, Mt Ord in the King Leopold Range, reaches only 936 metres above sea level—but the terrain is extremely rugged. Throughout the region there are gigantic rocky barriers, mostly sandstone but with substantial areas of granite, basalt and metamorphic rocks.

As the Kimberleys lie within the tropics, they are governed by a monsoonal climate of distinct Wet and Dry seasons which bring dramatic changes of mood to the landscape. In the Wet summer months from December to April, torrential rains thunder down, flooding the land and making access to vast areas virtually impossible. Swollen rivers pour furiously towards the sea and cyclones race across the land. The levels of the Ord and Fitzroy rivers, in particular, rise by many metres, making them Western Australia's largest volume-carrying rivers. Yet despite the severity of the Wet, it is a rejuvenating time. When the waters begin to recede, the land takes on a lush tropical softness, with new green growth and fresh streams and waterfalls. By May the rains stop, and the Dry of winter sets in. The muddy ground soon bakes hard in the warm sun and rivers gradually shrink, forming series of placid waterholes. Trees slowly lose their fresh mantle of green and grasses turn tinder yellow. A peace comes over the land . . . but with it comes an arid harshness which by October will beckon the coming Wet.

The climate and the resistant rocky terrain have enabled only very thin soils to develop over much of the Kimberleys. Some of the plains carry deeper red and black clay soils, but good alluvial lands are restricted to river flats and estuaries. These limitations of the soil, together with the fact that the vegetation must be able to cope with both flood and drought, has led to the evolution of many highly specialised plants, some of them unique to the Kimberleys.

The most distinctive tree is the lovely boab, or baobab (*Adansonia gregorii*), which grows in great numbers all over the region but is not found anywhere else. Its gleaming silvery-grey trunk varies in shape from a long bottle with a tapered neck to a bulbous carafe or flagon, giving rise to the common name "bottle tree". (It is not related, however, to the *Brachychiton* bottle trees of Queensland, although it does have related

Wandjina painting, Galvan's Gorge

species in Africa, India and Madagascar.) Other unique trees in the Kimberleys are less easily identifiable and include a bloodwood (*Eucalyptus collina*) and several species of hibiscus, acacia and pandanus.

A wide variety of sharp and prickly grasses are conspicuous throughout the region, including species of spinifex, Mitchell grass, Flinders grass, kangaroo grass and spear grass. The shorter of these grass types tend to dominate the western part of the Kimberleys, while the tall species favour the eastern sector. Intriguingly, hidden among these wild grasses are numerous tiny, exquisite wildflowers of intricate shapes and colourings.

Animal life in the Kimberleys is abundant, though it is relatively inconspicuous because of the great size and ruggedness of the region. Termite mounds dot the landscape and birds, especially flocks of white sulphur-crested cockatoos (*Cacatua galerita*), are often seen in flight overhead. Insects, too, are prolific, with some, such as grasshoppers and locusts, reaching plague proportions. A great variety of small lizards with beautiful colourings are found in rocky areas, but snakes, although

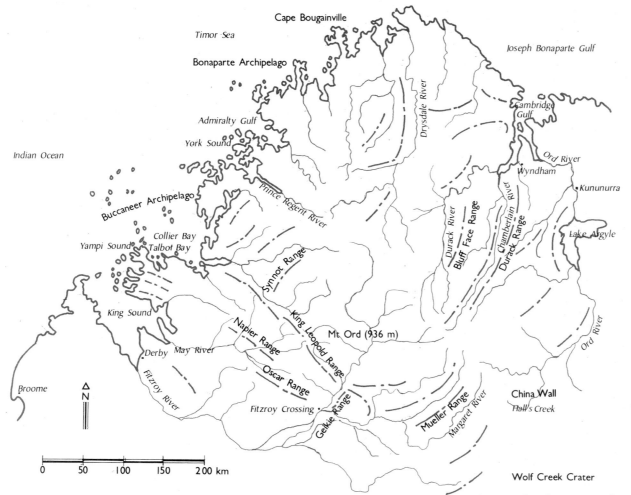

present, are seldom seen. Most of the marsupials inhabiting the region are nocturnal, and generally only euros (*Macropus robustus*) and wallabies, notably the agile wallaby (*Macropus agilis*), show themselves by day. More commonly seen are introduced animals—cattle, donkeys, buffaloes and feral cats —and occasional dingoes.

The gorges, with their permanent waters, are important refuges for many of these species and they also support numerous other animals which could not otherwise survive in the Kimberleys. Tiny frogs with camouflage colourings, tortoises, and waterbirds such as ibis, herons and cormorants crowd many of the waterways. The cool waters of larger gorges provide a home for several fascinating species of fish, which over millions of years have adapted from a marine or estuarine existence to a freshwater one. Stingrays, sharks, sawfish and strange little freshwater prawns called cherrabuns (*Cherax sp.*) are the most notable of these creatures. Another interesting fish is the silver archer fish (*Toxotes oligolepis*), which sprays a jet of water to catch insects from the foliage above. The freshwater Johnston crocodile (*Crocodylus johnstoni*), which is harmless to man, is also common in the large gorges, while the man-eating saltwater crocodile (*Crocodylus porosus*) lives in the estuaries and other coastal areas.

The Kimberley was one of the last major areas of Australia to be infiltrated by European settlers. However, the climate and the environment always proved to be such obstacles to their endeavours that even today a large part of this vast, rugged region is remote and untouched.

But while the land remains much as it always was, the white man's impact on the widespread groups of Aborigines who inhabited the Kimberleys has been devastating. For centuries these traditional owners of the land had traded peacefully with fishermen and other visitors from Asia. They regarded Europeans as the worst of beings, who killed and injured people, and they fought hard to prevent the invasion of their land. But their spears were no match for the white man's gun and today many of the tribes are extinct. The descendants of other tribes live mainly in the few scattered towns and Aboriginal settlements which dot the edges of the region, their cultural identity all but lost.

A map by Coronelli of Venice, dated 1618, gives the first indication of European knowledge, or summation, of the existence of the Kimberleys as a distinct region. Showing the coastline reasonably accurately, it calls the area *Terra de Concordia* —"land of peace and harmony". The earliest navigators known to have seen the coast, however, had a less favourable impression, and two centuries were to pass before any European showed a liking for the place.

The first of the known European visitors to the region was the Dutchman Abel Tasman, who in 1644 sailed along the entire Kimberley coast with a fleet of three tiny boats, looking for trade or for riches such as the Spanish had found in the Americas. Instead, he found only a treacherous coastline with huge tides and rips and countless hidden reefs. The failure of his mission discouraged further Dutch interest in the continent and more than 40 years elapsed before another European ventured to the Kimberley shores.

This next visitor was the British buccaneer William Dampier, who arrived at King Sound in 1688 aboard the privateer *Cygnet*, commanded by Captain John Read. On his return to England, Dampier wrote a book called *A New Voyage Around the World*, which became one of the most popular adventure stories of its day. Although his comments about New Holland (as Australia was still called) were disparaging, his knowledge so impressed the British Admiralty that they gave him command of HMS *Roebuck* and sent him to investigate New Holland further. In 1699 Dampier anchored at the southernmost part of the Kimberley coast, which he named Roebuck Bay, but he saw nothing to change his unfavourable opinion of the country.

Not until some years after the establishment of the British penal colony at Sydney Cove on the continent's east coast in 1788 did Europeans show any further interest in the Kimberley region. The scattering of French names on the coast date from 1801 when Nicolas Baudin, in the *Geographe*, conducted a cartographic exploration of the area. He was followed by Phillip Parker King, who in the cutter *Mermaid* charted many sections of the Australian coastline in 1818-21, finishing the detailed English mapping of the continent which had been started nearly 20 years before by Matthew Flinders. King discovered Cambridge Gulf in May 1819 and, thinking it must end in a river, he sailed up to the point where the town of Wyndham now stands. Finding only mud flats, poor soils and undrinkable water, he did not pursue his search and thereby missed dis-

1. Rugged plateau country,
north-eastern Kimberleys
2. Tiered waterfalls on the Mitchell
River in the north-western Kimberleys,
during the Dry season

covering several big rivers, including the Ord, which empty into the sea near there. He was, however, impressed by the natural beauty of other parts of the coastline, especially the Prince Regent River area which he discovered in 1821.

Up until this time European knowledge of the Kimberleys was confined to the coastline. Then, in January 1838, the 25-year-old George Grey anchored his schooner *Lynher* in Hanover Bay, just south of the Prince Regent River, and set out to explore the hinterland. It was the rainy season, and travel was difficult for both horses and men, but nonetheless Grey was enthusiastic about "... the wild beauty of the scenery, which was as lovely and picturesque as impetuous torrents, foaming cascades, lofty rocks and a rich tropical vegetation could render." Despite encounters with hostile Aborigines, during one of which Grey was speared, he persevered with his exploration and made several important discoveries including the Glenelg River and the first examples of the elegant *Wandjina* rock paintings of mouthless figures in large head-dresses, which have since become among the most famous Aboriginal works of art. Overall, Grey reported favourably on the region, especially on the apparent richness of the land.

The first attempts at settlement in the Kimberleys region were made in the mid-1860s by sheepmen hoping to establish pastoral empires around Roebuck Bay and in the areas found by Grey. But the oppressive climate, attacks by Aborigines, and heavy stock losses due to the unsuitability of native grasses, led to the abandonment of their activities.

This failure, however, did not deter the explorer Alexander Forrest. In 1879 he undertook to explore the Kimberleys from the south. Unable to pass the King Leopold Range, he turned east and followed the Margaret River to the Ord country, discovering the excellent grazing lands of the Fitzroy plains. It was Forrest who recommended that the region be named the Kimberley Range, after the British Colonial Secretary, the Earl of Kimberley.

Forrest's glowing report was somewhat over-optimistic concerning the amount of pastoral country available, but it came at a time when there was a hunger for land, especially in eastern Australia. As a result, the 1880s saw the epic overland cattle drives of people such as the Duracks, Emanuels, Buchanans and MacDonalds who set out from Queensland and New South Wales and settled in the Ord region. And while the cattlemen claimed the eastern Kimberleys, sheepmen from the south-west of Western Australia brought their stock by ship and settled in the western Kimberleys. Within the decade the townships of Broome, Derby, Wyndham and Hall's Creek had sprung up, shortly to be joined by Fitzroy Crossing which was originally administered from Derby. Although these towns are now all centres serving the beef cattle industry—which since the earliest days has been the economic mainstay of the region —they were not all founded on beef.

Broome's fortune was earned from pearls, which had been

taken from the north-western coast since the late 1860s. In its heyday the town boasted a multicultural population of 5500 people (Japanese, Chinese, Malays, Filipinos and others) and had a pearling fleet of more than 400 luggers. It was a wild town, with such entertainments as opium dens, fan-tan gambling parlours and brothels to cater for the divers on their annual lay-up.

Mother-of-pearl shell, used principally for making buttons and ornaments, was the mainstay of the pearling industry and for a time Australia supplied 80 per cent of the world's requirements. Buyers from all over the world also came to Broome to purchase the fabulous natural pearls found in these northern waters. Australia's largest pearl, the drop-shaped "Star of the West" which weighed 6.48 grams, and the unique "Southern Cross", a pearl-compound formation with nine pearls forming the shape of a crucifix, were both found near Broome. But by World War II a decline of the pearling beds in shallow waters, together with the withdrawal of the Japanese divers and a prohibition on the export of pearlshell, brought the industry almost to a standstill. It picked up again after the war, but the increased use of plastics in the manufacture of buttons in the 1950s caused it to slowly decline again. Today cultured pearls, not shell, are the basis of pearling in the Kimberleys. The main centre of activities is a thriving pearl farm at remote Kuri Bay, further north.

On the other side of the Kimberleys, Hall's Creek also began as a boom town, but here the prize was gold. The likelihood of this mineral existing in payable quantities had been suggested by several people since the beginning of the 1880s, and in 1883 Charles Hall and Jack Slattery struck good alluvial deposits near the little creek that came to bear the former's name. By 1886 their discovery had sparked off Western Australia's first major goldrush and a shanty town with a population of about 3000 quickly sprang up. At the same time Wyndham was established as a port to service the goldfields. But the rush was short-lived and within five years the gold had petered out.

Since then, the Kimberleys have remained sparsely settled. The total population of the region today is around 15 000, about half of whom live in the towns. The beef cattle industry remains the mainstay of the region's economy, with meatworks operating from the ports of Wyndham, Derby and Broome.

In the 1960s the ambitious Ord River Scheme was mounted in an attempt to further utilise the area, especially for agriculture. This scheme was the first major effort to harness the Kimberleys' plentiful summer rains for irrigation, flood mitigation and, eventually, the generation of hydro-electricity. Two huge dams were constructed: one holding back the main reservoir, Lake Argyle, which covers more than 700 square kilometres and in terms of area is Australia's largest lake, and the other creating a diversion reservoir, Lake Kununurra (an Aboriginal word meaning "big waters"). The settlement built at Kununurra to service the scheme became the only new town

to be established in the Kimberleys this century.

The first farms dependent on the Ord Scheme were taken up in 1970-2 on the Packsaddle Plains near Kununurra. Crops grown have included cotton, rice, sorghum, peanuts, safflower and kenaf (a maize-like plant used for the production of bags and paper pulp). However insect plagues, transport and other problems have been found to be insurmountable, and the scheme has yet to prove economically viable.

Despite the experiences at the Ord, the Kimberley is still regarded by many people as an area of potential economic wealth. Other activities in the region in recent years include the mining of bauxite, large-scale exploration for diamonds, and an increase in tourism.

Such exploitation could bring drastic changes to the Kimberleys and must be stringently controlled if the region is to be preserved as one of Earth's great wild places. To date man's intrusion has been limited, but only small areas around some of the major scenic attractions and a larger area around the Drysdale River are protected as national parks.

The Tidal Waterfalls

The Kimberley coastline is a panorama of sheer sandstone cliffs and basalt promontories, indented by many deep inlets and bays. Offshore are beautiful coral reefs and countless tiny islands, some totally barren, others supporting low vegetation and abundant animal and bird life.

But for man the beauty of this coastline is tempered by gigantic tides which fluctuate up to 10 metres. The biggest tides in Australia, they swirl furiously around the many islands and reefs, and around hundreds of pinnacle rocks that lie hidden beneath the surface of the water.

As this maze of land, reef and water is largely unsurveyed, it is easily one of the most treacherous coastlines in the world. It is unlit and unsounded, making navigation extremely hazardous, especially in the monsoon season when cyclonic storms may suddenly hit. As a result, almost the entire coast is uninhabited and seldom visited by man.

Guarded by the forces of nature, this great coastline harbours some of Earth's least-known spectacular scenery—wild rivers, fantastically sculptured cliffs, and, most remarkable of all, tidal "waterfalls". They are not waterfalls in the normal sense of the word, but strong currents rushing through narrow coastal gorges at such incredible speeds that they look like waterfalls flowing horizontally.

There are several of these waterfalls along the Kimberley coast, but at Talbot Bay, north of King Sound, the phenomenon occurs on an especially grand scale. Here there is an almost landlocked inlet whose only entrance is a long and narrow gorge leading to a small drowned valley, which in turn breaks into another, even narrower gorge leading to a second drowned valley. The narrowness of both gorges restricts the amount of

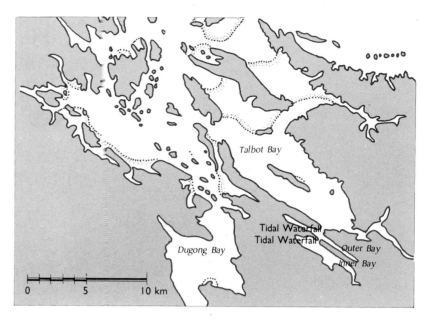

1. Ebb tide in the inner gorge, Tidal
Waterfalls
2. Aerial view from Talbot Bay towards
the inner gorge
3. The inner drowned valley
4. The inner gorge

Talbot Bay

Tidal Waterfall
Tidal Waterfall

Dugong Bay

Outer Bay
Inner Bay

0   5   10 km

water able to pass through, thus creating differences of up to a metre in the water levels between the open bay and the first valley, and of up to 2 metres between the first valley and the second valley. Consequently this forms not one, but two fierce tidal waterfalls.

The sheer cliffs of both gorges are composed of a very hard, yellowy-white sandstone and are about 30 metres high. The outer gorge has a wide entrance section and then tapers in to a narrow, 70-metre-long gap, where the first waterfall forms.

But the most impressive waterfall is in the 100-metre-long inner gorge. The thunder of the torrent (which reaches a speed of perhaps 20 or 30 knots) continues for almost the full 24 hours of the day, with only a few minutes of relative calm between each tide change. About half an hour before the change it is possible to detect a slight dimming in the roar of the torrent, then 2-3 minutes before the change it drops to a gurgle. Finally, and lasting for only one minute, there is complete silence as the water slows to a halt. Then the water starts to run again in the other direction, very slowly at first, but gathering momentum quickly so that soon the gurgling can be heard again and the whole pattern is repeated in reverse.

During the few minutes of semi-stillness as the water slows to a halt, floating patterns of leaves and debris gather in the gorge and huge fish cruise alongside its walls, looking for food. Squadrons of pied and sooty oyster catchers (*Haematopus ostralegus* and *H. fuliginosus*) swoop through the gorge in tight formation, low over the water, and occasionally sharks wait on the other side for fish washed out with the new flow of the tide.

The depth of the water in this gorge is thought to be at least 20 metres below the low water mark. Local Aboriginal people recall that there was once a natural rock bridge joining the two cliffs. Exactly when it collapsed into the tumultuous waters below is not certain, but some of the older Aboriginal people think that it was about 70 years ago.

Although awesome, the outer gorge is less turbulent than the inner gorge. In fact, there are times when the inner gorge is still churning with white foaming water, while the outer one is completely flat and still. However, for most of the day both gorges are utterly unnavigable.

The two valleys of this remarkable inlet are extremely pretty, especially the inner one, where the pool is about a kilometre wide and five times as long. At the far ends of the valley, the land is fairly open and slopes gently, but elsewhere it is bordered by cliffs. The water is fringed with mangroves and spinifex, and various small stunted trees grow further back. The native yam (*Dioscorea spp.*) also grows in abundance. Animal life is varied: apart from many species of fish, there are turtles and other sea creatures, and numerous birds.

The water is not very deep and low tide reveals mud banks standing free from the shore. During an incoming flow of the tide, choppy waters are carried almost to the other side of the valley, like waves coming in to a beach. Near the gorge there are giant whirlpools and boiling mushrooms of foam.

The area of the tidal waterfalls is known to the Aboriginal people of the Kimberleys as *Wolbunum*. It was once inhabited by the now-extinct Meda tribe and was also visited by the Worora people who still live in the southern Kimberleys. In the past these people maintained cross-country tracks to the valleys, but they have long been overgrown.

Today the few visitors to the inlet usually see it only from a plane, although occasionally a boatman will risk travelling through the gorges during the short periods of tidal change. The landward journey to the region is now considered far more difficult than the treacherous seaward entry. Apart from the heat and a lack of fresh water, the terrain is harsh, precipitous and tangled with thorny creepers and vines.

Despite the difficulty of access, the Kimberley coast has the world's greatest physical potential for the harnessing of tidal power. Studies have been made at various places where tidal waterfalls form, including Talbot Bay, but the most suitable sites for such a scheme are considered to be further north at Walcott Inlet and Secure Bay. However, as there is no nearby market, a venture of this type would not be economically viable at present, and hopefully the wild and beautiful Kimberley coast will remain untouched.

An Ancient Barrier Reef

The Kimberley plateau is cradled by an ancient barrier reef which loops around the coast in a giant U-shape from Wyndham to Derby and then extends inland for some 300 kilometres. Regarded as one of the best-preserved fossil reefs in the world, it is visible in several places, principally in one long, narrow ridge called the Napier Range.

The reef developed some 350 million years ago, when a shallow sea bordered the western Kimberleys. In geological terms this time is called the Devonian Period and consequently the reef is usually referred to as the Devonian Barrier Reef. It was constructed by various lime-secreting and binding organisms, primarily calcareous algae, stromatoporoids (an ancient form of life, now extinct) and corals. As these organisms were able to keep pace with a slow subsidence that occurred in the area during Devonian times, they formed very thick platforms of limestone which rose more than 200 metres above the surrounding sea floor.

The Napier Range of today rises vertically, like a fortress wall, about 60 metres above the adjacent plain. Extending some 100 kilometres, its grey limestone rocks present a strange and shadowy outline against the clear sky. The contours of this ancient reef are much as they would have been when the sea was there and in many places they produce grotesquely picturesque landscapes. In one notable section east of Yammera

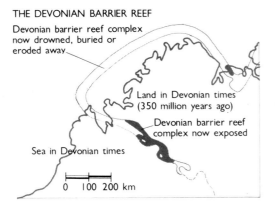

THE DEVONIAN BARRIER REEF

Devonian barrier reef complex
now drowned, buried or
eroded away

Land in Devonian times
(350 million years ago)

Devonian barrier reef
complex now exposed

Sea in Devonian times

0 100 200 km

*Strange dark spires
stand in great profusion . . .*

Napier Range

Gap, strange dark spires about 3-4 metres tall stand in great profusion on a plateau totally devoid of soils or vegetation. Ranging in colour from misty grey to charcoal black, they have a dull surface that shows no trace of glisten or shine. They are extremely sharp and very hard, and make a ringing sound when tapped with stone or metal. The only obvious inhabitants in this eerie environment are thousands of tiny black bees.

Elsewhere in the Napier Range rainwater and streams have hollowed out gorges and extensive cave systems.

Windjana Gorge

Windjana Gorge, which breaks into the Napier Range, is one of the prettiest gorges in the Kimberleys and also provides geologists with a classic cross-section for studying the ancient Devonian Barrier Reef. About 4 kilometres long and averaging 180 metres in width, it is framed by beautiful 60-metre-high orange cliffs. The upper sections of the cliffs are streaked with black rainwater marks and patterned by shadows where caves have developed, but their base is even more captivating, having been washed white and sculptured with tiny grottoes by the wild floodwaters of the Lennard River which rush through the gorge during the Wet season.

The deep riverbed is flanked on either side by a white sandbank that stretches right to the cliffs and in some places supports quite large eucalypts and tropical trees, most of them leaning gently. During the long months of the Dry, several permanent but very muddy pools maintain a home for Johnston crocodiles, freshwater sharks and several species of fish, and provide a watering place for numerous birds and ground animals.

Windjana (pronounced *Winj*-ana) is the name given to the gorge by the Unggumi and Bunaba people who frequented the area for countless generations. Although their music and laughter can no longer be heard, they have left many paintings of birds, animals and sacred *Wandjina* beings, and a number of burial niches high in the cliffs.

For a time many Europeans feared this lovely place and called it "Devil's Pass", because it was a main camp of the 1890s Aboriginal guerrilla leader, Pigeon (also known by his tribal name, *Sandamara*). A former police tracker, Pigeon was instrumental in mounting a fierce Aboriginal campaign to rid the western Kimberleys of the white man. With a band of about 50 warriors, he killed four Europeans and terrorised numerous others. Two of his major skirmishes were fought at Windjana Gorge, and it is here, also, that he had one of his safest hideouts —a cave high on the northern face of the gorge, near the entrance, which gave him a fine vantage point to watch for approaching police parties. However, because of his earlier allegiance to the white man, Pigeon had lost credibility with many Aborigines and on several occasions his own countrymen helped the police to avoid ambushes he had set.

Tunnel Creek

Tunnel Creek is a perfect storybook cave. With beautifully sculptured grey limestone walls and a sandy white floor, it forms an enchanting natural passage running straight through the Napier Range. From the northern entrance, which is partly hidden by huge boulders, it is possible to walk along the tunnel's entire 750-metre length, emerging on the southern side at a serene pool shaded by fig and pandanus trees.

Along most of its length the tunnel is about 15 metres wide, but the height of the ceiling varies between 3 and 12 metres. Several patches of thick dry stalactite formations hang from the higher sections and there are also a few faint remnants of Aboriginal paintings on the walls.

For the most part the tunnel is extremely dark, sometimes pitch black. However, about halfway along, the roof has collapsed, flooding the central section with light. On one side of the collapse the rocks form a sloping pile and it is possible to climb to the top of the range, but the rest of the wall is sheer. A curtain of hanging roots from native fig trees fringes the gaping hole, some of the larger ones having become plaited together to form giant wooden ropes which reach down many metres. In some seasons raucous fruit bats (or flying foxes), attracted by the fig trees, inhabit this part of the tunnel and hence it is often called the "Cave of Bats".

The stream that over aeons has created this beautiful tunnel is today full-flowing only during the Wet season, when flash floods may also occur. But even in the Dry there is always water. The permanent pools are fed by a cool, clean spring which continually runs into the tunnel through a wrist-sized hole in a side wall near the central cave-in.

Hidden within the wild mountain range, the tunnel has all the romantic charm needed to make it an ideal setting for an adventure story. But no fiction could surpass the real-life drama which was played out there.

In the 1890s Pigeon, the Aboriginal outlaw who had his main camp at Windjana Gorge, saw the advantages of hiding out in a secluded cave with three exit points. He lived at Tunnel Creek intermittently over a two-year period, safe from his white pursuers. But Pigeon, a former police tracker, had made a fatal mistake. When he turned his back on the law he took with him a young lubra, Calamvira, who had been promised to another man. The forsaken lover, Marawon, determined to have his revenge. In 1895 he tracked Pigeon to Windjana Gorge and informed the police. The ingenious Pigeon managed to escape, although Calamvira was caught. Not long after, however, Pigeon returned to Tunnel Creek, where he was again tracked by Marawon. This time he was unable to elude the police patrol that came to find him. There are several versions of the story about how he died, the most likely being that he was shot by an Aboriginal tracker during a running gun battle in Tunnel Creek, but survived for two days before being finished off by another tracker.

*. . . A cross-section of
an ancient barrier reef*

1. The Napier Range
2–4. Windjana Gorge

A perfect storybook cave . . .

1. The southern entrance, Tunnel Creek
2. The central cave-in, Tunnel Creek
3. A plaited fig-root hanging from the central cave-in
4. Pool at the southern end of Tunnel Creek

*Carved by the roaring
torrents of the Wet . . .*

Geikie Gorge during the Dry

Geikie Gorge

With beautiful cliffs, lush riverine vegetation and deep permanent waters, Geikie Gorge is one of the richest and most vibrant places in the Kimberleys. Whereas other parts of the region become yellowed and parched during the Dry season, Geikie remains green and fresh.

The gorge has been cut by the big Fitzroy River at the junction of the Oscar and Geikie ranges, both of which are remnants of the ancient Devonian Barrier Reef that once grew around the Kimberleys. Here, for about 6 kilometres, the river passes between 30-metre-high limestone cliffs, superbly patterned with three horizontal bands of colour. On the lower sections the floodwaters of centuries have washed the cliffs creamy-white, but at flood level they change abruptly to a wide band of red-stained rock, which then merges into a weathered upper strip of dark grey. Like a painted facsimile, these beauti-

ful colours are reflected with glimmering, mirror-like intensity in the still green waters below.

Throughout the gorge, the river is about 200 metres wide. The cliffs are not particularly high in comparison, but their grandeur is accentuated by prominent vertical jointing which gives them an exquisite sculptural appearance. The waters in the gorge rise up to 16.5 metres during the Wet season and they have deeply undercut the base of the cliffs, forming beautifully shaped clefts and grottoes, and exposing intricate patterns of shells and other marine organisms. In the Dry the tranquil waters lapping against the walls of these recesses make a soothing, hollow clapping sound, contrasting with the deafening roars of the wild torrents which create them.

The permanent waters do not always extend right to the cliff walls. In many areas they are separated by alluvial banks sup-

1. Water-sculptured grottoes, Geikie Gorge
2. Lennard Gorge, King Leopold Range
3. Folded rock strata, King Leopold Range
4. The China Wall

1

porting graceful river gums and dense stands of tropical trees such as cadjeputs, freshwater mangroves, native figs and occasional Leichhardt trees (*Nauclea coadnata*). Lovely pandanus palms with hanging green leaves also grow in patches along the gorge, giving brilliant colour relief to the stony backdrop of the cliffs. Of the smaller growth, the most prominent are a bright green passionfruit vine (*Passiflora foetida*) which spreads wildly over trees and shrubs, and a tall tropical reed (*Phragmites karka*) which grows in clumps by the edge of the water.

In the Wet, the high waters drown both the river and its vegetation, but in the Dry the area is crowded with wildlife. Commonly seen animals include marsupials, lizards, snakes, tortoises and the freshwater Johnston crocodile. The most prolific inhabitants of the gorge, however, are the countless bird species, especially waterbirds such as ibis, herons and cormorants.

An abundant food source, Geikie Gorge has always been an important place for the Aboriginal people of the Kimberleys. It was first seen by white men in 1883 when the government Surveyor-General, John Forrest (brother of Alexander, and later to become the first Premier of Western Australia) explored the area, accompanied by Edward Hardman, the government geologist. Hardman was so impressed by the beauty and structure of the cliffs that he named the gorge in honour of the famous British geologist, Sir Archibald Geikie.

King Leopold Range

"We found ourselves at the foot of a lofty perpendicular range, extending for an unknown distance," wrote the explorer Alexander Forrest in May 1879. "The scenery here was amazingly beautiful. It is impossible to describe the loveliness of the gorges, covered with a luxuriant growth of tall trees and a tangle of exquisitely-coloured creepers, with waterfalls and streams of crystal purity flowing down them. I felt as if I had found my way into an earthly paradise."

The King Leopold Range, named by Alexander Forrest in recognition of King Leopold II of Belgium's interest in exploration, is the most majestic mountain range in the Kimberleys. It extends 225 kilometres and includes the region's highest peaks, Mt Ord (936 metres) and Mt Broome (927 metres). Forming the southern border of the ancient Kimberley plateau, the Leopolds are flanked to the south only by the ridges of the Devonian Barrier Reef and the plains of the Fitzroy River. Directly to the north are numerous smaller ranges, which like the Leopolds are studded with idyllic oases such as Forrest describes.

Typical of these oases is Galvan's Gorge, in the nearby Phillips Range. Here a small, pretty rock pool at the foot of a tiered waterfall appears unexpectedly among rough, thick bushland which on one side grows right to the water's edge. On the other side, a semicircle of high red cliffs tapers down from the waterfall, finally giving way to overhanging pandanus, fig and eucalypt trees.

However, not all the gorges in this part of the Kimberleys are so delicate. Manning Gorge in the Packsaddle Range, for example, is jungle-like. Wide and winding, it has fairly low, sheer orange walls enclosing white sandbanks, lush vegetation and pools covered with waterlilies. In contrast, the dramatic Lennard Gorge in the Leopolds is a very deep and barren opening, like a sculptured stone corridor. Eerie and dark, it leans on a slight angle and is deeply undercut on one side.

Secluded, and accessible only via rough dirt roads and rudimentary walking tracks, these and the many other gorges in the Leopold region retain an almost magical, wild beauty which has been lost in many other parts of the continent. And equally impressive are the wide mountain panoramas of untouched stony hills and green valleys sprawling grandly, far into the distance.

China Wall

Looking for all the world like a man-made structure, the China Wall near Hall's Creek is a fantastic freak of nature. Formed 300 million years ago, it is one of the oldest exposed veins of quartz in Australia. It was originally precipitated into a fracture in ancient sandstone, but being more resilient it has resisted the forces of weathering while the softer sandstone has been eroded away. Today it projects above the ground, forming a natural white stone wall with a block-like appearance.

The quartz appears in several patches, winding over a distance of some tens of kilometres. The finest section stands above a picturesque creek, just 6 kilometres from the township of Hall's Creek. Opaque and brilliantly white against a red and green bush background, it resembles the remnants of a miniature Great Wall of China.

4

2

3

Wolf Creek Crater

Seen from the air, Wolf Creek Crater appears as an extraordinary scar on the smooth south-eastern Kimberleys landscape. One of the largest and most impressive landforms of its type in the world, it was created by the impact of a huge nickel-iron meteorite which plunged to Earth perhaps as much as 2 million years ago. It is renowned for its perfect circular shape and uneroded condition, and measures approximately 850 metres in diameter across the top of the crater rim and 107 metres deep, although the bottom 55 metres have been filled in with deposits of wind-blown sediments.

Approached from the ground, the crater appears at first as a long, low hill rising 30 metres above an otherwise flat and featureless plain. The spectacular circular symmetry cannot be seen until the top of the steep, rocky red rim is reached.

Composed of shattered angular blocks of very hard sandstone and quartzite, the rim is flat-topped, almost uniform, and lightly vegetated with tufts of spinifex. It descends abruptly to a flat gypsum floor, which is extremely porous and broken by numerous sinkholes. In the very centre of the floor there is a circular patch of fine greyish-white sand (almost like dust) which supports a variety of trees, but towards the walls of the crater the soil becomes increasingly coarse and is only sparsely covered by spinifex and occasional shrubs.

The meteoritic origins of the crater were not identified by geologists until the late 1940s, though the landform has been known to Europeans since the end of the last century. It takes its name from a small creek nearby.

At one stage it was suggested that the crater be utilised as a reservoir to service both local cattle stations and the Canning Stock Route which passes nearby. But its floor was found to be too porous to hold water, and today the crater still stands bold and intact. □

EPILOGUE

Laughing kookaburra (*Dacelo gigas*)

THROUGHOUT the world, the concept of the value of wilderness is gathering momentum. A growing number of people are becoming alarmed at the accelerated rate at which modern man, with technological know-how, is modifying and altering the land. For although our grand civilisations offer many advantages, they do not provide substitutes for the raw beauty and ecological balance that can be found in natural environments . . . in which all living things have a right. ☐

Acknowledgements

THE AUTHOR and photographer are acutely aware that it would not have been possible to produce this book in its present form without the generous help of a great many people and organisations. To everyone who assisted us, we extend our sincerest thanks.

Our special thanks to:

Scientists of the Australian Museum, Sydney, especially: Dr Alex Ritchie, Curator of Palaeontology; Dr Lin Sutherland, Curator of Mineralogy and Petrology; Dr Harold Cogger, Curator of Reptiles and Deputy Director of the Museum; Dr Ron Lampert, Curator of Anthropology; and Dr Pat Hutchings, Curator of Marine Invertebrates.

Dr Brian Logan of the Department of Geology, University of Western Australia, for explaining the structure of the Shark Bay Stromatolites, providing copies of research papers and checking the manuscript for this chapter; and also to Dr John Bauld, Research Scientist, Baas-Becking Geobiological Laboratory, Canberra, for supplying valuable data on the same subject.

Chester Shaw and Vic Fahey, Rangers with the Tasmanian National Parks and Wildlife Service, Mole Creek, for organising the photography sessions in Kubla Khan Cave and for providing generous help and hospitality.

Stephen Opper and Peter Culley, for help and kind hospitality in photographing the Jenolan Caves.

Staff of the Royal Botanic Gardens, Sydney, especially Tony Rodd, Horticultural Botanist.

Rangers of National Parks throughout Australia.

Staff of the State Herbariums of Western Australia, New South Wales, Victoria, Tasmania, South Australia and Queensland for assistance in identifying flora.

For providing transportation, grateful thanks to:

John Rodgers of THIESS TOYOTA PTY LTD, Sydney; Boyd Gluyas, John Corcoran, Richard Kennedy and Carolyn Love of ANSETT.; Geoffrey Selby-Adams of ESSO AUSTRALIA LTD; and Bill King, Don Nayler, Vivien Leisk, Peter Webster and Annette Heppell of BILL KING'S NORTHERN SAFARIS.

Warmest thanks also to:

TAS: (Hobart) Tasmanian National Parks and Wildlife Service; Tasmanian Wilderness Society; Tasmanian Department of the Environment; Tasmanian Museum and Art Gallery; Tasmanian Department of Mines; Tasmanian Department of Tourism. (Country) Andrew Simmons, Remarkable Tours, Port Arthur; Jim Hayward and Louise Turner, Australian-Pacific Tours.

VIC: (Melbourne) Dr Bill Birch, Curator of Minerals, and Kerryn Robinson, Mineralogy Assistant, National Museum of Victoria; Pam MacKenzie, Information Services, Victorian Government Travel Authority; Victorian National Parks Service. (Country) Stawell and Grampians Tourist Information Centre; Bob Jones, Ian Threadgold and Steve Voros, rangers, Wilson's Promontory National Park.

NSW: (Sydney) Alan Catford, Project Officer, Australian Conservation Foundation; David Roberts; Densey Clyne; Max Peatman; Grahame Harrison, Department of History, University of Sydney; Graeme Pattison, University of New South Wales Speleological Society; Craig Leighton; Vicki Harriott and Elizabeth Pope, marine biologists; Phil Alderslade, marine biologist, Roche Products; the Mitchell Library; the Stanton Library; the Royal Australian Historical Society; New South Wales Geological Survey, Department of Mineral Resources; Australian Bureau of Statistics; Australian Military Establishments (Army), Victoria Barracks; New South Wales Department of Tourism. (Country) Ann Jelinek, Blue Mountains National Park; John Culley, Jenolan Caves.

QLD: (Brisbane) Queensland National Parks and Wildlife Service; Geological Survey of Queensland; Queensland Tourist and Travel Corporation; Queensland Museum. (Country) Great Barrier Reef Marine Park Authority, Townsville, especially R.T. Williams, Assistant Executive Officer, and Len Zell, photographer; Dave Barnes, Australian Institute of Marine Science, Cape Ferguson; Dr Barry and Lois Goldman, Lizard Island Research Station; Roger Watters, geologist, Cairns; Grahame Walsh, National Parks ranger, Carnarvon region; Paul and Harriet Watson, Sea Life Aquarium, Magnetic Island; Jim and Jo Wallace, the MV Matthew Brady, Port Douglas.

NT: George Chaloupka and Dr Colin Jack-Hinton, Northern Territory Museum and Art Galleries, Darwin; Alex Carter, Bill Neiiji and Ian Morris, rangers, Kakadu National Park; Chris Haynes, Australian National Parks and Wildlife Service, Darwin; Damian Bourne, Principal Information Officer, Department of Aboriginal Affairs, Darwin; R.B. Thompson, Resident Geologist, Department of Mines and Energy, Alice Springs; Derek Roff, ranger-in-charge, Uluru National Park; Peter Kingston, ranger, Finke Gorge National Park; Heather MacDonald, ranger, Chambers Pillar Scenic Reserve; Jim Cotterill, Wallara Ranch Motel; Gilbert Green, Ross River Tourist Ranch; Australian National Parks and Wildlife Service, Canberra; Territory Parks and Wildlife Service, Alice Springs; Northern Territory Government Tourist Bureau, Sydney.

SA: (Adelaide) South Australian National Parks and Wildlife Service; South Australian Museum, especially Neville Pledge, Curator of Palaeontology; South Australian Government Tourist Bureau; South Australian Department of Mines and Energy; South Australian Department of Lands; Kevin Mott, Cave Exploration Society of South Australia. (Country) Griselda Sprigg, Arkaroola–Mt Painter Sanctuary, Flinders Ranges; Cyril Gurney, Koonalda Station.

WA: (Perth) Richard May, Barry Muir, John Hunter and Joy Christian of the National Parks Authority of Western Australia; Ron Wright and Charles Charlesworth of the Royal Western Australian Historical Society; Rosemary Frazer; K.J. McNamara, Curator of Palaeontology, and Jeanne d'Espeissis, Assistant Curator of Anthropology, Western Australian Museum; Western Australian Geological Survey, Department of Mines; State Energy Commission of Western Australia; Battye Library; Forests Department of Western Australia; Harbour and Light Department, Fremantle. (Country) Sam and Elkun Umbagai, Elders, and Milton Newman, Project Officer, Mowanjum Aboriginal Community, Derby; Dampier Mining Company; Rob Sherwood, Koolan Island; Alan and Rae Walter, Carranya Station, near Wolf Creek Crater; Linda Ottaway, Wave Rock Caravan Park; District Officer, Fitzroy Crossing; Ron Spackman, Jewel Cave, Augusta; Port Hedland Public Library; Broome Public Library; Pemberton–Northcliffe Tourist Bureau; Augusta–Margaret River Tourist Bureau.

Finally, our most appreciative thanks to:

Walter and Jean Stone for help and advice; Oliver Chalmers for painstakingly checking the manuscript and offering many valuable suggestions and corrections; Jackie Kent for enthusiasm, encouragement and reliable editing; Anita Jacoby and Audrey Down for generous assistance when deadlines were looming; Joan Clarke for carefully compiling the index and for much encouragement; Joan Hempenstall for help with picture cataloguing, encouragement and kind assistance with library needs; members of our Publisher's staff who gave us much-needed support throughout the many months of working on this book; Maggie for help and for caring; and, most of all, Bruno Grasswill for his design and sensitive interpretation of the pictures and text, and for invaluable help in countless other ways. □

Select bibliography

WHEREVER possible, original historical journals, correspondence, published accounts and maps have been consulted during the research of this book, and almost all quotations are taken directly from these sources. Scientific data has been obtained principally from professional journals, specialised technical sources and private research papers. Nevertheless, we are indebted to the authors and photographers of many excellent general and reference publications for providing either inspiration or information. It would be impossible to acknowledge them all here; however, those listed below merit special appreciation.

Alderman, A.R., *Southern Aspect*, South Australian Museum, Adelaide 1973
Béchervaise, John, *Australia: World of Difference*, Rigby, Adelaide 1967
Béchervaise, John, and Burt, Jocelyn, *Wilson's Promontory*, Rigby, Adelaide 1976
Béchervaise, John, and Hay, Fraser, *Grampians Sketchbook*, Rigby, Adelaide 1971
Blombery, Alec M., *What Wildflower Is That?*, Paul Hamlyn, Sydney 1972
Brown, D.A., Campbell, K.S.W., and Crook, K.A.W., *The Geological Evolution of Australia and New Zealand*, Pergamon Press, London 1968
Brownlie, Sue and John, *Wilson's Promontory National Park*, Algona Guides, Montrose Vic 1973
Cogger, H.G., *Reptiles and Amphibians of Australia*, A.H. & A.W. Reed, Sydney 1979
Dulhunty, Roma, *The Spell of Lake Eyre*, Lowden, Kilmore Vic 1975
Dulhunty, Roma, *When the Dead Heart Beats Lake Eyre Lives*, Lowdon, Kilmore Vic 1979
Dutton, Geoffrey, *The Hero as Murderer: The Life of Edward John Eyre*, Collins, Sydney 1967
Fairley, Alan, *A Complete Guide to Warrumbungle National Park*, Murray Child, Sydney 1977
Fox, Allan M., *Warrumbungle National Park*, National Parks and Wildlife Service, Sydney 1972
Fuller, Basil, *The Nullarbor Story*, Rigby, Adelaide 1970
Gee, Helen, and Fenton, Janet (Eds.), *The South West Book*, Australian Conservation Foundation, Melbourne 1978
Hodgson, Margaret, and Paine, Roland, *A Field Guide to Australian Wildflowers*, Vols I and II, Rigby, Adelaide 1971, 1972

Holliday, Ivan, and Hill, Ron, *A Field Guide to Australian Trees*, Rigby, Adelaide 1975
Holliday, Ivan, and Watton, Geoffrey, *A Field Guide to Native Shrubs*, Rigby, Adelaide 1978
Isaacs, Jennifer (Ed.), *Australian Dreaming: 40 000 Years of Aboriginal History*, Lansdowne Press, Sydney 1980
Laseron, Charles Francis, *The Face of Australia*, Angus and Robertson, Sydney 1972
Mincham, Hans, *The Story of the Flinders Ranges*, Rigby, Adelaide 1967
Morcombe, Michael, *Australia's National Parks*, Lansdowne Press, Melbourne 1969
Mountford, Charles, *Brown Men and Red Sand*, Angus and Robertson, Sydney 1950
Mullins, Barbara, Martin, Margaret, and Baglin, Douglass, *Warrumbungle National Park*, A.H. & A.W. Reed, Sydney 1976
Rees, Coralie and Leslie, *Spinifex Walkabout*, Australasian Publishing Co. and G.G. Harrap, Sydney 1953
Ride, W.D.L., *A Guide to the Native Mammals of Australia*, Oxford University Press, Melbourne 1970
Roff, Derek, *Ayers Rock and the Olgas*, Ure Smith, Sydney 1979
Rolsh Photographics, *Cave Wonderlands of Western Australia*, c. 1979
Simpson, Colin, *Adam in Ochre*, Angus and Robertson, Sydney 1962
Siseman, John, and Chapman, John, *Cradle Mountain National Park*, Algona Guides, Montrose Vic 1979
Slater, Peter, *A Field Guide to Australian Birds*, Vols I and II, Rigby, Adelaide 1972, 1974
Sprigg, Reg and Griselda, *Arkaroola–Mt Painter in the Flinders Ranges, South Australia*, Arkaroola Travel Centre, Adelaide 1976
Thomas, Tyrone, *50 Walks in the Grampians*, Hill of Content Publishing, Melbourne 1977
Woolley, D.R., *A Layman's Guide to the Geology of Central Australia*, Alice Springs Tourist Promotion Association, Alice Springs 1977
Wynd, Ian, and Wood, Joyce, *A Map History of Australia*, Oxford University Press, Melbourne 1978
The Australian Encyclopaedia, The Grolier Society of Australia, Sydney 1977
Australia's Heritage, Paul Hamlyn, Sydney 1970
Australia's Wildlife Heritage, Paul Hamlyn, Sydney 1974

Index

Numbers in *italics* indicate a
picture only; numbers in **bold**
indicate a major chapter.
Entries in *italics* with an
asterisk (*) signify an
Aboriginal name.